對外經濟貿易大學
远程教育系列教材

U0833816

日常商务E-mail

Everyday Business E-mail

张二虎　主编
Fanny Fangfang　Lu Zhang　Barbara Resch 张二虎　编者

对外经济贸易大学出版社
中国·北京

内 容 简 介

本书是一本具有特定目标及内容、集日常商务词汇、英文写作技巧及北美相关社会文化知识为一体的教材。全书共十三课。每课均配有两篇实例电邮及学习目标、相关词汇、语法、句法、文化背景、写作指南、参考译文、多种练习及答案。

图书在版编目（CIP）数据

日常商务 E-mail / 张二虎主编. —北京：对外经济贸易大学出版社，2011

对外经济贸易大学远程教育系列教材

ISBN 978-7-5663-0188-8

Ⅰ.①日… Ⅱ.①张… Ⅲ.①商务－英语－电子邮件－写作－高等教育：远程教育－教材 Ⅳ.①H315

中国版本图书馆 CIP 数据核字（2011）第 217595 号

日常商务 E-mail
Everyday Business E-mail

张二虎 **主编**

责任编辑：朱笑妍 戴 菲

对 外 经 济 贸 易 大 学 出 版 社

北京市朝阳区惠新东街 10 号　　邮政编码：100029

邮购电话：010－64492338　　发行部电话：010－64492342

网址：http://www.uibep.com　　E-mail：uibep@126.com

北京山华苑印刷有限责任公司印装　　新华书店北京发行所发行

成品尺寸：185mm×230mm　　20 印张　　401 千字

2011 年 10 月北京第 1 版　　2011 年 10 月第 1 次印刷

ISBN 978-7-5663-0188-8

印数：0 001－5 000 册　　定价：30.00 元

对外经济贸易大学远程教育系列教材

编审委员会名单

总　序

中国远程教育的发展经历了三代：第一代是函授教育；第二代是广播电视教育；20 世纪 90 年代，随着现代信息技术的发展，以网络为基础的第三代现代远程教育应运而生。到目前为止，教育部批准开展现代远程教育试点的高校共67 所。对外经济贸易大学远程教育学院（简称“贸大远程”）是在中国加入 WTO 后的第一年，于2002 年3 月正式成立的。

现代远程教育作为新生事物，对传统的教学模式、学习习惯、获取新知的途径等产生了巨大的冲击。如何在网络时代打造学习型社会，构筑终身教育体系，是当今时代的重大课题。现代远程教育试点高校为此进行了许多卓有成效的探索。在网络教育的具体实践中，贸大远程始终坚持依托学校的整体优势和特色，坚持知识的内在逻辑性与职业、行业的市场需求的统一，坚持开展面向广大在职人员的现代远程教育，逐步形成了独具我校特色的“7 + 1”学习模式（即网络课堂、网上答疑、课程光盘、教材资料、适量面授、网上串讲、成绩检测，以及第二课堂活动），为学生个性化学习提供了广阔的空间。自2003 年起，贸大远程连续三年蝉联新浪网、择校网、搜狐网和《中国电脑教育报》联合评出的全国“十佳网络教育学院（机构）”称号。值得一提的是，“国际贸易实务”课程荣获国家级奖项，“商务英语”等七门课程荣获北京市优秀教材一等奖和精品课程称号，另有十余门课程在全国性的远程教育课程展示会上获得大奖。

几年来丰富的现代远程教育实践和教学经验积累，为我们出版成龙配套的贸大远程系列教材奠定了厚实的基础。目前，普通高等学校的现有教材并不完全适合远程教学，市面上真正用于现代远程教育的成规模的网络教材还不多见，与网络课件相配套的系列教材更是寥寥无几，因而为接受远程教育的广大莘莘学子专门设计符合他们需要的教材已成为现代远程教育发展的迫切需求。

基于以上原因，贸大远程按照学校一级教学管理体制，本着为社会、为学生服务的宗旨，致力于教学质量的保证和提高，特组织了国际经济与贸易学院、金融学院、国际商学院、英语学院、公共管理学院等学院的优秀教师，以目前开设的两个学历层次的十个专业为依据，以现有的导学课件为基础，编写了这套远程教育系列教材。本套教材共分为外语、经济贸易、工商管理、法律、金融与会计、行政管理、综合十大系列，全面覆盖两个学历层次十个专业的上百门课程。为了打造贸大远程优质教材品牌，我们与清华大学出版社和对外经济贸易大学出版社达成协议，计划三年之内全部出齐。

本套教材在策划编写过程中，严格遵循现代远程教育人才培养的模式与教学规律，充分考虑到远程学生在职和成人继续教育业余学习的实际情况，专门为远程学生量身定制而成，具有较强的针对性、实用性和可操作性。本套教材的编写具有以下特点：

一、在教材体系和章节的安排上，严格遵循循序渐进、由浅入深的教学规律；在对内容深度的把握上，考虑远程教育教学对象的培养要求和接受基础，其专业深度比本科有所降低，基础面相对拓宽，不是盲目将内容加深加多，而是做到深浅适中，难易适度。

二、在每章开篇给出明确的学习目标与重点难点提示，涵盖了教学大纲的重点或主要内容。相对于传统的学校教育，远程教育更倚重于学生的自学能力和自控能力。明确的教学目标有利于学生带着任务有目的地学习。同时，教材中充分考虑到了学生学习时可能遇到的问题，给他们以提示和建议。本套教材的作者都是经过挑选的具有长期教学经验的优秀教师，且大多数作者都来自远程教学的第一线，是远程网络课件的主讲老师，能够为学生提供比较丰富的切中要害的问题解答，从而可使远程学生在学习时少走弯路。

三、在章后和书后分别设置有"同步测练与解析"和"综合测练与解析"，它们涵盖了本章及本书的重要知识点，并给出了详尽的参考答案，对难题还进行了分析点评，列出解题思路与要点，从而更加方便学生自学。测验是检验教学目标是否达到的有效手段。远程学生是在虚拟的网络课堂上课，远离教师，处于相对独立的学习环境；教师不能通过直接交流，了解学生对学习内容的掌握情况；学生也由于与教师、同学的分离，无法判断自己的学习状况，因此，我们在教材中设置了大量自测自练题目，旨在通过这种自测自练方式，积极引导学生及时消化和吸收所学知识，不断加深对教材内容的理解，阶段性检查学习效果，全面复习和掌握所学知识，综合评判自己对知识的掌握程度，巩固最终学习成果。

四、考虑到有些专业课程具有较强的社会实践性，在教材的编写上也力争做到理论联系实际，注重案例的引入，尽可能安排一个或多个案例，并进行详细的分析讲解，旨在通过案例教学，对课程重点难点进行深化分析和实操训练，加强学生对知识点的理解和记忆，强化学生分析问题、解决问题的能力以及动手操作的能力。

本套教材的编写与出版得到了众多业界专家学者的真诚理解与支持，得到了清华大学出版社与对外经济贸易大学出版社的通力合作，在此向他们一并致以衷心的感谢。在前所未有的战略机遇期和“十一五”期间，相信本套教材的出版，必将是全国远程教育界一件很有意义的事情。衷心祝愿现代远程教育在建立学习型社会、构筑终身教育体系的进程中，在推动中国教育事业向现代化大教育形态的历史转变中，迈出更大更坚实的脚步。

对外经济贸易大学远程教育学院院长

谢毅斌

2006年7月于北京

前　言

当今是信息时代，无可置疑商务电子邮件的往来又是信息传播的主要渠道。由此英语商务电子邮件成为了商务领域中不可替代的沟通工具，也是将从事商务贸易的高校学生的必修之课。

为此编写，出版适合在校教学及远程教学所需的教材尤为迫切，这也是我们酝酿，策划，拟定，编写《日常商务 E-mail》一书的初衷。以下简称“商邮”。

此书的主要对象应定位为已达到初等英文程度群体，如大学远程一，二年级学生。“商邮”一书是一本具有特定目标及内容、集日常商务词汇、英文写作技巧及北美相关社会文化知识为一体的教材。它不但能培养学生用实际英语表达“日常实用商务”活动所需要的语言交流技能，同时将北美文化背景、风俗民情、社交礼仪乃至西方人的思维，沟通方式也融入此书，因而提高学生对学习实用英语的兴趣。

基于以上构思，我们在“商邮”一书的总体安排和细节编写上做了与目前高校英语教材风格截然不同的设计。

首先，在选题上力求概括最具代表性，最有普遍意义的实用商务英文电子邮件。每篇实例电邮的编写力求真实、生动、实用、风趣，尽可能避免“老生常谈”的书本语言，每课练习的设计，也本着鼓励，激发学生主动互动的宗旨，提供多种形式的练习去运用乃至灵活掌握该课词汇、语法、写作特点等机会，达到学以致用的目的。

二、我们认为语言的学习与社会文化应融为一体，使学生通过了解北美文化提高英语水平。而“商邮”通过每课逐一地介绍了美国的人文、地理、时事、休闲、风俗、民情、礼仪及家庭等文化背景，有助于学生在实际商务电子邮件沟通时，避免由于缺乏文化背景知识所造成的误解。

三、我们在编写框架上，将“商邮”一书合理地分为十三课。每课均配有两篇实例电邮及学习目标、相关词汇、语法、句法、文化背景、写作指南、参考译文、多种练习，在其内容上前后衔接又相对独立，使用者可根据难易程度及教学对象的需要调整安排课程。我们根据词汇的使用频率，仔细慎重地考虑了词、词组及专用名的挑选。它们将是大学英语一、二年级学生首先应该掌握的日常实用商务英语词汇。学生通过此教材的学习有助于掌握：

- 有效的写作模式；
- 电子邮件交流要素；
- 电子邮件交流的典型词汇，语法及句型，句法；
- 电子邮件交流中的文字处理技能；
- 撰写有特定要求的文章。

在此我们想说明，尽管我们都分别在中国和美国有着十几年到几十年的高校教书及著书经历，但由于此书是在新趋势、新模式下编著的，因此本书存在尚可提高，完善的地方，我们真诚地期盼读者提出改进意见。

《日常商务 E-mail》一书的文字、插图由张二虎，吕方方（Fanny Zhang）和 Barbara Resch 拟定。张二虎主要负责全书策划，统稿及审阅、出版、部分练习及文字注释。吕方方（Fanny Zhang）和 Barbara Resch 负责设计、编写实例电邮、撰写人文信息、词汇表、文字语法注释、文化背景注释、互动练习、写作指南、中文译文、专业英汉对译、中英对照、全书审阅及插图绘制。

我们也借此机会感谢北京对外经济贸易大学远程学院和美国科罗拉多学院（Colorado College）对此书出版及编著的支持。

编　者

2011 年 9 月于北京对外经济贸易大学，
美国科罗拉多学院

A Letter to Teachers

Welcome to *Everyday Business E-mail*. The University of International Business and Economics has created this student textbook to expand your students' use of business English in an authentic way. The 13 lessons in this book draw students into engaging scenarios that will teach them new vocabulary as well as the way Americans use e-mails in their personal and/or professional business.

Each lesson begins with learning objectives that highlight what students should learn in that lesson. Two sets of e-mails appear in each lesson; we have based the e-mail dialogs on actual e-mails. As Americans intermix their business and personal lives, we have provided a range of e-mail styles, from formal e-mails that companies send to customers, to informal e-mails sent at work, to personal e-mails that involve electronic commerce. We have also included e-mails from many areas of business and employment, such as large corporations, small businesses, colleges and universities, freelance workers, and private shoppers. These e-mails also reflect American culture. For example, we have used an assortment of personal names to reflect the diversity in American life and the types of names your students may encounter in real life.

Following each set of e-mails are lists of vocabulary and notes. The notes explain common business and Internet terms and aspects of the American culture. They also clarify the grammar and usage in the e-mails. One feature of the notes is the extensive examples, written in both English and Chinese, of vocabulary and expressions and their variations.

Exercises give students a variety of ways to work with the new words and grammar. In each lesson, students have two opportunities to practice writing in English, by answering questions about the e-mails, and then summarizing the dialogs. Then they are to complete two sets of fill-in-the-blank exercises, which emphasize the vocabulary. The multiple-choice exercises require students to concentrate on subtle issues like prepositions, homonyms, spelling, and idioms. The last two exercises are for students to translate sentences from English to Chinese, and vice versa.

We have also included drawings to illustrate the dialogs in the e-mails. We suggest you ask students to use the lessons' vocabulary to describe the drawings. Consider, for example, having students retell a dialog by referring to images in a drawing. Or ask them to use the drawings to create their own dialogs.

Each lesson has a "Writing Tips" chart. Some tips elaborate on a grammar point found in the lesson, such as capitalization or hyphenation. Others discuss a finer point of e-mail usage, like texting abbreviations or the types of e-mail attachments. Finally, answer keys and translations of the e-mails are provided for students to check their work.

We hope that you and your students will find *Everyday Business E-mail* to be an innovative textbook for studying contemporary English.

C

CONTENTS

Contents

Lesson 1

Basic E-mail Greetings
基本电子邮件问候

Learning Objectives

In this lesson, you will learn the following:

- How to tell friends and family about a new address and phone number
  告知亲友新电话及地址
- How to respond to an e-mail about a new address and phone number
  电邮回复新电话及地址的变更
- How to tell work colleagues about a new employee
  通报新员工的聘用
- How to introduce yourself to a new employee
  向新员工自我介绍
- How to write personal and business e-mails
  撰写个人及商务邮件
- What the basic etiquette rules for e-mails are
  电子邮件基本规范

E-mail Thread 1

Subject: New Address and Phone Number
From: Lisa@cmail.com
Date: November 9, 2012
To: Mary@cmail.com; Michael@cmail.com; Suzanne@cmail.com; Jimmy@cmail.com
Hello everyone, I am excited to tell you that my husband, Phil, and I have moved to a log cabin in the beautiful mountains outside of Aspen, Colorado. We are looking forward to the challenges and rewards of living in the mountains! Our new address is 226 Green River Rd., Aspen, CO 81611. Our new phone number is 555-555-0190. My e-mail address is the same (Lisa@cmail.com). I hope all is well with you. Please visit us! Sincerely, Lisa

Subject: Re: New Address and Phone Number
From: Suzanne@cmail.com
Date: November 9, 2012
To: Lisa@cmail.com
Hi Lisa, Thanks for the update. I'm very happy for you and Phil. Enjoy this new adventure! Best, Suzanne

New Words 1

1.	address	[ə'dres]	*n.*	住址，地址
2.	adventure	[əd'ventʃə]	*n.*	令人激动的活动
3.	basic	['beisik]	*adj.*	基本的
4.	challenge	['tʃælindʒ]	*n.*	挑战
5.	employee	[ˌemplɔi'iː]	*n.*	雇员；员工
6.	excite	[ik'sait]	*v.*	使兴奋；使激动
7.	following	['fɔləuiŋ]	*adj.*	下面的，下述的
8.	introduce	[ˌintrə'djuːs]	*v.*	介绍，引见
9.	objective	[əb'dʒektiv]	*n.*	目的，目标
10.	reward	[ri'wɔːd]	*n.*	奖赏；奖励
11.	sincerely	[sin'siəli]	*adv.*	真诚地，诚恳地，真挚地
12.	subject	['sʌbdʒikt]	*n.*	主题；题目
13.	update	[ʌp'deit]	*n.*	最新的情况，最新的信息

Phrases and Expressions 1

1.	e-mail greetings	电子邮件的问候
2.	etiquette rules	基本礼仪规范
3.	log cabin	小木屋
4.	moved to	搬到
5.	respond to	对……的回应
6.	work colleagues	工作同事

Proper Names 1

1.	Aspen	阿斯彭
2.	Colorado	科罗拉多
3.	Green River Rd.	绿河路
4.	Jimmy	吉米

5. Lisa 丽莎
6. Mary 玛丽
7. Michael 麦克尔
8. Phil 菲尔
9. Suzanne 苏珊

Notes 1

1. *e-mail accounts* (电子邮件账户): E-mail accounts are available through companies, schools, and Internet service providers (ISPs). Some providers, like Google, offer accounts that let users send e-mails, pictures, and documents for free. Other providers charge a monthly fee for sending and storing unlimited e-mails. After setting up the account, the user can send, receive, reply to, and save e-mails. Users can receive domestic e-mails almost immediately; international e-mails are also received quickly.
网络服务机构，各公司，学校均可为用户提供电子邮件账户。有些提供者，如“谷歌”可为用户免费发送电子邮件、照片及文件。 有些提供者会收取月费，但其发送及存储电子邮件是无数量限制的。电子邮件账户建立后，用户即可发送、收阅、回复和存储电子邮件。用户能即刻收到国内电子邮件，而且国际电子邮件也能很快收到。

1.1. *personal e-mails* (私人电子邮件): Personal e-mails can be as simple as one or two sentences. They can also be written like a personal letter, with a salutation (e.g., “Dear,” or “Hi,”) and a closing (e.g., “Best,” “Thanks,” or “Love,”).
撰写私人电子邮件可以简单到一两个句子，也可以像私人信件以“亲爱的”、“你好”开始，以“祝好”、“谢谢”或“爱你的”结束。

1.2. *business e-mails* (商务电子邮件): Business e-mails are more formal than personal e-mails. The initial business e-mails that are sent between an individual and a company or between two companies are written like formal letters, with the following parts:
商务电子邮件比私人电子邮件要正式得多。第一封个人与公司或者两家公司间的电邮相当于正式函电。以下是撰写的基本要点。

1) the recipient’s name and title (if the recipient’s name is not known, use a title, such as “Director of Human Resources”)

收件人的姓名和职务名；若不知收件人的姓名，可用职务名如“人力资源主管”

2) the recipient's company name

   收件人的公司名称

3) the recipient's address (optional)

   收件人地址（非固定格式）

4) a reference line (optional; e.g., "Re: Job Application")

   主题说明（非固定格式；如：回复工作申请）

5) a formal salutation (e.g., "Dear Ms. Smith,"; if the recipient's name is not known, use "Dear Sir or Madam," or a specific title such as "Dear Director of Human Resources,")

   正式的称呼（如：“亲爱的史密斯女士”若不知收件人的姓名，可用“亲爱的先生或女士”或具体的职务名，如：“人力资源主管”）

6) the body of the letter

   信的具体内容

7) a formal closing (e.g.,"Sincerely," "Best regards," or "Yours truly,"; note that the second word is lowercase)

   正式结束语（如：“真诚的”、“致敬”、“忠实于你的”。注意，第二个词的第一个字母要用小写。）

8) your name, title, address, and phone number

   你的名字、职务名、地址及电话号码

Don't include a date, since the e-mail program automatically includes one.

每一个电子邮件自动带有日期，所以不必写发送邮件的日期。

These e-mails often become less formal as the business relationship develops. For example, writers may exclude the company names and addresses. They may also address each other by first name and use informal salutations and closings.

随着商业关系的不断发展，电子邮件的往来逐渐趋于非正式。比如，撰写电子邮件的人可能不再罗列公司名称及地址。他们也可能仅用相互的名字称呼对方，非正式的称呼语句及结束语句。

E-mails sent between colleagues at the same company are also less formal. Colleagues who work closely with each other often send e-mails that are similar to personal e-mails. The tone of all business e-mails should remain professional, however.

在同一公司同事中的电子邮件的往来，都是采用非正式的形式。在一起工作同事间的电子邮件的往来与私人电子邮件相似。然而，所有商业电子邮件都应保持其专业格式。

2. *e-mail rules* (电子邮件规则): Follow these rules when writing and answering personal and business e-mails:
撰写商业电子邮件及私人电子邮件时应遵守以下几点：

2.1. These etiquette rules apply to all e-mails:
这些规范适用于所有的电子邮件：

1) Don't send private or secure information.
不要发送与个人隐私和安全有关的信息。
2) Don't send e-mails that you don't want anyone else to read. (Your e-mail could be forwarded without your knowledge.) Don't send e-mails when you are angry; wait before sending them.
不要发送你希望不被收信人以外的其他人阅读的电子邮件。（在你不知情时，你发送的电子邮件可能被转发。）在你气愤的时候不要发送电子邮件，应先等一下后发送。
3) Have a colleague or friend review important e-mails for clarity and accuracy before you send them.
在你发送重要的电子邮件前，请同事或朋友帮你复阅一下它的清晰度及准确度。
4) Always include a concise, informative subject line. This helps recipients find messages in their in-boxes and encourages them to respond sooner.
总是包含一个简明扼要的标题，这样可帮助收信人了解信息内容，促使他们尽早回复。
5) Use the e-mail program's return receipt or delivery confirmation feature only when necessary.
只在需要时才使用电子邮件程序里回复或递送确认功能。

2.2. Following these guidelines will help you write effective e-mails:
运用这些指南可帮你撰写有效的电子邮件：

1) Present yourself in the best way by using correct spelling, grammar, and punctuation, especially for business e-mails.
要想呈现最佳的自我，尤其是在撰写商业电子邮件时，要通过使用准确无误的拼写、语法、标点符号来实现。
2) Use active voice (e.g., "I am sending you this message because...") instead of passive voice ("This message is being sent to you because...").

采用主动语气，（如：我发送这个信息是因为……）而避免采用被动语气。（如：你之所以收到这个信息是因为……）。

3) Put the key point of your message at the beginning.
电子邮件的信息重点要放在前面。

4) Avoid long sentences; be concise.
避免长句；力求简明。

5) When writing about people in general, don't use singular pronouns or terms that refer to one gender. Instead, use plural pronouns, which include all people, and gender-neutral terms. For example, don't write: "Give the customer his receipt and thank him for shopping with us." Do write: "Give the customers their receipts and thank them for shopping with us." Similarly, don't use "mankind" but do use "humankind."
当撰写与人物有关的电子邮件时，避免使用单数的人物代词或仅代表一种性别的词汇。相反采用复数人物代词及男性、女性均可接受的词汇，来包括整个群体。比方说，不要写，"给这位顾客他的发票并感谢他在我们这里购物"。而要写，"给顾客们发票并感谢他们在我们这里购物"。同样，用"humankind"一词，而避免用"mankind"一词泛指"人类"。

6) Ask specific questions that require a yes or no answer (e.g., "Can we meet at 10:00?") rather than open-ended questions ("Let me know when you can meet.")
邮件可用一般疑问句。（如："我们能十点见吗？"）而不用祈使句。（如："告诉我，我们什么时候能见面？"）

7) Use the spell-check feature but also proofread your e-mail. (Spell-checkers don't catch every mistake.)
在利用电脑拼写检查功能纠错的同时，也要校读自己的电子邮件。

2.3. Use simple formatting so your e-mails are easy to read:
采用简明格式，以便你的电子邮件易读：

1) Separate paragraphs with blank lines, which gives an uncluttered appearance.
展现整齐有序的电子邮件，应以空行分隔段落。

2) Align text on the left margin and avoid indents.
避免使用缩格式书写，文字应全部向左对齐。

3) Avoid uncommon fonts, italics and bold, and special characters such as "—" or "1/2," because some e-mail programs can't display them.

有些电子邮件程序不能显示不常用的字体，如斜体、黑体和特别的字体符号“——”或“1/2”，因此应该避免使用。

4) Use emoticons and abbreviations sparingly. Don't use them in business e-mails unless you know the recipient well.
谨慎使用字符图像和缩写词。除非你对收件人十分了解，商业电子邮件不能使用字符图像和缩写词。

5) Avoid typing in all capital letters because it sometimes indicates yelling.
有时全部使用大写字母会暗示信息带有较强的情绪，因此应避免全部使用大写字母。

6) Choose professional-looking fonts and conservative colors for business e-mails and make sure the font isn't too small.
选择看起来非常职业化的字体和传统的颜色，并注意字体不要太小。

2.4. These guidelines for replying and forwarding will ensure courteous e-mail correspondence:
以下提示会使你有礼貌地回复和转发电子邮件：

1) Reply soon after receiving the e-mail. When you don't have time to write a complete reply, briefly acknowledge the e-mail by writing, "I received your e-mail and will get back to you soon."
收到电子邮件尽快回复。若没有时间回复邮件，可简短告知“收到你的电子邮件并将尽快回复”。

2) Include previous responses (called "e-mail threads") when replying so that all correspondence is available for reference.
当回复邮件时应包括以前的相关电子邮件（称为电子邮件主题），以利于参考。

3) Make sure you don't use the reply-all feature when you want to reply to only one person.
当仅希望回复一人时，不要用电子邮件程序回复群体的功能。

4) When forwarding a message, write a brief note explaining why you are forwarding it. Don't forward offensive or personal e-mails, hoaxes, and viruses.
当转发信息时，应写简明扼要标题解释转发缘由。不要转发无礼或私人电子邮件，及欺骗或有病毒的电子邮件。

3. *Log cabins* are small houses made of round or rough-hewn logs that are stacked on top of each other. The gaps between the logs are filled with "chinking" (mud, rocks, and other

materials). The inside walls look like the outside walls because they are not covered with plaster. Log cabins were a common type of house on the American frontier.
原木造的小木屋是由一根根砍下并去皮的原木搭成。原木间的缝隙由泥、碎石或其他填充物填充。由于屋内没有抹灰的墙壁，屋内看起来与屋外相似。原木造的小木屋曾在美国边远地区非常流行。

4. *possessives* (名词所有格): Possessives indicate ownership or association, as in "Lisa's cabin." In English, a possessive is formed by adding an apostrophe (') and the letter *s* to the end of the noun that "owns" the object. The placement of the apostrophe depends on whether the noun is singular or plural and on the meaning.
英文名词所有格由所有格符号（'）和英文字母（s）组成。所有格符号（'）位置跟随不同名词及意思而定。

4.1. To form the possessive of a singular noun (including proper nouns, numbers, and letters), add *'s*:
单数名词包括专有名词、数字及字母的所有格直接其后加*'s*。
例：1) Lisa + 's = Lisa's cabin　丽莎的小木屋
2) California + 's = California's governor　加州州长
3) 2012 + 's = 2012's hurricane season　2012 年的飓风季节

4.2. To form the possessive of a plural noun that ends in *s*, add an *'* after the *s*:
例：the mountains + ' = the mountains' beauty　群山的美丽

4.3. To form the possessive of a plural noun that doesn't end in *s*, add *'s*:
例：children + 's = children's toys　儿童玩具

4.4. To form the possessive of two nouns that form a unit and possess the same thing (such as a married couple possessing a house), add *'s* after the second noun:
例：Lisa and Phil + 's = Lisa and Phil's cabin　丽莎和菲尔的小木屋

4.5 To form the possessive of two separate nouns that possess separate things, add *'s* or an *'* to both nouns:
例：Singular nouns: Aspen and Denver + 's + 's = Aspen's and Denver's airports

阿斯彭和丹佛的飞机场

Plural nouns: children and teenagers + 's or ' = children's and teenagers' clothing

儿童和青少年的衣服

5. 在美国，房屋的种类很多，因此描述房子的名词也不少。

例：1) cabin 小木屋

2) cottage 乡村小石屋

3) villa 别墅

4) house 洋房，独幢房，单体屋

5) semidetached house 半独立式洋房

6) town house 联排别墅，连栋屋

7) bungalow 有游廊的平房

6.1. *same* 一词常用于形容词，但在课文中当 same 同 the 连用时，same 是代词，意思是“我的 e-mail 地址没有变，同以前的 e-mail 地址一样”。

另外 the same 还可用作副词。

例：I think the same of him as you do.

我对他的看法和你一样。

6.2. *the* 用在形容词前时还有名词作用。

例：1) the poor 穷人

2) the wounded 伤员

3) the homeless 无家可归者

7.1. *well* 常用于副词，意思是“好”。

例：The kids are doing well at school.

孩子们在学校学习、生活都挺好的。

7.2. *well* 在课文中是形容词。well 用于形容词时主要有两个意思“健康的和令人满意的”，它后面常用介词“with”。

例：1) I knew that all was well with her.

我知道她一切称心如意。

2) I'm not well today.
我今天不舒服。

Exercises 1

I. Answer the following questions.

1. Who is Phil?
2. What type of house did Phil and Lisa move into?
3. Where is the house?
4. What are Phil and Lisa looking forward to?
5. What is Phil and Lisa's new address?
6. Did Phil and Lisa's phone number change?
7. Did Lisa's e-mail address change?
8. Who replied to Lisa's e-mail?

II. Write the key points of this e-mail thread.

III. Fill in the blanks.

1. I am excited to ________ you that I have moved to the mountains.
2. Badaling is in the mountains ________ of Beijing.
3. I am looking ________ to the challenges and rewards of being a parent.
4. You moved? Please tell me your ________ address.
5. My phone number didn't change; it is the ________.
6. We hope ________ is well with you and your family.
7. They moved into a new house; I am very ________ for them.
8. ________ your new adventure in the mountains!

IV. Fill in the missing information.

Hi Felicia,

I wanted to give you an update. My husband and I have moved to our new home in the mountains. Our new address is 948 Acorn Drive. Please visit us!

Best,

Sarah

Hi Sarah,

I'm very happy ________ you and your husband. Is your phone number ________ same?

I am looking forward to ________ you!

Thanks,

Felicia

V. Choose the correct answer. Only one answer is correct.

1. Everybody was ________ the news of victory.
   A. excited in B. exciting by C. excited by D. exciting in
2. The cabin ________, so we get morning sun.
   A. look to east B. face east C. face to the east D. faces east
3. The bar was so crowded you could ________.
   A. hardly talk B. hardly move C. talk D. move
4. I'm happy that everything ________ in the end.
   A. worked out well B. works well C. worked out good D. works good
5. We're very happy ________.
   A. for taking part B. to be taking part C. for take part D. to take part in
6. The president faces a strong ________ from rival groups.
   A. thing B. work C. change D. challenge
7. Usually a school has its own system of ________ and punishments to encourage good behavior.
   A. reward B. rewards C. gift D. gifts
8. The report provides a ________ on the progress of the project.
   A. brief update B. brief news C. brief information D. brief advice

VI. Translate the following from English into Chinese.

1. When do you think you will move to Washington?

2. Please set up an e-mail account for the new employee.
3. I sent e-mails to more than 10 people.
4. President Abraham Lincoln was born in a log cabin.
5. I can't go this evening. I've got a lot of e-mails to reply to.

VII. Translate the following from Chinese into English.

1. 电子邮件主题是什么？
2. 你在找什么呢？
3. 请把她的地址转发给我。
4. 我现在很穷，还不能买房子。
5. 他想找一个有挑战性的工作。

Writing Tips

Parts of an E-mail	
Subject line:	Describes the content of the e-mail. Some e-mail programs block e-mails with empty subject lines or with subject lines that contain words often used in advertisements (for example, "Rx," "prescription," and "free shipping").
From:	Identifies the sender. The sender's "username," or "screen name," comes before the @ sign. Usernames are often the first name or first initial and the last name of the sender (for example, JohnSmith@cmail.com or JSmith@cmail.com). They can also be an alias that reflects the person's interests (for example, foodlover@cmail.com). Don't use inappropriate or unprofessional usernames.
Date and time:	Inserted automatically by the e-mail program to record when the message was sent.
To:	Lists the recipient or recipients, who can be individual people or groups.

Cc:	Lists people who will receive a copy of the e-mail. Use this feature sparingly. "CC:" is the abbreviation for "carbon copy" and refers to copies made on typewriters by inserting carbon paper between sheets of typing paper. The term also means "courtesy copy."
Bcc:	Secretly sends a copy of the e-mail to people. Use this feature sparingly. "BCC:" is the abbreviation for "blind carbon copy."
Message body	Is the main text.
Signature	Identifies the sender; some e-mail programs can be set up to automatically insert the sender's name. Business e-mails should also include contact information.
Attachments	Attaches separate documents, photographs, and other files to the e-mail. Attachments should have meaningful files names to help the recipient save and retrieve them, such as LiuResume2012.pdf.

E-mail Thread 2

Subject: Welcome Kathy Masterson
From: ECohen@widget.com
Date: July 16, 2012
To: <All Staff>
Ladies and Gentlemen, We are pleased to announce a new face in the main office: Kathy Masterson. Kathy previously worked at various local companies. She has assumed the accounting duties for Widget Corporation. Contact Kathy at Kmasterson@widget.com or 555-555-0110 if you have accounting questions. Please welcome Kathy to our company. I am very happy to have her working with us, and I know you will be, too. Elaine Cohen, Director ECohen@widget.com Phone: 555-555-0111

Subject: Welcome!
From: JRosen@widget.com
Date: July 16, 2012
To: Kmasterson@widget.com
Dear Kathy, Welcome aboard. You will find Widget Corporation to be a great company to work for. I am the manager of the Sales Department and will be working with you on monthly sales reports. I am looking forward to meeting you.

With best regards,

Joe Rosen, Manager
JRosen@widget.com
Phone: 555-555-0114

New Words 2

1.	accounting	[ə'kauntiŋ]	*n.*	会计；会计学
2.	assume	[ə'sjuːm]	*v.*	承担；就任
3.	contact	['kɔntækt]	*v.*	联系
4.	director	[di'rektə]	*n.*	主管
5.	previously	['priːvjəsli]	*adv.*	以前
6.	staff	[stɑːf]	*n.*	职员；工作人员
7.	various	['veəriəs]	*adj.*	各种各样的
8.	welcome	['welkəm]	*v.*	欢迎

Phrases and Expressions 2

1. accounting duty 会计职责
2. main office 综合办公室；总部
3. sales department 销售部
4. sales report 销售报告
5. welcome aboard 欢迎加入我们的团队

Proper Names 2

1. Elaine Cohen 伊莱恩·库恩
2. Joe Rosen 乔·罗森
3. Kathy Masterson 凯茜·马斯特森
4. Widget Corporation 威洁特公司

Notes 2

1. *to have her working with us* 意思是“有她同我们在一起工作”。

另外在英语中还有两个常用句型：*to have somebody do something* 和 *to have something done by somebody*:

例：1) I don't really want to go, so I will have my sister go instead.

我实在不想去，所以我会让我妹妹去。

（*to have somebody do something* 有命令口气。）

2) I went downtown to have my hair cut. 我到城里理发了。

（to have something done 是被动语态，是别人给我理发。）

2.1. director 在公司同 *manager* 一样都可译为经理，但 director 往往负责范围更广，既负责行政也负责业务，而 manager 主要负责业务。此外，director 还有公司董事的意思。在公司，表示负责人的词还有：

例：1) CEO 行政主管，行政总裁；总裁，首席执行官

2) executive 总经理（大公司）

3) administrator 主管

2.2. *director* 在政府部门通常译为处长。在中国政府里，表示部门领导的词有：

例：1) premier 总理

2) minister 部长

3) general director 局长

4) director 处长

5) section chief 科长

3. *sale* 是名词。*sales* 是形容词。

例：1) sales manager 销售经理

2) sales meeting 销售会议

3) sales figure 销售数字

4. *monthly* 是形容词，表示时间，意思是“每月一次的”。在英语中表示时间的类似词有：

例：1) daily 每日的

2) weekly 一周一次的
3) fortnightly 两周一次的
4) quarterly 一季度一次
5) yearly 一年一次的

Exercises 2

I. Answer the following questions.

1. Who is the "new face" in the office?
2. Where did she work previously?
3. What duties has she assumed for Widget Corporation?
4. How do work colleagues contact her?
5. Who is happy to have her joining Widget Corporation?
6. Who welcomed her?
7. What department does he work in?
8. What kind of reports will they be working on?

II. Write an e-mail that tells friends, family, or work colleagues about your new address and phone number.

Key to E-mail Thread 1 Exercises (for Reference)

I. Answer the following questions.

1. Phil is Lisa's husband.
2. Phil and Lisa moved into a log cabin.
3. The house is in the mountains outside of Aspen, Colorado.
4. Phil and Lisa are looking forward to the challenges and rewards of living in the mountains.
5. Phil and Lisa's new address is 226 Green River Rd., Aspen, CO 81611.
6. Yes, Phil and Lisa's phone number changed.
7. No, Lisa's e-mail address did not change.

8. Suzanne replied to Lisa's e-mail.

II. Write the key points of this e-mail thread.

- Lisa sent an e-mail telling friends and family that she and her husband, Phil, moved.
- Lisa and Phil moved to a log cabin in the mountains outside of Aspen, Colorado.
- Lisa and Phil are looking forward to the challenges and rewards of living in the mountains.
- Lisa and Phil's new address is 226 Green River Rd., Aspen, CO 81611, and their new phone number is 555-555-0190.
- Lisa's e-mail address is the same.
- Suzanne replied to Lisa's e-mail. Suzanne thanked Lisa for the update and said she was happy for Lisa and Phil.

III. Fill in the blanks.

1. I am excited to tell you that I have moved to the mountains.
2. Badaling is in the mountains outside of Beijing.
3. I am looking forward to the challenges and rewards of being a parent.
4. You moved? Please tell me your new address.
5. My phone number didn't change; it is the same.
6. We hope all is well with you and your family.
7. They moved into a new house; I am very happy for them.
8. Enjoy your new adventure in the mountains!

IV. Fill in the missing information.

Hi Felicia,

I wanted to give you an update. My husband and I have moved to our new home in the mountains. Our new address is 948 Acorn Drive. Please visit us!

Best,

Sarah

Hi Sarah,

I'm very happy for you and your husband. Is your phone number the same?

I am looking forward to visiting you!

Thanks,

Felicia

V. Choose the correct answer. Only one answer is correct.

1. C 2. D 3. B 4. A 5. B 6. D 7. B 8. A

VI. Translate the following from English into Chinese.

1. 你什么时候会搬到华盛顿去？
2. 请帮新员工建个电子邮件账户。
3. 我给十多个人发送了电子邮件。
4. 林肯总统就出生在一个小木屋。
5. 今晚我去不了，我有许多电子邮件需要回复。

VII. Translate the following from Chinese into English.

1. What is the e-mail's subject?
2. What are you looking for?
3. Please forward her address to me.
4. Right now I am very poor; I won't be able to buy a house.
5. He wants a job that offers a challenge.

Translation of E-mail Thread 1 (for Reference)

译文：

邮件 1-1

主题：新地址；新电话
发件人：Lisa@cmail.com

日期：2012 年 11 月 9 日
收件人：Mary@cmail.com；Michael@cmail.com；Suzanne@cmail.com；Jimmy@cmail.com

大家好，

我非常兴奋地告诉大家，我和我丈夫吉姆搬到了小木屋，它坐落于科罗拉多州阿斯彭郊外的美丽群山之中。我们期待着住在群山中的挑战和享受。

我们的新地址是科罗拉多州阿斯彭市绿河路 226 号，邮编：81611
新电话号码为：555-555-0190
我的电子邮件信箱没变，仍为 Lisa@cmail.com

祝福你们，请拜访我们。

真诚地，

丽莎

邮件 1-2

主题：回复：新地址；新电话
发件人：Suzanne@cmail.com
日期：2012 年 11 月 9 日
收件人：Lisa@cmail.com

你好，丽莎，

谢谢你的最新信息。我非常为你和菲尔高兴。尽情享受这一新尝试吧。

最好的，

苏珊

Key to E-mail Thread 2 Exercises (for Reference)

I. Answer the following questions.

1. The "new face" in the office is Kathy Masterson.
2. Kathy previously worked at various local companies.
3. Kathy has assumed the accounting duties for Widget Corporation.
4. Work colleagues can contact her at Kmasterson@widget.com or 555-555-0110.
5. Elaine Cohen, a director, is happy to have her joining Widget Corporation.
6. Joe Rosen, a manager, welcomed her.
7. Joe works in the Sales Department.
8. Joe and Kathy will be working on monthly sales reports.

Translation of E-mail Thread 2 (for Reference)

译文:

邮件 2-1

主题：欢迎凯茜·马斯特森
发件人：伊莱恩·库恩
日期：2012 年 7 月 16 日
收件人：全体公司员工

先生们，女士们：

我非常荣幸地通知大家，凯茜·马斯特森是综合办公室的新雇员。凯茜以前曾在不同的本地公司工作过。她将承担威洁特公司会计职责。若你有财会方面的问题请用此邮件地址 Kmasterson@widget.com 或电话 555-555-0110 与凯茜联系。

请大家欢迎凯茜加入我们公司，我非常高兴她能和我们一起工作， 我知道你们也有同感。

伊莱恩·库恩（公司主管）
ECohen@widget.com
电话：555-555-0111

邮件 2-2

主题：欢迎
发件人：乔·罗森
日期：2012 年 7 月 16 日
收件人：凯茜·马斯特森

亲爱的凯茜，

欢迎加入我们的团队。你将发现你所工作的威洁特公司是一家特别优秀的公司。

我是销售部的经理。我将就月销售报告一事与你共同商议。我期待着认识你。

诚挚的问候，

乔·罗森（经理）
JRosen@widget.com
电话：555-555-0114

Lesson 2

Family Events
家庭活动

Learning Objectives

In this lesson, you will learn the following:

- How to write an e-mail invitation and an announcement
  电子邮件邀请信及通告
- How Americans celebrate a baby's birth
  庆祝新生命的诞生
- How to congratulate someone
  贺喜
- What names and colors Americans use to indicate gender
  名字、颜色与性别
- How to send a gift for a newborn
  新生儿的礼品
- What a car seat is for
  儿童乘车安全椅

E-mail Thread 1

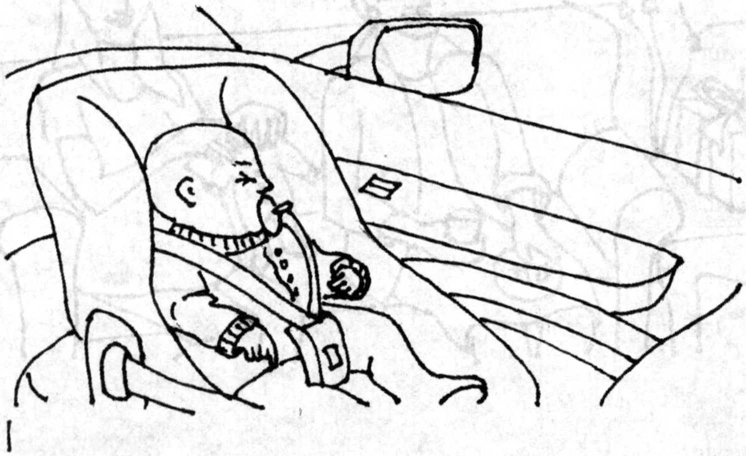

Subject: Surprise Baby Shower for Stephanie
From: Amber@cmail.com
Date: March 15, 2012
To: Laura@cmail.com
Dear Aunt Laura, I will be hosting a surprise baby shower at my house for my sister Stephanie on April 8. I hope you and Grandma can come. (I've invited Stephanie's friends, too.) Here are the details: April 8, 1:00-4:00 p.m. 123 Sumac St., Boston, MA Please RSVP by April 1. Stephanie is registered with the Baby Gear store in Boston. Love, Amber

Subject: Re: Surprise Baby Shower for Stephanie
From: Laura@cmail.com
Date: March 18, 2012
To: Amber@cmail.com
Hi Amber, Grandma and I would love to attend Stephanie's baby shower! I ordered two gifts from the Baby Gear store—a car seat from Grandma and baby clothes from me. The store will ship them to your house. Would you watch for the shipment?

I noticed that the baby items that Stephanie chose are either pink or yellow, not blue. She must be having a girl. (Although either a girl or a boy would be wonderful.)

Love,

Aunt Laura

New Words 1

1.	although	[ɔːl'ðəu]	*conj.*	虽然
2.	attend	[ə'tend]	*v.*	参加；出席
3.	choose	[tʃuːz]	*v.*	选择；挑选
4.	details	['diːteils]	*n.*	具体细节；详细情况
5.	gift	[gift]	*n.*	礼物；赠品
6.	host	[həust]	*v.*	主持；操办；主办；举办
7.	item	['aitəm]	*n.*	商品；货物
8.	notice	['nəutis]	*v.*	意识到；注意
9.	order	['ɔːdə]	*v.*	订购；下订单
10.	ship	[ʃip]	*v.*	运货；交货
11.	shipment	['ʃipmənt]	*n.*	货物；物品
12.	store	[stɔː]	*n.*	商店
13.	surprise	[sə'praiz]	*v. & n.*	意外；使惊讶
14.	wonderful	['wʌndəfəl]	*adj.*	极好的

Phrases and Expressions 1

1.	baby shower	为准妈妈所举办的聚会
2.	car seat	儿童乘车安全椅
3.	either...or	是……或是……，……或……
4.	must be having	一定有（怀）了
5.	to register with	登记；注册
6.	to RSVP	请回复

7. to watch for (something) 注意等待；关注
8. would love to 非常愿意

Proper Names 1

1. Amber 安布尔
2. Aunt Laura 劳拉婶婶；劳拉姑妈
3. Baby Gear 婴儿用品店
4. Boston, Massachusetts (MA) 马彦诸塞州（麻省）波士顿
5. Stephanie 斯蒂芬妮

Notes 1

1.1. *dear* 用在邮件的开始，常用于称呼，表示客气。
一个陌生人在通信中一般以“Dear Sir,”或“Dear Madam,”开始。另外，dear 需大写，称呼后面用逗号，关系亲近则用“Dear Laura or Dear Amber”。

1.2. *love* 则用于邮件的结尾，可在给密友和亲戚的邮件中使用。在写给公司或陌生人的邮件中用“Yours truly,”“Sincerely,”or “Best regards,”。在写给一般朋友的邮件中用“Best,”。第一个字母大写，末尾用逗号。

2.1. *a surprise baby shower*: American people have a variety of ways for celebrating the coming of a new baby, and the popular one is to have a baby shower. Usually it is difficult for a mother to buy everything needed for the new baby, and the shower allows others to help her. If it is a surprise party, her friends will find out from her husband or a family member whether or not the date of the party is good for her. Only women attend baby showers, where they play games, eat cakes, and watch the mother open presents.
美国人有许多庆祝新生儿诞生的方式。最常见的是为准妈妈所举办的给婴儿送礼物的聚会。通常一位母亲很难买齐新生儿所需的一切，因此这种聚会就为亲友提供了帮她的机会。如是一个让准妈妈意外惊喜的聚会，她的亲友会从她的家人或丈夫那儿了解到适合她举办聚会的日子。这种聚会只有女性亲朋参加，大家一起玩游戏，吃蛋糕，看准妈妈打开给婴儿的礼物。

2.2. Many mothers often register their baby items with their favorite stores or even online. This is a good way for her friends to find out what kind of gifts she wants. If the items are expensive, several people will go together to purchase one gift.
许多母亲常常在她们喜欢的商店，甚至在网上登记购买婴儿商品。这样十分有利于她的朋友了解到她想要什么礼品。如果东西贵，就几个人一起为她买一个礼物。

2.3. Formal shower invitations often include a picture of an umbrella, which may symbolize that the mother will be "showered" with gifts. Showers are held about three months before the baby is born.
正式的 *baby shower* 请柬常常带有小雨伞的插图，它意味着给准妈妈的礼物犹如绵绵细雨纷纷而至。这种聚会一般都在婴儿出生前三个月举办。

3. *RSVP* 是四个法文字的缩写，在课文里是动词。相当于"Please reply to this invitation"。意思是"请予回复"。在邀请函中，RSVP 后面是电话号码。所以在接到邀请邮件后，出于礼节你必须确认你是否参加。

4. *to register with a store*（在商店注册礼品账户）连锁商店通常以会员注册的方式为消费者提供信息和个性化的服务。另外随着生活节奏的加快，客户可以向商家发送购物信息，并约定送货时间，得到商家的快捷、省时、方便的服务。

5.1. *store* 译为商店，是常用词。在美国无论大的、小的、各种商品的商店都用此词。

例：

1) grocery store	食品杂货店	2) sporting goods store	体育用品店
3) toy store	玩具店	4) electronics store	电器用品店
5) pet store	宠物店	6) home improvement store	建材用品店
7) department store	百货店	8) liquor store	酒店
9) natural food store	绿色食品店	10) import shop	进口商品店
11) dollar store	一元店	12) bookstore	书店
13) furniture store	家具店	14) shoe store	鞋店
15) candy store	糖果店	16) clothing store	衣服店
17) appliance store	家用电器店	18) gift shop	礼品店
19) jewelry store	珠宝店	20) cookware store	厨房用具店

5.2. 此外，在美国还有许多常用的描述商店的词。

例： 1) supermarket 超市 2) pharmacy or drugstore 药店
3) mall 购物中心 4) outlet 厂家直销店
5) farmer's market 农贸市场 5) thrift store 旧货店；廉价店

6. *car seat* (儿童乘车安全椅) is a special seat for a baby or young child that protects the child while traveling in a car. US federal law requires all children to be strapped into a car seat, and each state has specific laws about its use.
它是放在汽车内的儿童安全座。为保证儿童的乘车安全，北美国家要求的一种在汽车内使用并可移动的儿童座椅。美国联邦政府规定儿童乘车过程中必须坐在由汽车安全带固定好的儿童安全乘车椅中，各州的法律也有对此相应的具体规定。

7.1. *ship* 在课文中是动词，译为运送；运输。to ship means to send the goods by ship, plane, or truck. to ship 并不完全是海运，其他方式的运输也可用 ship。

7.2. *shipment* 为装载的货物。
例： Several shipments of books arrived at the bookstore.
几批书籍已运到了书店。

8. *to watch for* 表示等候，对……等待；关注。
例： 1) The crossing guard watches for students to cross the road safely.
交通协管员关注小学生安全过马路。
2) We must watch for forest fires.
我们一定要警惕森林火灾。

9. *blue, pink, yellow* 在美国，若即将出世的是个男婴，那么房间布置,服装置办都将会以蓝色调为主；若将出世的是女婴，则是以粉色调为主。若是婴儿出生前未知其性别，则先选用黄色和浅绿色置办衣物，等婴儿出生后，再使用蓝色或者粉色调。

10.1. *either* 可用作形容词、代词、副词和连词。

10.1.1. 用作形容词。起定语作用，常放在单数名词前。
例： You may use either book.
两本书你可以随便用一本。

10.1.2. 用作代词。范围多限定于两者之间，常用作主语。

例：Either of the knives is useful.

两把刀都有用。

10.1.3. 用作副词，只用于否定句中，表示“也（不）”。

例：I don’t know how to speak French. She doesn’t either.

我不会讲法语，她也不会。

10.2.1. *either...or...* 是连词词组，在连接两个并列的单数名词作主语时后面动词用单数。

例：Either be quiet or leave the hospital, please.

要么保持安静，要么离开医院。

10.2.2. 此外，*either...or...* 还可连接两个并列谓语。

例：You can either ride a bike or take a bus there.

你可以骑车或坐公共汽车去那里。

11. *although* —“regardless the fact that”引导的从句放在主句前后均可，有时还可放在句中。although 不能与“but；however”连用，但可与“yet，still”连用。

例：1) Although I ate a big lunch, I was hungry again very soon.

尽管我午饭吃了很多，可是我很快又饿了。

2) He often helps me with my English, although he is quite busy.

他尽管相当忙，但是还常常帮我学英语。

Exercises 1

I. Answer the following questions.

1. Who is hosting the baby shower?
2. When is the baby shower?
3. Who is attending the baby shower?
4. Does Stephanie know about the shower?
5. Why does Aunt Laura think the baby is a girl?

6. How many gifts did Aunt Laura buy?
7. Who is the car seat from?
8. What store did Stephanie register with?

II. Write the key points of this e-mail thread.

III. Fill in the blanks.

1. Her best friend ________ two gifts for her.
2. A good ________ for a baby shower is a car seat.
3. Stores will ship the gifts ________ the baby shower.
4. He hopes his aunt ________ attend.
5. Blue baby items are for a ________.
6. Laura asks her to watch ________ the shipment.
7. Don't tell her about the baby shower; it's a ________.
8. She noticed all the clothes ________ pink.

IV. Fill in the missing information.

Dear Marie,

I am hosting a baby shower for Megan on March 3 at 2:00 p.m. It would be wonderful if you could attend.

Love,

________ Ashley,

I would love ________ attend. Is it ________ surprise baby shower? Is Megan registered ________ a store?

________,

Marie

V. Choose the correct answer. Only one answer is correct.

1. Before their baby shower, mothers usually ________ their favorite stores.
   A. register from　B. register with　C. register to　D. register for
2. Blue clothing means the parents are ________.
   A. having a girl　B. hating a boy　C. having a boy　D. having the boy
3. Baby showers are usually held ________ house.
   A. in a sisters　B. at a sister's　C. for a sister's　D. to a sisters
4. What color are items for baby girls?
   A. They are pink.　B. They are blue.　C. They are yellow.　D. It's pink.
5. Did Aunt Laura order four gifts?
   A. No, she ordered two.　B. No, she ordered one.
   C. No, she ordered three.　D. No, she ordered two for herself.
6. The car seat is too expensive. I can only afford to buy ________ clothing ________ a blanket.
   A. neither, or　B. either, nor　C. either, or　D. neither, nor
7. The store will ________ gifts to the baby shower.
   A. ship　B. ships　C. shipped　D. shipping
8. What did you ________ to buy as a gift?
   A. follow　B. work　C. go　D. choose

VI. Translate the following from English into Chinese.

1. I will be hosting a surprise baby shower at my house for my sister Stephanie on April 10.
2. I did not take much notice of her suggestions at the meeting.
3. I'll put up a notice about the meeting soon.
4. He received two month's notice from the landlord.
5. She watches the kids for us occasionally.

VII. Translate the following from Chinese into English.

1. 安妮又点了一杯红葡萄酒。
2. 请把桌子上的所有报纸整理好。
3. 这张邮票是姑妈给我的礼物。

4. 你发现他早早就离开了晚会了吗？
5. 美国公司正密切关注中国的发展。

Writing Tips

Punctuation in E-mails	
ALL CAPITAL LETTERS	Indicate yelling (usually inappropriate); also emphasize something
: Colon	Used as punctuation after formal and business salutations ("Dear Mr. Smith:"); also introduces lists and information that is set off
, Comma	Used as punctuation after a informal salutation ("Dear Mom,") and after a closing ("Sincerely,"); also separates a series of items
... Ellipsis point	Indicates an interruption in thought, a pause, or a sense of sadness, irony, or frustration
! Exclamation point	Indicates surprise, excitement, irony, or happiness
- Hyphen	Separates ranges of numbers
—Dash	Set off explanations; also indicate an interruption in thought or a quick comment
( ) Parentheses	Set off information
? Question mark	Indicates a question
" " Quotation marks	Indicate a phrase, quotation, or irony
!!, ?? Repeated punctuation	Used informally to express extreme surprise or confusion

E-mail Thread 2

Subject: Emma Grace Smith!
From: Amber@cmail.com
Date: June 28, 2012
To: Laura@cmail.com
Aunt Laura, Joshua and Stephanie went to the hospital yesterday morning. Joshua sent an e-mail at midnight with the news, "It's a girl." (We knew that was coming!) This just in: **Emma Grace Smith 6/27/12 @ 11:16 p.m., 6 pounds, 12 ounces, 18.25 inches**

Joshua said Stephanie is tired, but she and the baby are healthy and happy. Emma has 10 fingers and 10 toes and lots of hair. They will be in the hospital till tomorrow. I visited them this afternoon and will send you pictures. Love, Amber

Subject: Congratulations!
From: Laura@cmail.com
Date: June 28, 2012
To: Stephanie@cmail.com
Stephanie and Joshua— Amber just sent me pictures of Emma from her cell phone. Your daughter is a cutie! Uncle Mark, Grandma, and I will visit you tonight to see your "new arrival." Congratulations to both of you! Love, Aunt Laura & Uncle Mark

New Words 2

1. congratulation [kənˌgrætju'leiʃən] *n.* 庆贺；祝贺
2. cutie ['kjuːti] *n.* 可爱的孩子
3. ounce [auns] *n.* 盎司
4. toe [təu] *n.* 脚趾头

Phrases and Expressions 2

1. cell phone 手机
2. new arrival 新来者；新生儿

Proper Names 2

1. Emma Grace Smith 史艾玛
2. Joshua 乔舒亚
3. Uncle Mark 马克叔叔

Notes 2

1. *cutie* 在这里作名词，指可爱的人。cutie 的形容词是“cute”，意思是形容女孩子是“可爱的，漂亮的”。在英语中，形容人长得好看的形容词有很多。常用的对女性有“beautiful，pretty”而对男性则是“handsome，cool，sharp”。最常用的词是 *cute*，因为 cute 只是夸奖某人逗人可爱，没有那些敏感的意思。

Exercises 2

I. Answer the following questions.

1. When did Stephanie have the baby?
2. What is the baby's name?
3. When did Joshua send Amber an e-mail?
4. Is the baby a girl or a boy?
5. What does the baby look like?
6. Who visited the new parents in the afternoon?
7. Who will visit the new parents tonight?
8. How did Amber send pictures of Emma to Aunt Laura?

II. Write an e-mail to your friend after she just had a baby girl.

Key to E-mail Thread 1 Exercises (for Reference)

I. Answer the following questions.

1. Stephanie's sister Amber is hosting the baby shower.
2. The baby shower is on April 8, from 1:00 to 4:00 p.m.
3. Grandma, Aunt Laura, and Stephanie's friends are attending the baby shower.
4. No, Stephanie does not know about the baby shower; it's a surprise.
5. Aunt Laura thinks the baby is a girl because most of the baby items are pink.
6. Aunt Laura bought two gifts, one from her and one from Grandma.
7. The car seat is from Grandma.
8. Stephanie registered with the Baby Gear store.

II. Write the key points of this e-mail thread.

- Amber is hosting a surprise baby shower at her house for her sister Stephanie.
- The shower is on the afternoon of April 8.
- Amber invited Grandma, Aunt Laura, and Stephanie's friends to the baby shower.
- Stephanie is registered with the Baby Gear store in Boston, Massachusetts.
- Aunt Laura and Grandma said they would attend the shower.
- Aunt Laura ordered two gifts from the Baby Gear store. The car seat is from Grandma, and the clothing is from Aunt Laura.
- Amber will watch for the store's shipment of the gifts.
- Aunt Laura thinks the baby is a girl because the baby items are pink.

III. Fill in the blanks.

1. Her best friend <u>ordered</u> two gifts for her.
2. A good <u>gift</u> for a baby shower is a car seat.
3. Stores will ship the gifts <u>to</u> the baby shower.
4. He hopes his aunt <u>will</u> attend.
5. Blue baby items are for a <u>boy</u>.
6. Laura asks her to watch <u>for</u> the shipment.

7. Don't tell her about the baby shower; it's a surprise.
8. She noticed all the clothes were pink.

IV. Fill in the missing information.

Dear Ashley,

I would love to attend. Is it a surprise baby shower? Is Megan registered with a store?

Love,

Marie

V. Choose the correct answer. Only one answer is correct.

1. B　2. C　3. B　4. A　5. A　6. C　7. A　8. D

VI. Translate the following from English into Chinese.

1. 四月十号我将在我家为姐姐斯蒂芬妮举办一个让她惊喜的宝宝庆生会。
2. 我没太注意她在会上的提议。
3. 我一会儿把会议通知贴出去。
4. 他收到了房东让他两个月后搬出的通知。
5. 她有时帮我们照看一下孩子们。

VII. Translate the following from Chinese into English.

1. Anne ordered another glass of red wine.
2. Put all the newspapers on the table in order please.
3. The stamp is a gift from my aunt.
4. Did you notice him leaving the party early?
5. American companies are watching Chinese developments closely.

Translation of E-mail Thread 1 (for Reference)

译文：

邮件 1-1

主题：意外惊喜的庆生会
发件人：安布尔
日期：2012 年 3 月 15 日
收件人：劳拉

亲爱的劳拉姑妈，

四月八号我将在我家为姐姐斯蒂芬妮举办一个让她惊喜的宝宝庆生会。希望你和奶奶能来参加。(我也邀请了斯蒂芬妮的一些朋友)。

这是具体时间和地址：

四月八号下午一点到四点
麻省波士顿苏麦客街 123 号
请在四月一日前答复。

另外，斯蒂芬妮已在波士顿的盖尔婴儿用品店注册了一个礼品账户。

爱你们的，

安布尔

邮件 1-2

主题：意外惊喜的庆生会
发件人：劳拉
日期：2012 年 3 月 18 日
收件人：安布尔

你好，安布尔，

我和奶奶很愿意来参加这个为斯蒂芬妮举办的聚会。

我从盖尔婴儿用品店订购了两件礼物。他们会将奶奶送的儿童安全乘车座和我送的婴儿套装送到你们家。你能否关注一下这些物品？

我还注意到斯蒂芬妮所选的婴儿用品不是粉色就是黄色调的。她一定怀的是女孩吧。我们都觉得无论是男孩还是女孩都非常好。

爱你的，

劳拉姑妈

Key to E-mail Thread 2 Exercises (for Reference)

I. Answer the following questions.

1. Stephanie had the baby at 11:16 p.m. on June 27, 2012.
2. The baby's name is Emma Grace Smith.
3. Joshua sent Amber an e-mail at midnight.
4. The baby is a girl.
5. The baby has 10 fingers, 10 toes, and lots of hair; she is a cutie.
6. Amber visited the new parents in the afternoon.
7. Aunt Laura, Uncle Mark, and Grandma will visit the new parents tonight.
8. Amber used her cell phone to send pictures of Emma to Aunt Laura.

Translation of E-mail Thread 2 (for Reference)

译文：

邮件 2-1

主题：史艾玛
发件人：安布尔
日期：2012 年 6 月 28 日
收件人：劳拉

劳拉姑妈，

乔舒亚和斯蒂芬妮昨天早上去了医院，午夜的时候他送来了这条消息：“是个女孩儿！”（我们早就有这个预感。）

下面是刚收到的消息：

史艾玛
出生日期和时间：2012/6/27 晚上 11:16
体重：6 磅 12 盎司
身长：18.25 英寸

乔舒亚说，“虽然斯蒂芬妮有些疲倦，可是她和宝宝都很健康，愉快。艾玛有十个手指，十个脚趾和浓密的头发。她们后天出院。”我今天下午去医院看望了她们母女。我会发些她们的照片给你们。

爱你的，

安布尔

邮件 2-2

主题：祝贺！
发件人：劳拉
日期：2012 年 6 月 28 日
收件人：斯蒂芬妮

斯蒂芬妮，乔舒亚：

安布尔刚刚用她的手机发了几张照片。你们的女儿是个非常可爱的小家伙。我、奶奶和马克叔叔今晚会去探望你们，也要看看新来的“小公主”。

祝贺你们！

爱你的，

马克叔叔，劳拉姑妈

Lesson 3

Entertainment
休闲活动

Learning Objectives

In this lesson, you will learn the following:

- How to invite someone to have dinner or attend an event at a home
  私人晚餐或活动邀请
- How to accept an invitation
  接受邀请
- How to give directions
  讲解行程路线
- How to pay for a private event
  私人活动的费用
- What some American social activities are
  美国人的社交活动

E-mail Thread 1

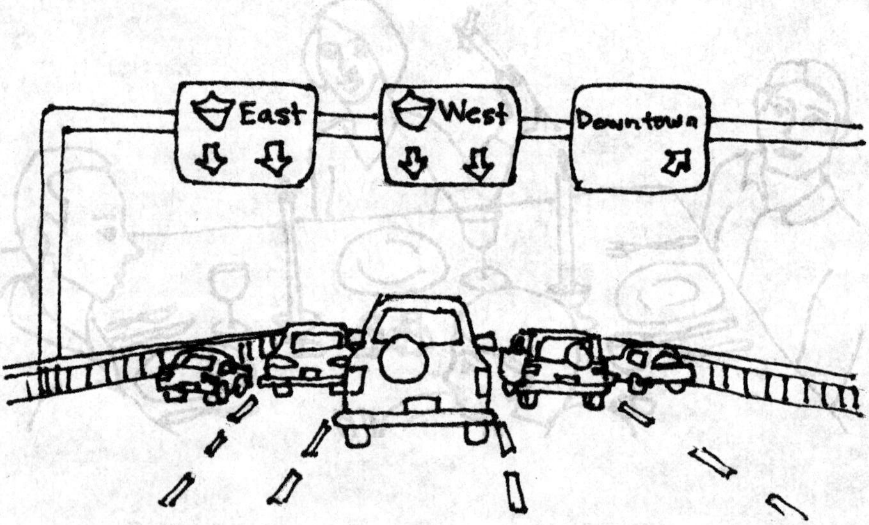

Subject: Evening of Dinner and Chinese Culture
From: Maria@cmail.com
Date: January 8, 2012
To: Donald@cmail.com
Dear Donald, Your daughter Sophia told us that you and Anita will be taking a tour to China next month and you'd like to know a little more about Chinese culture before you leave. We had a great time in China last year, and we'd love to share some travel tips. I could even teach you a few Chinese phrases. We can show you pictures, too. I love talking about China! Can you make it this Saturday, January 14, at 6:00 p.m.? Sunday is also open for us. I'll make a Chinese dinner and green tea. (Let me know if there's anything you can't eat.) We live off Washington Blvd. From the highway, take the downtown exit and go west. Turn right (north) onto Washington. Turn right onto Pine Tree Rd. (across from the supermarket). Turn left onto Peony Dr. Turn right onto Meadow Dr. Our house is number 2254, and it is the first house on the left after the corner. Maria & Carl 2254 Meadow Dr. 555-0102

Subject: Re: Evening of Dinner and Chinese Culture
From: Donald@cmail.com
Date: Maria@cmail.com
To: January 9, 2012
Maria and Carl, Thank you for your generous offer to share your China travel experiences with us before we

leave for our tour. We would love to get together to see your pictures and learn a little Chinese. Saturday the 14th would be great!!

We eat everything. Can we bring something?

Thanks again,

Don and Anita Jones
Phone: 555-0151

P.S. Thanks for the great directions. We live on the Westside, so you are an easy drive.

New Words 1

1.	corner	['kɔːnə]	*n.*	街角；拐角处
2.	culture	['kʌltʃə]	*n.*	文化
3.	phrase	[freiz]	*n.*	短语
4.	share	[ʃɛə]	*v.*	交流；分享
5.	supermarket	['sjuːpəˌmɑːkit]	*n.*	超市
6.	tour	[tuə]	*n.*	旅游

Phrases and Expressions 1

1.	downtown exit	市区出口路
2.	generous offer	慷慨帮助；盛情邀请
3.	to get together	聚在一起
4.	to have a great time	玩得很开心
5.	to take a tour	去旅游
6.	travel tips	旅游提示；旅游建议

Proper Names 1

1.	Anita Jones	艾妮塔·琼斯

2. Carl 卡尔
3. Donald (Don) 唐纳德（唐）
4. Maria 玛丽亚
5. Meadow Dr. 原野路
6. Peony Dr. 牡丹路
7. Pine Tree Rd. 松树街
8. Sophia 索菲娅
9. Washington Blvd. 华盛顿大道
10. Westside 城西边

Notes 1

1. *food habits* (饮食习惯): Planning a dinner party can be difficult because many Americans exclude different foods from their diets for health and philosophical reasons. Vegetarians don't eat meat because they object to killing animals or to using large amounts natural resources to raise cattle. Vegans don't eat meat and any products produced by animals, including honey, eggs, dairy products, and fish sauce. People with heart problems limit how much fat they eat, and those with diabetes limit how much sugar they eat. Others concerned about their health may only eat organic foods, or they may only eat "raw foods," which are not heated above 118 degrees Fahrenheit (48 degrees Celsius).
不少美国人因为健康和心理因素不食用某些食品，所以准备一顿请客的晚餐则是一件并不容易的事。比方说，有些素食者禁食肉类，是因为他们对宰杀牲畜的方式或对畜牧业耗费了大量的自然资源有异议。有些素食甚至禁食畜牧业的副产品像蜂蜜、蛋类、奶制品及鱼露。患心脏疾病的人对脂肪的摄取量有限制，而患有糖尿病的人对糖的摄取量也有限制。另一些人出于为自身健康而考虑，仅食用绿色食品，或者烹调温度未超过 48 摄氏度（118 华氏度）的食品。

2. *giving directions* (行程路线): Americans like complete directions that contain distances, landmarks, compass directions, street names, and every turn.
美国人喜欢讲解完整细致的行程路线，具体到距离、特别地形标志、方向、街道名称及每个转弯。

3. *street names* (街名): Many American streets are named after presidents, trees and plants, and historical people or places. Streets can also be numbered (for example, "Fifteenth Street"). In suburban areas, the street names may not have any meaning and merely sound like nice places to live (for example, "Carefree Circle," "Happy Way"). Street names end in various suffixes, more or less indicating their size or shape.

许多美国街道常常以总统的名字、树名、植物名或历史上的名人、地方命名。也有些是按数字顺序命名的。例如，第十五街。在市郊，街道名称则仅仅本着听起来是个人人向往并愿意居住的街道，例如，无忧街、开心路。

此外用于路/街/大道的词也有不少，通常与它的长短、形状有关。常用的词有：

例： 1) Rd. = road (A road that goes between cities, towns, and rural areas) 连接城市、城镇及乡村的公路）

2) Ave. = avenue (A wide road within a city or town; it may indicate roads that go only north-south or east-west) 城市里的大道

3) Blvd. = boulevard (较宽的市区大路)

4) St. = street (A road that goes in both directions within a city or town) 城市内的街道

5) Dr. = drive (A road in a residential area) 通往私人住宅的路

6) Cir. = circle (只有一个入口街道)

7) Ct. = court (只有一个入口弯行街道)

8) Ln. = lane (较窄的街道或胡同)

9) Way = way (路线)

4. *foreign languages* (*外语*): Most Americans don't speak a second language, and if they do, it is probably Spanish because of the many immigrants from Latin America. Americans are used to traveling to places where English is spoken, and many are uncomfortable traveling in countries where English is not common.

多数美国人除了英文以外，不会说第二种语言。要是会说，也很可能是西班牙语。因为这样的美国人多半是拉美后裔。由于在非英语国家旅游之不便，美国人通常去英语国家旅游。

5. *bringing a gift to a dinner party*: When invited to a dinner party, it is polite to ask whether you can bring anything, such as a side dish or alcoholic beverage. Most hosts will decline the offer, but guests usually bring a bottle of wine or flowers anyway.

当被邀请参加晚宴时，最礼貌的行为是问一下邀请人是否需要带样小菜或酒水。大多数主人都会婉言谢绝，但是作为客人通常还是应带一瓶红酒或一束花为佳。

6. *Chinese culture*: 美国人最想了解中国文化的具体内容有中国人的礼仪和习俗，我国各种各样的传统节日，特别是民族节日。另外还想知道中国的传统事物：比如武术、书法、中国结、京戏脸谱、兵马俑、景泰蓝、玉雕、中国红灯笼等。

7. *to make* 是及物动词，又是多义词，用法很多。在课文中，*make it this Saturday* 意思是约在周六。*to make a dinner and tea* 意思则是准备晚餐和茶。

例：1) Mary made a beautiful cake.
玛丽做了一个漂亮的蛋糕。
2) I didn't make any promises.
我没有作任何承诺。
3) We just made the last bus.
我们正好赶上末班公交车。
4) He makes $700 a week before taxes.
他每周税前的收入是七百美元。
5) Peter hopes to make the debate team this year.
彼得希望今年能成为辩论队的成员。

8. *to be open* 在课文中是形容词，意思是有空闲时间（"to be free" or "not engaged"）。还有以下意思："not shut；free to be used；ready to take in new ideas；available"。

例：1) The assistant manager job at Walmart is still open.
沃尔玛的助理经理的职位仍是个空缺。
2) This question is still open.
这仍然是一个尚未解决的问题。
3) Is the store open from 9 a.m. to 7 p.m.?
那家商店是从上午九点营业到晚上七点吗？
4) Jim has a very open mind.
吉姆的思想很开放。
5) He is always open to suggestions.
他总是愿意接受各种建议。

9. *to live off* 和 *to be off* 在课文中 *off* 相当于"on"，意思是住在华盛顿大道。此外，*live off* 又是一个固定动词词组，意思是"to subsist on"；以……为生；维持。它也有"附近区域"意思。

例：1) Most Asians live off rice.
多数亚洲人以大米为主食。
2) My grandmother lives just off Central Avenue.
我祖母就住在中心大街附近。
3) The museum is just off the highway. It's right next to the highway exit.
博物馆离高速公路很近。就在高速公路出口旁边。

10. *highway* 在这里指高速公路时速 55 英里/小时到 75 英里。各州根据车的密度而定。在美国用于公路或高速公路的词很多。常用词有：
1) expressway
2) freeway
3) parkway
4) superhighway

11. *to turn (right/north/etc.) onto* 和 *to turn into*: "to turn onto" is used when giving directions and means to exit one road and enter another. "To turn into" means to become or change into something else.
"*to turn onto*" 在解释行程路线时所用，即从某条路拐上另一条路。"*to turn into*" 某种东西或事物演变成另外一种东西或事物。

例：1) Turn north onto Main Street.
往北拐上市区主路。
2) When she is angry, she turns into a monster.
她生气的时候就变成"怪物"。

12. *corner* 意思是拐角处，常用于说明某一地方的方位。常同 corner 搭配的介词。

例：1) in the corner (内角，室内的角落)
2) after the corner (拐弯后；路口)
3) at/on the street corner (街角；路口)

13. *China travel* 是指在中国旅游的整体概念，也可以讲 *travel in China*。如果两个词都是大写，则指中国旅行社。

14. *experiences* 在这里指经历，是可数名词（something that a person has done or taken part in）。*experience* 作不可数名词时是指经验“to feel; to undergo”。

例：1) The two experiences aren't comparable.
这两次经历不能相提并论。
2) I have gained some experience while teaching here.
在这儿教书，让我获得了一些经验。
3) Tom already has two years' experience as a salesperson.
汤姆已有两年做销售员的工作经验。
4) I didn't experience much pain when the dentist took out my tooth.
牙医为我拔牙的时候，我没感到非常疼。

15. *P.S.* 是 postscript 的缩写，中文意思就是附笔、备注，又可解释为附言、后记。最开始是指用在信尾的补充内容，现在用途更广泛了，凡是补充说明都可以用。

16. *you are an easy drive*: 在句子中，*you* 是指你居住的地方。*drive* 在这里是名词，意思是驾车。*easy* 是定语，修饰 drive，意思是很容易就开到了。在这儿 *easy* 意思还是“简单；快捷；省事”。

例：1) Macaroni and cheese is an easy meal to fix.
做奶酪意大利面是很省事的饭。
2) Because it's only one stop on the subway, it's an easy trip.
因为乘地铁只一站，所以很快就到。

Exercises 1

I. Answer the following questions.

1. Who is hosting the dinner party?
2. Besides eating dinner, what is the purpose of getting together?
3. What days are open for Maria and Carl to host the dinner party?
4. Is there any food that Donald and Anita cannot eat?
5. What street do Maria and Carl live off?

6. What part of town do Donald and Anita live on?
7. What did Donald and Anita ask?
8. Is it a difficult drive from Donald and Anita's house to Maria and Carl's house?

II. Write the key points of this e-mail thread.

III. Fill in the blanks.

1. Before I travel, I like to learn ________ a country's culture.
2. The only Chinese ________ I know are *ni hao* and *zai jian*.
3. Thank you for inviting us—we had ________ great time at your dinner party.
4. The guidebook ________ good travel tips for traveling in China.
5. I live at the ________ of First and Main Streets.
6. When you travel to China, will you ________ a tour or travel by yourself?
7. A spoiled child doesn't like to share toys ________ other kids.
8. The party is Friday. Can you make ________?

IV. Fill in the missing information.

Hi Brandy,

You mentioned that you would like to learn a few Chinese phrases. I could teach you some at 2:00 p.m. on Saturday at my house. Can you make it then?

Best,

Julie

Hi Julie,

Thank you for your generous ________. Yes, I can make it then.

Do you live ________ Fillmore Street? That's ________ easy drive for me. I can ________ the downtown exit off the highway.

Thanks again,

Brandy

V. Choose the correct answer. Only one answer is correct.

1. The supermarket is ________.

   A. on the corner B. in the corner C. on a corner D. in a corner

2. I haven't seen Stacey since we ________ last month.

   A. made together B. went together C. had together D. got together

3. From the highway, take the downtown ________.

   A. emit B. outlet C. exit D. way out

4. Did you take ________ of New York City?

   A. a travel B. a tour C. a visit D. a sight

5. Everyone had ________.

   A. the great time B. a big time C. a great time D. the good time

6. She made me ________.

   A. the happy invitation B. the happy offer

   C. a generous invitation D. a generous offer

7. To save money, we ________ a hotel room.

   A. have to share B. would better share

   C. will live D. are going to live

8. Sorry, I don't ________.

   A. speak British B. speak Chinese C. say British D. say Chinese

VI. Translate the following from English into Chinese.

1. We live off Washington Blvd. From the highway, take the downtown exit and go west.
2. Can we take a cycling tour in Hang Zhou next month?
3. It's full here and can I share the table with you?
4. He felt he couldn't offer what she wanted.
5. The couple are quite open with each other about their feelings.

VII. Translate the following from Chinese into English.

1. 汤姆去年夏天在华盛顿做导游。
2. 我们可以租个房子分摊一下房租费用。
3. 房间的一角放着一个桌子。
4. 你每天起床后叠被子吗？
5. 我无法拒绝给我提供的北京免费行程！

Writing Tips

Invitations	
Who	Identify who is invited, including children.
What	State the type of event, for example, a formal or informal party, a dinner, an evening of drinks and dessert, or a special event or fund-raiser.
When	State the date and time (and include the ending time of formal events).
Where	Give the address and directions or a map.
Why	Explain whether the event is being held for a special reason, such as a birthday, a surprise party, or a fund-raiser.
How much	For events that cost money (for example, house concerts and fund-raisers), state the cost or suggested donation.
How to pay	For events that cost money, identify when and where to send the payment and what type of payments are accepted.
What to bring	State whether guests are expected to contribute anything to the event.

E-mail Thread 2

Subject: House Concert: Irish Musician Sean Murphy, August 17
From: Jason@cmail.com
Date: July 28, 2012
To: Tiffany@cmail.com

To All Our Neighbors and Friends,

This is to let you know about a concert we will host at our house on August 17. It is a rare opportunity to hear Irish musician extraordinaire Sean Murphy. He loves the intimate setting of a house concert.

If you've seen him live in concert before, then you know what a great evening this will be! He's made a new album—not yet out—and there may be some sneak previews at this concert...

We hope to have a good turnout because these concerts are how Sean pays for his trip around

the US. It should be a great evening! The details are: August 17, 7:00 p.m. 36 Bach Monument Ave., Houston, TX 77000 Tickets: $15 IN ADVANCE; $18 at the door Please make your check out to Sean Murphy and send it to us at the address above. Because this is a private residence, there are a limited number of chairs; we'd appreciate your bringing folding chairs to sit on. We're having a potluck, so please bring whatever you'd like to drink and a dish of munchies to contribute to the evening's festivities. —Jason and Nikki Please share this with/forward to anyone who might be interested. Thanks!

Subject: Re: House Concert: Irish Musician Sean Murphy, August 17
From: Tiffany@cmail.com
Date: August 1, 2012
To: Jason@cmail.com
Hi Jason, Thanks for the invitation. We're sending in our check today. I haven't heard of Sean Murphy, so I asked my brother about him. (He always recommends music to me). He said, "GO!" Tiffany

New Words 2

1. contribute [kən'tribjuːt] *v.* 提供；捐助
2. extraordinary [ekstrɔːdiː'nεə] *adj.* 杰出的

3.	festivity	[fes'tiviti]	*n.*	庆祝活动
4.	intimate	['intimit]	*adj.*	亲切的；舒适的
5.	munchies/snacks	['mʌntʃiz/snæks]	*n.*	点心；零食
6.	musician	[mjuː'ziʃən]	*n.*	音乐家
7.	opportunity	[ˌɔpə'tjuːniti]	*n.*	时机，机会
8.	rare	[rɛə]	*adj.*	稀有的；罕见的
9.	turnout	['təːn'aut]	*n.*	出席者

Phrases and Expressions 2

1. a new album 新专辑
2. a potluck “百家宴”
3. a private residence 私人住宅区
4. folding chairs 折叠椅
5. sneak previews 先睹（为快）

Proper Names 2

1. Irish 爱尔兰的
2. Jason 杰森
3. Nikki 妮可
4. Sean Murphy 肖恩·墨菲
5. Tiffany 蒂法尼

Notes 2

1. *house concert* (家庭音乐会): House concerts have become popular in America. Hosts invite a small group to their house to hear a traveling musician perform. The guests bring food and beverages to share, and they pay the musician at the concert. The musician keeps all or most of the money (unlike at a concert, where the sponsor takes a percentage), and the guests enjoy the intimate setting.

在美国越来越流行家庭音乐会。主办者邀请一部分人到家里聆听旅行音乐家的表演。大家一起享用各自带来食品和饮料，并分摊付给音乐家的费用。与通常的音乐会不同，没有中间人参与，由此音乐家将得到全部或绝大部分酬劳。与此同时，听众也享受这种亲近音乐家及音乐的形式。

2. *potlucks*: Americans frequently host informal "potlucks," in which the hosts invite friends to their home for a party or event and ask each guest to bring a beverage (usually alcoholic) and/or whatever side dish they wish to make. Guests share the food; the "luck" is that something tasty is in each pot.
美国人常常喜爱举办由客人们各自带来一个拿手菜及酒水的聚餐活动。大家都可以品尝每个人带来的美食。"幸运—美味"取之于每个盘子。

3. *limited space available* (空间有限，位置有限) means that only a certain number of tickets will be sold or seats will be available, and people should buy their tickets early.
意思是只出售一定数量的票或只能提供一定数量的座位，因此你应尽早购票。

Exercises 2

I. Answer the following questions.

1. Who is invited to the house concert?
2. What kind of music does Sean Murphy play?
3. How does Sean pay for his trip around the United States?
4. What is the cost of a ticket that is bought in advance?
5. What should guests bring?
6. Will Sean play any new songs?
7. Can neighbors and friends share the e-mail with anyone else?
8. Who recommended that Tiffany see Sean?

II. Write an e-mail announcing an event you will host at your home.

Key to E-mail Thread 1 Exercises (for Reference)

I. Answer the following questions.

1. Maria and Carl are hosting the dinner party.
2. Besides eating dinner, the purpose of getting together is for Donald and Anita to learn about Chinese culture.
3. Saturday or Sunday are open for Maria and Carl to host the dinner party.
4. Donald and Anita eat everything.
5. Maria and Carl live off Washington Blvd.
6. Donald and Anita live on the Westside.
7. Donald and Anita asked if they could bring something.
8. No, it is an easy drive from Donald and Anita's house to Maria and Carl's house.

II. Write the key points of this e-mail thread.

- Donald and Anita Jones have a daughter named Sophia. Sophia told Maria that her parents would be taking a tour to China next month. Sophia also said her parents would like to learn about Chinese culture.
- Maria invited Donald and Anita to her house so she could share travel tips and taught them a few Chinese phrases. She loves to talk about China.
- Maria asked Donald and Anita if they could make it for dinner on Saturday, January 14, at 6:00 p.m. She said that Sunday was also open to get together.
- Maria will make a Chinese dinner and green tea. She asked if there was anything Donald and Maria couldn't eat.
- Maria gave Donald and Anita directions to her house.
- Donald thanked Maria for her generous offer.
- Donald and Anita can get together on Saturday the 14th.
- Donald said he and Anita ate everything. He asked if they could bring something.

III. Fill in the blanks.

1. Before I travel, I like to learn <u>about</u> a country's culture.
2. The only Chinese <u>phrases</u> I know are *ni hao* and *zai jian*.

3. Thank you for inviting us—we had a great time at your dinner party.
4. The guidebook has good travel tips for traveling in China.
5. I live at the corner of First and Main Streets.
6. When you travel to China, will you take a tour or travel by yourself?
7. A spoiled child doesn't like to share toys with other kids.
8. The party is Friday. Can you make it?

IV. Fill in the missing information.

Hi Julie,

Thank you for your generous offer. Yes, I can make it then.

Do you live off Fillmore Street? That's an easy drive for me. I can take the downtown exit off the highway.

Thanks again,

Brandy

V. Choose the correct answer. Only one answer is correct.

1. A 2. D 3. C 4. B 5. C 6. D 7. A 8. B

VI. Translate the following from English into Chinese.

1. 我们住在华盛顿大街附近。从高速公路的出市区出口下高速公路，然后往西。
2. 下个月我们能否骑自行车游杭州？
3. 这的餐桌都被坐满了，我能同你拼桌吗？
4. 他感到他无法满足她的需求。
5. 这对夫妻在感情上是相互坦诚的。

VII. Translate the following from Chinese into English.

1. Tom worked as a tour guide in Washington last summer.
2. We can rent a house and share the rent.
3. A table sits in a corner of the room.

4. Do you make the bed every day?
5. I can't turn down the offer of a free trip to Beijing!

Translation of E-mail Thread 1 (for Reference)

译文：

邮件 1-1

主题：晚宴及中国文化
发件人：玛丽亚
日期：2012 年 1 月 8 日
收件人：唐纳德

亲爱的唐纳德，

你的女儿索菲娅告诉我们，下个月你和安妮塔要去中国旅行，并希望能在走之前了解一些有关的中国文化。去年我们在中国度过了一段非常愉快的时光，我们十分愿意与你们分享一些旅行经验。我甚至能教你说几句中国话。我们还可以给你看我们中国之行的照片。我很愿意与你们聊聊中国！

一月十五号星期六下午六点你们能来吗？我们星期日也有空。我会准备中餐并用绿茶招待你们。（请告知你们有没有什么忌口的。）

我们住在华盛顿大道附近。从高速公路市区出口下高速公路往西开，右拐（朝北）进入华盛顿。右拐接松树街（对面是个超市）。左拐接牡丹路，再右拐接草坪路，我家的门牌号是 2254，街角左边第一家。

玛丽亚，卡尔
原野路 2254 号
电话号码：555-0102

邮件 1-2

主题：回复：晚宴及中国文化
发件人：唐纳德
日期：2012 年 1 月 9 日
收件人：玛丽亚

玛丽亚，卡尔，

谢谢你们这样盛情地在我们中国之行前，提供与你们分享中国游经验的机会。我们非常愿意与你们聚在一起，看些照片和学几句中国话。你们所选定的（十五号星期六）时间相当合适。

我们没有任何忌口的。我们能带点什么嘛？

再致谢意，

唐纳德，安妮塔·琼斯
电话号码：555-0151

附言：谢谢你清楚的行程路线。我们住在城西，因此很容易就开到你家了。

Key to E-mail Thread 2 Exercises (for Reference)

I. Answer the following questions.

1. Neighbors, friends, and anyone who might be interested are invited to the house concert.
2. Sean Murphy plays Irish music.
3. House concerts pay for Sean's his trips around the United States.
4. A ticket bought in advance costs $15.
5. Guests should bring folding chairs, whatever they would like to drink, and a dish of munchies.
6. Sean may have a sneak preview of songs from his new album.

7. Yes, neighbors and friends can share the e-mail with anyone who might be interested.
8. Tiffany's brother recommended that she see Sean.

Translation of E-mail Thread 2 (for Reference)

译文:

邮件 2-1

主题：家庭音乐；爱尔兰音乐家—申墨菲—8/17
发件人：杰森
日期：2012 年 7 月 28 日
收件人：蒂法尼

邻居们和朋友们，

我们要告诉大家，八月十七号,我们将在家里举办一个家庭音乐会。这是聆听爱尔兰奇才音乐家肖恩·墨菲难得的机会。他非常喜爱这种亲切形式的音乐会。

如果你以前观看过他本人的音乐会，你能想象得出这将是一个多么美妙的夜晚。在这个音乐会上你可能会欣赏到一些他尚未公演的最新音乐专辑……

我们希望这是一场座无虚席的音乐会，因为这些音乐会的收入将用于支付肖恩·墨菲在美的旅行。你将会有一个令人难忘的夜晚！

具体安排如下：
时间：八月十七日晚七点
地址：得州休士顿巴哈纪念碑街 36 号，邮编 77000
票价：提前购票十五元；入场时购票十八元
请将抬头为肖恩·墨菲的支票寄到以上地址。

座位有限。

由于私人寓所椅子有限，我们非常感谢若你能用自带的折椅。我们还会有一个庆祝晚餐，所以请你为这个晚间庆祝活动带你喜爱的饮料和小吃。

——杰森和妮可

请与对此有兴趣的朋友分享这个信息。谢谢!

邮件 2-2

主题：回复：家庭音乐；爱尔兰音乐家——肖恩·墨菲—8/17
发件人：蒂法尼
日期：2012 年 8 月 1 日
收件人：杰森

你好，杰森：

谢谢你的邀请。今天我们就会把支票寄出来。因为我没听说过肖恩·墨菲，所以问了我弟弟（他总是向我推荐好音乐)。弟弟说，很值得去听。

蒂法尼

Lesson 4

Sports
运动

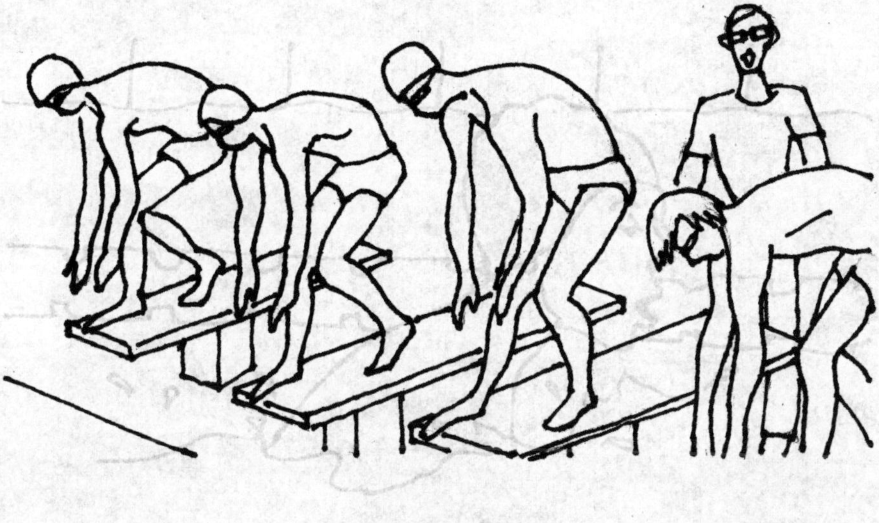

Learning Objectives

In this lesson, you will learn the following:

- How recreational sports teams coordinate team activities
  组织业余运动队活动
- How to order apparel for a sports team
  订购运动队队服
- How to schedule recreational sports events
  安排业余体育活动
- What some swimming terms are
  游泳运动术语

E-mail Thread 1

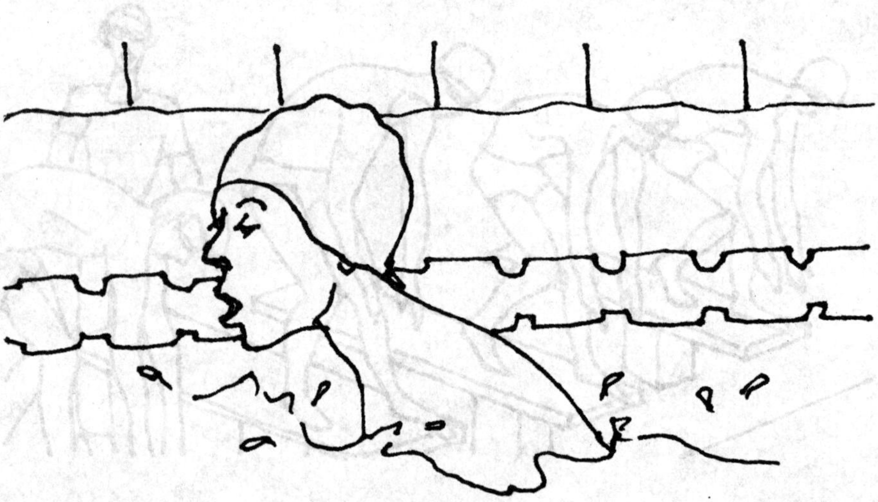

Subject: Team Caps and T-Shirts Are In
From: TeamCoach@cmail.com
Date: June 8, 2012
To: <Parents>
Dear Parents, We just received a new supply of team swimming caps in both latex and silicone, as well as a new supply of team T-shirts. If you are a recent addition to the team and haven't received your cap and T-shirt, please see your group coach, who will have a supply of these. Or go see Assistant Coach Devin at the pool at Lincoln High School during swimming-lesson hours (4:30-6:30 p.m.); he will be able to help you. Regards, Coach Jim

Subject: Re: Team Caps and T-Shirts Are In
From: SwimmingMom@cmail.com
Date: June 11, 2012
To: CoachJim@cmail.com
Dear Coach Jim, My son Ryan lost his original cap, and he needs a larger T-shirt. (He just keeps growing!) Are replacements available for purchase? If so, I'd like to order 1 silicone cap and 1 large T-shirt. Please send me the price of each, and I will bring a check to the next swimming lesson. Thank you! Angela P.S. The team is doing great—thanks for your hard work!

New Words 1

1.	addition	[ə'dɪʃən]	*n.*	附加
2.	apparel	[ə'pærəl]	*n.*	衣服；服装；衣着
3.	available	[ə'veiləbl]	*adj.*	有空的；可得到的
4.	check	[tʃek]	*n.*	支票
5.	latex	['leitɛks]	*n.*	天然橡胶；乳胶；乳液
6.	order	['ɔːdə]	*v.*	订购；订货
7.	original	[ə'ridʒənl]	*adj.*	最初的；本来的
8.	parent	['pɛrənt]	*n.*	父亲；母亲；家长
9.	purchase	['pɜtʃəs]	*n.*	买；购买
10.	replacement	[rɪ'pleismənt]	*n.*	代替者；代替物
11.	silicone	['sɪlɪˌkon]	*n.*	硅胶
12.	supply	[sə'plaɪ]	*n.*	生活用品；供应品
13.	terminology	[tɜmə'nɑlədʒɪ]	*n.*	术语；专门用语
14.	T-shirt	[ti-ʃɜt]	*n.*	短袖圆领运动衫；T 恤

Phrases and Expressions 1

1. group coach 小组教练
2. swimming cap 游泳帽
3. swimming-lesson hour 游泳课时间表
4. team cap 队帽（统一设计并购置的队帽）
5. team coach 总队教练

Proper Names 1

1. Angela 安吉拉
2. Devin 戴文
3. Jim 吉姆
4. Lincoln High School 林肯高中
5. Ryan 瑞恩

Notes 1

1. *recreational sports* (业余体育运动): Many American adults and children play sports through recreational teams that are coordinated by schools, local governments, or local or national sports organizations. Popular recreational sports are soccer, softball, T-ball, swimming, and hockey. These teams usually require members to buy a uniform or a T-shirt in the team's colors.
很多美国成人，孩子都会参加业余体育运动队。这些运动队通常是由全国或者地方的体育协会、地方政府、学校出面组织。最普及的体育运动有足球、女子棒球、儿童棒球、游泳和曲棍球。一般各个运动队都要求队员购置队服或者代表各自运动队颜色的 T 恤衫。

2. *e-mailing groups of people* (给设定小组群发信息): Many e-mail programs let the sender put the e-mail addresses of many people under a group name, so that the sender only has to type the group name in the recipient line instead of each person's e-mail address. For example, a team coach would create a group called "Parents," and the e-mail would be sent to each parent in the group. Each parent can reply to the coach separately.
不少电子邮件程序的设计都可让发信人建立一个专用名称，其专用名称包括的是一组个人电子邮件的地址，因而当发信人需给全组成员发同样信息时，仅在发送栏中列出专用名称即可。例如，若教练在网上建立了“家长”的专用名称，每位在“家长”上注册了电子邮件地址的家长都会在同一时间内收到教练发出的信息，然而只有教练才能收到各位家长的回复信息。

3. *numbers* (数字): In formal writing, such as business correspondence, the numbers one through nine are spelled out. In informal writing, the numerals 1–9 are often used.
在类似于商业信函的正式格式中，数字 1–9 要用英文拼写出来。而在非正式的格式中常常使用 1–9 这些阿拉伯数字。

4.1. *Team caps and T-shirts are in*: "Team caps and team T-shirts" 是指一个队统一购置的游泳帽和 T 恤衫。

4.2. *in* 在这里是副词，意思是“……到货了”。In 常用于介词，但作为副词 in 用法也较多。

例：1) Please come in.
请进。

2) I called on him, but he wasn't in.
我去拜访他，但他不在家。

3) The shipment is in at last.
货物终于来了。

4) Miniskirts are in again.
迷你裙又时髦起来了。

5. *addition* 是名词。作为可数名词时，该词在意思上不仅指物，还可指人。*addition* 通常同“latest”、“new”和“recent”组成词组，后面跟介词 to。

例：1) The baby is a new addition to our family.
这个婴儿是我们家新添的人丁。

2) My dad built an addition on our house because we need a study.
因为我们需要书房，我爸爸又在房子边上接出了个房间。

6. *go see* 是不符合语法的常用口语句型，表示“去找，去见，去联系”(“to visit”or“to meet with”)。该句型省掉了 *and* 一词。类似常用的流行语还有：“go get...”

例：1) Wow, how come your eyes are so red? You had better go see a doctor as soon as you can.
天啊，你的眼睛怎么那么红，你最好马上去看一下医生。

2) I will go get something for lunch.
我要去买点什么当午饭。

7. *He just keeps growing*: *To keep (doing something)* 又是常用口语句型，相对正规句型是“to keep on doing something”。该句型有两个概念：

7.1. 表示某状态

例：Nowadays, the price of food just keeps going up, and we have to watch every dime.
最近食品越来越贵，我们得省着点花钱。

7.2. 表示一直在做某事的动作

例：The 911 operator will keep talking to the lost child until the police officer can reach him.
在警察找到走失孩子之前，911（相当于中国的 120）值班员一直在电话上安慰他。

7.3. 此外，类似的常用句型还有“to keep somebody doing something”。

例：I'm keeping them waiting at the gate.
我让他们在大门口等候。

Exercises 1

I. Answer the following questions.

1. Who just received a supply of team caps and T-shirts?
2. What are the two kinds of team swimming caps?
3. What is this team's sport?
4. Who is the coach, and who is the assistant coach?
5. When are the swimming-lesson hours?
6. What do "new additions" do if they haven't received their caps and T-shirts?
7. Why does Ryan need a new cap?
8. How will Angela pay for the new cap and shirt?

II. Write the key points of this e-mail thread.

III. Fill in the blanks.

1. The team just received ________ new supply of T-shirts.
2. Jim is the team ________.
3. I ________ my cap and need to order a replacement cap.
4. Team swimming caps come in both latex and ________.
5. Are T-shirts ________ for purchase?
6. I need a ________ T- shirt because this one is small.
7. Is that your original ________ or a replacement cap?
8. Please send me the price of the T-shirt, and I will bring a ________ to the next lesson to pay for it.

IV. Fill in the missing information.

Dear Parents,

Team members are required to wear team T-shirts to all swimming events, including lessons. Please make sure your son or daughter has a T-shirt and wears it.

Thank you,

Coach Matthew

Dear Coach Matthew,

My daughter Rachel lost her ________. I'd like ________ order 1 T-shirt. Please send me the ________, and I will bring a ________ to the next swimming lesson.

Thank you,

Amy Jones

V. Choose the correct answer. Only one answer is correct.

1. Ryan is ________ to the swimming team.
   A. an old addition B. a new addition C. a new additional D. an old additional
2. Swimming-lesson ________ are 9:00–11:00 a.m.
   A. hours B. services C. groups D. class
3. I need to order a(n) ________ supply of T-shirts.
   A. other B. another C. recent D. new
4. What will Devin do?
   A. He will. B. He will help you. C. She helps you. D. He helps you.
5. Caps come in both latex and ________.
   A. sillycone B. silicon C. silicone D. selicon
6. Thanks for your hard ________.
   A. work B. job C. help D. order
7. She needs a ________ T-shirt than this one.
   A. large B. larger C. small D. largest

8. The team is doing ______.
   A. greatly   B. good   C. success   D. great

VI. Translate the following from English into Chinese.

1. Please send me the price, and I will bring a check to the next lesson.
2. The moment we saw the house, we knew we wanted to buy it.
3. I've only got a week's supply of tablets left.
4. I lost interest in go chess a year ago.
5. It is really depressing to see that she lost the final yesterday.

VII. Translate the following from Chinese into English.

1. 我看到他几分钟前走的。
2. 从这个塔望去你可以看到几英里远的地方。
3. 当地为我们提供食品。
4. 如果有问题请找我。
5. 编辑和校对者常常要加班工作。

Writing Tips

Common Types of Attachments*	
Documents (.doc, .pdf, .txt, .wpd)	Used for various document files; the file extensions (i.e., *.xxx*) indicate which software was used to prepare the files; the file extensions listed here indicate Word, Adobe Acrobat, text, and WordPerfect files, respectively.
Compressed files (.zip)	Used for one or more large files that are archived and compressed into one file. Zip files need to be unzipped before opening.
Executable files (.com, .exe)	Used for command and program files, respectively; may contain harmful programs or viruses.

Media files (.mov, .mpg, .ppt, .wav)	Used for multimedia files; the file extensions listed indicate QuickTime, compressed movie/audio, PowerPoint presentation, and sound files, respectively.
Picture files (.bmp, .gif, .jpg, .tif)	Used for digital photographs and scanned images; the file extension varies with the software and the settings used to save the image; TIFF files are usually too large to e-mail.
Spreadsheets (.xls)	Used for Microsoft Excel spreadsheet files.
Websites and links	Not attachments; include in an e-mail for the recipient to click on to access them.

*Be careful when opening attachments, because viruses and malware are often transmitted through them, particularly through executable files.

E-mail Thread 2

Subject: Mountain Swim League Championship Meet August 24-26; Entry Deadline August 10

From: TeamCoach@cmail.com

Date: August 2, 2012

To: <Parents>

Attachment: schedule.pdf

Dear Parents and Swimmers,

The attached PDF document has the meet information for the Mountain Swim League Championship scheduled for August 24-26 at Spruce High School. This year, the meet will also double as the Intermountain State Games, and it should be a lot of fun for all attendees. It is also the last chance to qualify for either the state championships in Grand City or the state seasonal championships here in town.

We would like to encourage our entire team to participate, so team members from any of our groups may attend. The only exception is team members who already have met the state time requirements in all their events. We would like them to sit this one out because they have automatically qualified for the state games.

The host team is expecting swimmers from six different states, and it needs time to coordinate this large event. Therefore, please sign up for this meet no later than next Friday, August 10. We will not be able to guarantee that the host team will accept entries received after that date.

The attachment gives you directions to Spruce High School and information about eligibility, entry fees, registration procedures, and the schedule. If you have any questions, please ask Assistant Coach Devin, via e-mail (ACDevin@cmail.com), as soon as possible.

Best regards,

Coach Jim

Subject: Re: Mountain Swim League Championship Meet August 24-26; Entry Deadline August 10
From: SwimmingMom@cmail.com
Date: August 4, 2012
To: ACDevin@cmail.com
Dear Devin, Both my son Ryan and daughter Morgan would like to participate in the Mountain Swim League Championship Meet. I'd like to check whether Morgan is eligible to participate, because she participated at the state meet. Did she meet the state time requirements in all her events? Please let me know as soon as possible so I can register both of them by August 10th. Thank you, Angela

New Words 2

1. attachment [ə'tætʃmənt] *n.* 附属物；附件
2. attendee [ə'tendiː] *n.* 出席者
3. automatically [ɔːtə'mætikəli] *adv.* 自动地
4. championship ['tʃæmpiənʃip] *n.* 冠军赛，锦标赛
5. check [tʃek] *v.* 检查；检验；核对
6. coordinate [kəu'ɔːdineit] *v.* 协调
7. deadline ['dedlain] *n.* 截止期限；最后限期
8. direction [di'rekʃən] *n.* 方向
9. eligibility [elidʒə'biliti] *n.* 合格；资格
10. eligible ['elidʒəbl] *adj.* 合格的；适宜的

11.	exception	[ik'sepʃən]	*n.*	例外；被除外
12.	guarantee	[gærən'tiː]	*v.*	保证；商品保证；保证书
13.	league	[liːg]	*n.*	俱乐部联合会
14.	participate	[pɑː'tisipeit]	*v.*	参加；与
15.	qualify	['kwɔlifai]	*v.*	能有资格
16.	schedule	['skedʒul]	*v.*	安排；预定
17.	via	['vaiə]	*prep.*	通过；凭借

Phrases and Expressions 2

1.	entire team	全队
2.	entry deadline	报名截止日期
3.	entry fee	报名费
4.	host team	主队
5.	meet information	比赛信息
6.	PDF document	可移植文档格式文件
7.	registration procedures	报名手续
8.	sign up	报名；注册
9.	state seasonal championship	全州的季赛
10.	state time requirement	达到参加州赛标准
11.	Swim League Championship Meet	游泳冠军联赛
12.	swimming event	游泳比赛项目
13.	to sit this one out	不出席；不参加

Proper Names 2

1.	Grand City	格兰德市
2.	Intermountain State Games	中部山区的联赛
3.	Morgan	摩根（女孩子的名字）
4.	Mountain Swim League Championship	山地游泳冠军联赛
5.	Spruce Mountain High School	云杉山高中

Notes 2

1. *dates*（日期）：正式的日期书写只用阿拉伯数字，不用序数。然而，非正式日期书写时可用序数表达，例如 10th。书写日期的顺序是：星期、月、日。

2. *league championship* 常译为联赛或季赛。*league* 一词本身是联盟或俱乐部的意思。league championship 是指在联盟或俱乐部成员内部举行的冠军赛。

3. *games* 常用于复数，有两个主要意思："游戏；运动会"。当它指运动会时，同"sports meet"意思一样，只是在规模和范围上，games 要更大一些。

4. *to sit this one out* 是不参加这次比赛。*sit out* 是固定词组，意思是"不参与，在一边看"。

例：1) He'll sit out the next dance.
下一个舞他不准备跳了。
2) Would you mind if I sit out this dance?
我不跳这个舞，你不介意吧？

Exercises 2

I. Answer the following questions.

1. When is the Mountain Swim League Championship?
2. Which high school will the meet be at?
3. Who is encouraged to participate?
4. Who should "sit this one out"?
5. How many different states is the host team expecting swimmers from?
6. What is the last day to sign up for this meet?
7. How should parents contact Assistant Coach Devin?
8. What does Angela want to check?

II. Write an e-mail to a coach that asks about a swimming meet.

Key to E-mail Thread 1 Exercises (for Reference)

I. Answer the following questions.

1. The swim team just received a supply of team caps and T-shirts.
2. The two kinds of team swimming caps are latex and silicone.
3. This team's sport is swimming.
4. Jim is the coach and Devin is the assistant coach.
5. Swimming-lesson hours are 4:30–6:30 p.m.
6. "New additions" who haven't received their caps and T-shirts can see their group coach or Assistant Coach Devin.
7. Ryan needs a new cap because he lost his original cap.
8. Angela will pay for the new cap and shirt by bringing a check to the next lesson.

II. Write the key points of this e-mail thread.

- The team received a new shipment of team swimming caps and T-shirts.
- New team members who didn't receive caps and T-shirts can get them by seeing their group coach or Assistant Coach Devin.
- Ryan needs new cap and a larger T-shirt.
- Ryan's mother, Angela, would like to purchase replacements. She will pay for them by bringing a check to the next swimming lesson.

III. Fill in the blanks.

1. The team just received <u>a</u> new supply of T-shirts.
2. Jim is the team <u>coach</u>.
3. I <u>lost</u> my cap and need to order a replacement cap.
4. Team swimming caps come in both latex and <u>silicone</u>.
5. Are T-shirts <u>available</u> for purchase?
6. I need a <u>larger</u> T- shirt because this one is small.
7. Is that your original <u>cap</u> or a replacement cap?
8. Please send me the price of the T-shirt, and I will bring a <u>check</u> to the next lesson to pay for it.

IV. Fill in the missing information.

Dear Coach Matthew,

My daughter Rachel lost her T-shirt. I'd like to order 1 medium T-shirt. Please send me the price, and I will bring a check to the next swimming lesson.

Thank you,

Amy Jones

V. Choose the correct answer. Only one answer is correct.

1. B 2. A 3. D 4. B 5. C 6. A 7. B 8. D

VI. Translate the following from English into Chinese.

1. 请告诉我价钱，我会在下次上游泳课的时候，把支票带给你。
2. 我们一看就知道这就是我们想要买的房子。
3. 我只剩下一周的药了。
4. 我一年前就不想下围棋了。
5. 看到她昨天在决赛中失利真令人难过。

VII. Translate the following from Chinese into English.

1. I saw him leave a few minutes ago.
2. You can see for miles from the tower.
3. We were given the local food.
4. Please see me if you have problems.
5. The editors as well as the proofreaders often work overtime.

Translation of E-mail Thread 1 (for Reference)

译文：

邮件 1-1

主题：队服和队帽
发件人：总队教练

日期：2012 年 6 月 8 日
收件人：家长们

亲爱的家长们，

我们刚购置了一批印有统一设计的游泳帽和 T 恤衫。（游泳帽有橡胶和硅胶两种。）

如果你是刚参加的新队员没有领到过游泳帽和 T 恤衫，请从你们组的教练那里领取。你还可以在林肯高中下午 4:30 到 6:30 上游泳课的这段时间里，在游泳池的场地内与戴文联系，他也能帮助你。

此致，

教练吉姆

邮件 1-2

主题：回复：队服和队帽
发件人：泳队妈妈
日期：2012 年 6 月 11 日
收件人：教练吉姆

亲爱的吉姆教练：

我儿子瑞恩把发给他的游泳帽弄丢了，而且也需要一件大号的 T 恤衫。（他还在不断地长个。）有没有备用的可以购买？如果有我想买一顶硅胶游泳帽和一件大号的 T 恤衫。请告诉我价钱，我会在下次上游泳课的时候，把支票带给你。

谢谢，

安吉拉
（附言）：这个队很棒，感谢您的辛勤付出。

Key to E-mail Thread 2 Exercises (for Reference)

I. Answer the following questions.

1. The Mountain Swim League Championship is from August 24 to 26.
2. The meet will be at Spruce High School.
3. The entire team is encouraged to participate.
4. Team members who already have met the state time requirements should “sit this one out.”
5. The host team is expecting swimmers from six different states.
6. The last day to sign up for this meet is Friday, August 10.
7. Parents should contact Assistant Coach Devin via e-mail.
8. Angela wants to check whether her daughter Morgan is eligible to participate in the championship.

Translation of E-mail Thread 2 (for Reference)

译文：

邮件 2-1

主题：8 月 24 日到 26 日的山地游泳冠军联赛；报名截止日期 8 月 10 日
发件人：泳队教练
日期：2012 年 8 月 2 日
收件人：家长们
附件：PDF 文件

亲爱的家长和队员，

附带的 PDF 文件有八月二十四到二十六日在云杉山高中山地游泳冠军联赛的时间安排。今年比赛的规模是以往中部山区的联赛的两倍。这对所有参赛者都是一件很兴奋的事。

同时，这也是能否被选入参加在格兰德市的全州冠军赛或者本市全州季赛的最后一次机会。

除了已经在所有项目上都达到州里标准的队员以外，我们鼓励全队各组的队员参加，我们希望成绩已自动达到参加州赛标准的队员不出席此冠军赛。

主办队将接待六个州的游泳队员，需要一些时间筹备这么大的活动。为此请在八月十日周五前报名。我们不能保证八月十日以后主办队还会接受报名事宜。

附件中，有到云杉山高中的路线指南、参赛资格及费用，注册手续和时间安排。若有问题，请尽快用电子邮件与助理教练戴文联系（ACDevin@cmail.com）。

祝好，

教练吉姆

邮件 2-2

主题：回复：8 月 24 日到 26 日的山地游泳冠军联赛；报名截止日期 8 月 10 日
发件人：泳队妈妈
日期：2012 年 8 月 4 日
收件人：戴文

亲爱的戴文，

我儿子瑞恩和女儿摩根都想参加山地游泳冠军联赛。因为摩根参加过州赛，我想知道她是否还有参加这个联赛的资格。她在所有项目上都达到州赛标准了吗?

请尽快告知我，以便我能在八月十日给他们报上名。

谢谢，

安吉拉

Lesson 5

Online Shopping
网上购物

Learning Objectives

In this lesson, you will learn the following:

- What an online order looks like
  网上订购
- How to track an order
  追踪订货
- How retailers' customer service departments handle problems with an order
  购物中问题的处理
- How retailers follow up on problems with an order
  问题处理的善后工作
- What online surveys and privacy settings are
  网上民意调查及隐私保护设置

E-mail Thread 1

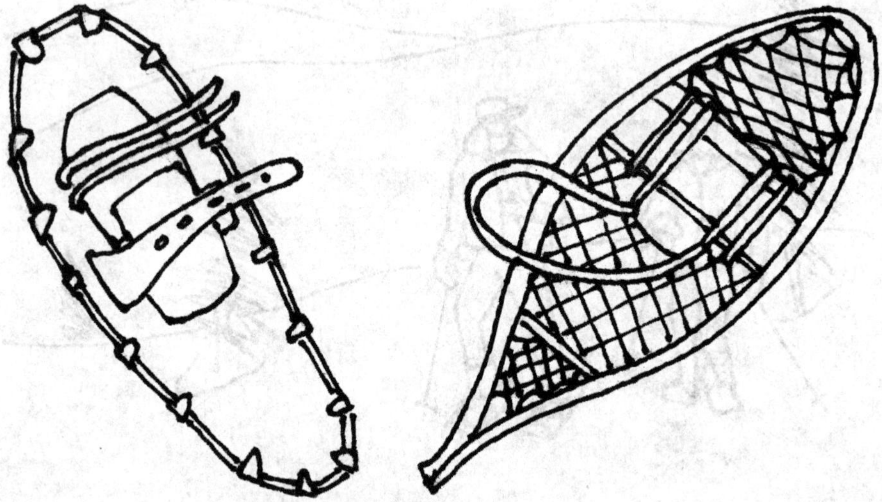

Subject: New Snowshoes!
From: RadBrad@cmail.com
Date: December 1, 2012
To: SnowshoerMiguel@cmail.com
Miguel, FYI, when we were talking about snowshoeing, you recommended two brands of snowshoes. Outdoor Gear's online outlet is having a sale this weekend on the Abominable Snowman brand, so I ordered a pair. You mentioned that the size of their snowshoes runs a little small, but I couldn't pass up 50 percent off. So I ordered them without trying them on at a store. I can't wait to use them—plan on going snowshoeing with me as soon as they arrive! Brad

Subject: Outdoor Gear Order Shipped: Order #70989
From: <Outdoor Gear Customer Service>
Date: December 3, 2012
To: RadBrad@cmail.com
Outdoor Gear 11 Stone Dr. #300 Austin, TX 78758 888-555-0175 customerservice@outdoorgear.com www.outdoorgear.com Dear Outdoor Gear Customer, We are happy to inform you that order #70989 has been shipped. We shipped your order via ground delivery, and you may track the shipment by clicking on the tracking number(s)

below. The shipper estimates that your order will take three business days to arrive, based on your shipping destination. Actual shipping time may vary.

Your tracking number is:
AZY5450057

If you have further questions, please do not hesitate to contact us at 888-555-0175.

Thank you for your order. We hope to be of service to you again soon.

Outdoor Gear
888-555-0175
www.outdoorgear.com

New Words 1

1.	brand	[brænd]	*n.*	商标；牌子
2.	estimate	['estimeit]	*v.*	估计；判断
3.	handle	['hændl]	*v.*	对待；处理
4.	hesitate	['heziteit]	*v.*	犹豫；有顾虑
5.	outlet	['autlet]	*n.*	销路；厂家直销店
6.	recommend	[rekə'mend]	*v.*	推荐；介绍
7.	residential	[rezi'denʃəl]	*adj.*	居住的；住宅的
8.	retailer	['riːteilə]	*n.*	零售商；零售店
9.	sale	[seil]	*n.*	卖；出售
10.	shipper	['ʃipə]	*n.*	发货人；运货人
11.	snowshoe	['snəuʃuː]	*n.*	雪鞋
12.	survey	[səː'vei]	*n.*	调查；向……作调查
13.	track	[træk]	*v.*	跟踪；追踪

Phrases and Expressions 1

1. 50 percent (%) off 打五折；半价
2. back-ordered item 延期交送货物
3. billing address 付款人的地址
4. business days 工作日，营业日
5. customer service 客户服务中心
6. FYI (for your information) 供你参考
7. gift card 礼物卡
8. grand total 总计
9. ground delivery 陆地/货车送货
10. online order 网上订货
11. online shopping 网上购物
12. privacy settings 私密保护设置
13. product description 产品描述
14. shipping destination 送货地点；终点
15. to base on 基于；以……（为）根据
16. to click on 点击
17. to follow up 跟踪服务；采取进一步措施
18. to pass up 放过；错过
19. to try something on 试穿

Proper Names 1

1. Abominable Snowman 雪人
2. Austin (Texas; TX) 奥斯汀
3. Brad Jones 布拉德·琼斯
4. Colorado Springs (Colorado, CO) 美国科罗拉多斯普林斯市
5. Miguel 米格尔
6. Outdoor Gear 户外用品店

Notes 1

1. *snowshoeing* 和 *snowshoes*: Snowshoeing has become a popular winter sport in America because it is easy to do and doesn't require much equipment. Modern snowshoes are made of a synthetic fabric stretched across a lightweight metal frame that straps onto boots. The snowshoes keep the snowshoer from sinking too deeply into the snow, and ski poles help with balance.
穿"雪地鞋滑雪"的运动在美国越来越流行。因为这个运动简单，不需要什么器械。现代的"雪地鞋"是网球拍状底和固定在靴子上的带子结合在一起的产品。这种"雪地鞋"能防止鞋在雪中陷得太深，滑雪杆则用来保持身体的平衡。

2. *Abominable Snowman* (雪人) is the mysterious Himalayan creature called the "Yeti." North America has its own version of this creature, called "Sasquatch" or "Bigfoot."
雪人是人们想象出的在神秘的喜玛拉雅山中的一种多毛怪物叫"野人"。北美版的叫"北美野人"或"大脚"。

3. *online outlet* (网上厂家直销) is a website where a retailer sells discounted and discontinued items.
销售商出售过时产品及减价产品的网页。

4. *ground delivery* (货车送货) indicates when items are shipped by truck, compared with two-day and overnight delivery, in which items are shipped by plane.
以货车送货的形式。两日和次日送货均为空运。

5. *tracking number* (追踪号): In this case, a *tracking number* is a number assigned to a shipment. Customers, shippers, and retailers enter it into the shipper's website to track where the shipment is and when it will be delivered.
在此处是专为这个出货的制定的一组号码。顾客、运货方及店家均可在网上用这组号码查询货物此刻所在地点和送到的时间。

6. *noun* + (*s*) (复数名词): In informal and scientific writing, "(s)" is used to indicate that there could be more than one of a given item. In formal writing, it is better to write out "noun or nouns" or to state the quantity.
在非正式和非文学书写格式中，名词后用"S"表示物品不止一件。而在正式英文书写格式中，最好写出物品的具体数量。

7. *recommend* 和 *introduce* 都有"介绍"之意，但意思不同。*recommend* 译为"推荐"，往往是你认为好的东西和好的人。显然，它的宾语不仅可以是人，也可以是物。而 *introduce* 只是客观地提供信息，不参与个人的意见。在社交中往往介绍两个陌生人互相了解和认识时，用 introduce。
例：1) I highly recommend Jason as a swimming coach.
我极力推荐杰森当游泳教练。
2) He introduced me to blues music.
他向我介绍了美国黑人音乐。

8. *tax* (税): Most US states apply sales tax to items sold within their jurisdiction.
差不多美国各州都有在本行政区内对出售商品加收销售税的规定。

9. *sale* 是个常用词，常常有降价的意思。另外，同 sale 组成的词组也很多。
例：1) a big sale 大甩卖
2) on sale 降价销售
3) Christmas sale 圣诞节促销
4) for sale 出售
5) yard sale 庭院销售

10. *off* 有低于……的价格的意思，因此 *50 percent off* 是低于原价 50%的意思，可译为打五折。如果是 30 percent off，应译为打七折。说到折扣，英汉表述法并不相同。

11. *I can't wait to...* 是常用口语句型，强调"某人迫不及待地想得到某东西或盼着某件事的发生"。
例：I can't wait to tell him the good news.
我迫不及待地想告诉他这个好消息。

12. *billing address* 和 *shipping address*: The billing address and the shipping address for an order can be different. For example, a person buying a gift will give his or her address as the billing address and the gift recipient's address as the shipping address.
付款人和收货人的地址可以不同。比方说，购买礼品的人要提供其地址作为付款人地址，而接受礼品人的地址则是收货人的地址。

13. *gift cards* (礼品券/卡): These popular gifts are similar to credit cards and are usually used at specific retailers. The person giving this gift buys a gift card that is worth a specific dollar amount (for example, $50) from a specific retailer. For example, the recipient can use a Walmart gift card only to buy items from Walmart. (But credit card companies offer gift cards that can be used anywhere the credit card is used.)
这种礼品卡非常流行，与信用卡相似并通常针对具体的零售商。通常一张某店家的礼品卡只能用于此店。送礼品卡有一定的金融面值。比方说 50 美元的礼品卡相当于 50 美元。但你若收到的是沃尔玛的礼品卡，那你只限于用在沃尔玛的购物。（信用卡公司也有礼品卡项目，这种礼品卡可在任何接受此种信用卡的店家使用。）

14.1. *order summary* (订货一览表): Retailers send customers an e-mail that confirms their online orders. Summaries may include the following information.
销售商发给顾客电子邮件，来确认顾客网上订购的货物。订货一览表包括以下信息：

Below is a summary of your order:	所订货物相关信息一览表：
Name: Brad Jones	名字：布拉德・琼斯
Outdoor Gear Order: #70989	户外用品订货序号：70989
Back-Ordered Items: No.___________	延期交货号：

Billing Address: 10 Green Dr., Colorado Springs, CO 80919
付款人地址：科州科泉市格林路 10 号，邮编 80919

Shipping Location: Residential	送货地点：居民区

Product Description: Abominable Snowman snowshoes
物品名称："雪人"牌雪鞋

Price:	+	220.00	价格：
Shipping:	+	15.00	运费：
Discounts:	–	110.00	折扣：

Tax:	+	12.50	税：
Gift Card(s):	–	0.00	礼卷（卡）：
Grand Total:	=	$137.50	总额：

14.2. *back-ordered item* (延期交送货物) is an item that is not in stock at the time of the order and will be shipped later. 目前没有库存，将晚些时间发货。

Exercises 1

I. Answer the following questions.

1. Why did Brad buy the snowshoes?
2. What brand of snowshoes did Brad buy?
3. What percentage was the discount?
4. Did Brad try on the snowshoes before ordering them?
5. When does Brad plan to go snowshoeing?
6. How was Brad's order shipped to him?
7. What is the tracking number for Brad's order?
8. What is the order number for Brad's order?

II. Write key points of this e-mail thread.

III. Fill in the blanks.

1. The online outlet is having a ________ this weekend.
2. I have to try on a bigger jacket; this brand's jackets run ________.
3. Click on the ________ to track your shipment.
4. If I ship it via ________, it will take five business days to arrive.
5. With tax and shipping, the ________ of my order is $11.
6. The snowshoes won't ship until next month ________ they are a back-ordered item.
7. Who do I ________ if I have questions?
8. I'm going to use my gift ________ to buy it. It will save me some money.

IV. Fill in the missing information.

Hey Anthony,

I'm planning to buy snowshoes at the end of winter, when they go on sale. Can you recommend a brand and where to buy them?

Melissa

Hi Melissa,

I recommend the Abominable Snowman brand. First, go to a store to try them on because they run a little ________. But order them from an online ________ because they usually give 50 ________ at the end of winter.

Have fun!

Anthony

V. Choose the correct answer. Only one answer is correct.

1. The store is having ________ this weekend.
   A. the large sale　B. sale　C. the sale　D. a big sale
2. You can't order one snowshoe; you have to order a ________!
   A. two snowshoes　B. pair
   C. pair snowshoes　D. pare of snowshoes
3. Your order ________ next month.
   A. will be shipped　B. has been shipped
   C. was shipped　D. is shipped
4. Can I use a ________ to purchase it?
   A. free card　B. gift　C. gift card　D. giftcard
5. Your order will take five ________ to arrive.
   A. work days　B. business days　C. work day　D. business day
6. We hope to be of service ________.
   A. to you soon　B. for you soon　C. with you soon　D. soon

7. Track your shipment by ________ on the link.
   A. pushing   B. pressing   C. clicking   D. klicking
8. I can't wait to ________ them!
   A. refuse   B. refusing   C. using   D. use

VI. Translate the following from English into Chinese.

1. If you have further questions, please do not hesitate to contact us at 888-555-0001.
2. Sleeping tablets are not recommended in this case.
3. December is the season for sales in Beijing.
4. We regret to inform you that your application has been rejected.
5. Most people are not very well-informed about the disease.

VII. Translate the following from Chinese into English.

1. 我推荐这个餐馆的火锅，很好吃。
2. 玛格丽特正在试穿你新买的外套呢。
3. 他们计划在五一节多休息三天。
4. 西安是许多外国人喜欢的旅游目的地。
5. 这个地区的气温常常变化。

Writing Tips

Types of Top-Level Domain Names*

.com	Used for companies and other commercial enterprises
.edu	Used for educational organizations
.net	Originally used for organizations providing network services but now also used for organizations and individuals
.org	Used mainly by nonprofit organizations but also used for organizations and individuals

*Domain names (for example, www.uibe.edu.cn) identify a computer, an organization, or an individual on the Internet. They have two main parts. Top-level domain names are the part on the right. Second-level domain names are the part on the left, and they reflect the name or mission of the organization or individual sponsoring the website.

E-mail Thread 2

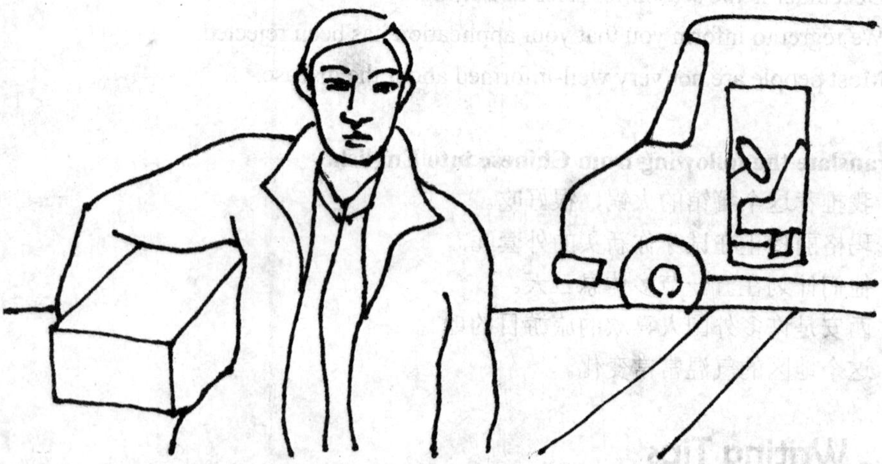

Subject: Customer Service Request
From: <Outdoor Gear Customer Service>
Date: December 10, 2012
To: RadBrad@cmail.com
Dear Outdoor Gear Customer, We received your request for assistance with order #70989 regarding exchanging your snowshoes for a larger size. An Outdoor Gear customer service agent will contact you by e-mail within 48 hours. The subject line of our agent's e-mail will contain the following information:

Customer Service Order #70989

If you do not see a customer service response in your in-box within 48 hours, please look in your spam or junk mail folder. (Many times our response ends up in these folders.) Our agent will provide you with a return authorization number, tell you whether replacement snowshoes are in stock, and give you return shipping instructions.

Thank you for contacting Outdoor Gear; we look forward to helping you resolve your problem.

Regards,

Customer Service
Outdoor Gear
888-555-0175
www.outdoorgear.com

Subject: Tell Us What You Think
From: <Outdoor Gear Customer Service Survey>
Date: December 29, 2012
To: RadBrad@cmail.com

We value your opinion! To ensure that you receive our e-mails, please add customerservicesurvey@outdoorgear.com to your address book.

Dear Outdoor Gear Customer,

At Outdoor Gear, your opinion is very important to us. As part of our commitment to excellence, we want to make sure our response met your needs. Please take a few moments to complete our survey. If you complete the survey by Tuesday, January 17, 2012, you will receive a free baseball cap wilh thc Outdoor Gear logo. Please follow the link below to take our survey:

www.outdoorgear.com/customerservicesurvey

Thank you for your interest in Outdoor Gear. We look forward to serving you again!

Customer Service
Outdoor Gear
888-555-0175
www.outdoorgear.com

Please do not reply to this e-mail. We cannot accept electronic replies to this e-mail address.

New Words 2

1.	assistance	[ə'sistəns]	*n.*	助理；协助
2.	commitment	[kə'mitmənt]	*n.*	承诺
3.	contact	['kɔntækt]	*v.*	联系；联络
4.	contain	[kən'tein]	*v.*	包含；包括
5.	ensure	[in'ʃuə]	*v.*	保证；确保
6.	link	[liŋk]	*n.&v.*	结合；连接
7.	logo	['lɔgəu]	*n.*	（公司）标志
8.	opinion	[ə'pinjən]	*n.*	见解；主张
9.	regard	[ri'gɑːd]	*n.&v.*	问候；致意
10.	request	[ri'kwest]	*n.*	要求；需求
11.	resolve	[ri'zɔlv]	*v.*	解决；解答
12.	response	[ri'spɔns]	*n.*	回答；答复
13.	spam	[spæm]	*n.&v.*	垃圾电子邮件
14.	survey	[səː'vei]	*n.*	调查；向……作调查
15.	value	['væljuː]	*n.&v.*	价值；重要性

Phrases and Expressions 2

1. authorization number 许可号码
2. baseball cap 棒球帽

3. customer service agent 客户服务代理
4. electronic reply 电子邮件回复
5. in stock 有库存
6. junk mail folder 垃圾电子邮件箱
7. replacement snowshoes 要更换的雪鞋
8. return instruction 退货须知
9. subject line 标题
10. to end up in 最终到达

Notes 2

1. *subject line* (标题) is the part of the heading that indicates the e-mail's main content.
是指电子邮件中的标题，标明邮件的主要内容。

2. *in-box* (收件箱) is the section of an e-mail program where incoming mail is viewed.
一般用来查看收到的电子邮件。

3.1 *to end up in* 是固定动词词组，后面的宾语表示一件事情的结果。
例：If you work like this, you will end up in the hospital.
如果你要这样做下去的话，你会病倒的。

4. *spam or junk mail folder* (垃圾电子邮件箱): Spam and junk mail are unsolicited e-mails, usually advertising products, that are sent to multiple mailing lists. Many e-mail providers have filters that put spam into a separate folder so that it doesn't clutter up the user's in-box.
垃圾邮件指未经要求送给大批有电子信箱的人群，其内容大多为产品所做的广告宣传。许多电子邮件服务网站都设立了存放垃圾邮件的独立邮箱，以避免收件箱中垃圾邮件的困扰。

5. *return authorization number* (退货许可号) is a number that retailers assign for approving and tracking returned items.
零售商提供的允许退货及跟踪退货的号码。

6. *address book* (通信录) is the section of an e-mail program that stores contact information.
用来汇集联系网址。

7.1. *to look forward to* 是动词短语，常在信函的结尾中使用。在这里 *to* 是介词，后面只能跟名词或动名词。

例：I am not looking forward to getting up early.
我不想早起床。

7.2. *to* 还有一个作用，就是连接动词不定式。

例：I'm trying to walk in my snowshoes.
我要试着穿雪鞋走一走。

Exercises 2

I. Answer the following questions.

1. What assistance does Brad need with his order?
2. Who will contact Brad and when?
3. Where should Brad look if he doesn't receive a customer service response in his in-box?
4. What will the customer service agent do?
5. Why did Outdoor Gear ask Brad to take a survey?
6. What will Brad receive if he takes the survey by Tuesday, January 17?
7. How long will it take Brad to complete the survey?
8. Can Brad reply to the e-mail that asked him to take the survey?

II. Write an e-mail from the customer service department that responds to a customer with a problem.

Key to E-mail Thread 1 Exercises (for Reference)

I. Answer the following questions.

1. Brad bought the snowshoes because Outdoor Gear's online outlet was having a sale that

weekend.

2. Brad bought the Abominable Snowman brand of snowshoes.
3. The discount was 50 percent off.
4. No, Brad didn't try on the snowshoes before ordering them.
5. Brad plans to go snowshoeing as soon as the snowshoes arrive.
6. Brad's order was shipped to him via ground delivery.
7. The tracking number for Brad's order is AZY5450057.
8. The order number for Brad's order is 70989.

II. Write the key points of this e-mail thread.

- Brad bought a pair of Abominable Snowman snowshoes that his friend recommended.
- Brad bought them at Outdoor Gear's online outlet.
- The snowshoes were 50 percent off that weekend.
- Outdoor Gear shipped his order via ground delivery.
- Brad's order should arrive in three business days.
- Brad can track the shipment by clicking on the tracking number.

III. Fill in the blanks.

1. The online outlet is having a <u>sale</u> this weekend.
2. I have to try on a bigger jacket; this brand's jackets run <u>small</u>.
3. Click on the <u>tracking number</u> to track your shipment.
4. If I ship it via <u>ground delivery</u>, it will take five business days to arrive.
5. With tax and shipping, the <u>grand total</u> of my order is $11.
6. The snowshoes won't ship until next month <u>because</u> they are a back-ordered item.
7. Who do I <u>contact</u> if I have questions?
8. I'm going to use my gift <u>card</u> to buy it. It will save me some money.

IV. Fill in the missing information.

Hi Melissa,

I recommend the Abominable Snowman brand. First, go to a store to try them on because they run a little <u>small</u>. But order them from an online <u>outlet</u> because they usually give 50 <u>percent off</u> at the end of winter.

Have fun!

Anthony

V. Choose the correct answer. Only one answer is correct.

1. D 2. B 3. A 4. C 5. B 6. A 7. C 8. D

VI. Translate the following from English into Chinese.

1. 您若有任何问题，请随时打这个电话：888-555-0001 跟我们联系。
2. 在这种情况下最好不用安眠药。
3. 在北京，十二月是大减价的季节。
4. 我们遗憾地通知你，你的申请没有通过。
5. 大多数人对这种疾病都不是十分了解。

VII. Translate the following from Chinese into English.

1. I recommend the hot pot in the restaurant—it's delicious.
2. Meg was trying on your new coat now.
3. They plan to take three more days off at May Day.
4. Xian is a popular tourist destination for many foreigners
5. The temperature in this region varies from time to time.

Translation of E-mail Thread 1 (for Reference)

译文：

邮件 1-1

主题：新雪鞋
发件人：拉德·布拉德
日期：2012 年 12 月 1 日
收件人：雪鞋滑雪人米格尔

米格尔，

你也知道当我们聊到买雪鞋时，你向我推荐了两种牌子。这个周末“雪人”牌的在户外用品网上减价出售，所以我就订了一双。我知道你提过他们的号比实际的小一点儿，可是我实在不想错过这个打五折的机会，没去店里试穿就订购了。

我期盼马上就能穿上新的雪鞋，你得准备好，我的雪鞋一到，我们就一起穿“雪鞋”滑雪去！

布拉德

邮件 1-2

主题：户外用品店购货发出：订货号 70989
发件人：户外用品店客户服务
日期：2012 年 12 月 3 日
收件人：拉德·布拉德

亲爱的顾客，

我们很高兴地通知您，订货号为#70989 的货物已用货车运送方式发出。您可以用下面的追踪号查询。根据您的地点，送货方估计大约在三个工作日后，您就能收到货物。实际上估计的运输时间并不百分之百准确。

您的追踪号是：AZY5450057

您若有任何问题，请随时用电话跟我们联系，我们希望今后能再次为您服务。

户外用品店
888-555-0175
www.outdoorgear.com

Key to E-mail Thread 2 Exercises (for Reference)

I. Answer the following questions.

1. Brad needs assistance exchanging his snowshoes for a larger size.
2. An Outdoor Gear customer service agent will contact Brad within 48 hours.
3. If Brad doesn't receive a customer service response, he should look in his spam or junk mail folder.
4. The customer service agent will provide a return authorization number, tell Brad whether replacement snowshoes are in stock, and give him return shipping instructions.
5. Outdoor Gear asked Brad to take a survey because his opinion was very important to the company; it is committed to excellence, and it wants to make sure it met his needs.
6. If Brad takes the survey by Tuesday, January 17, he will receive a free baseball cap with the Outdoor Gear logo.
7. It will take Brad a few moments to complete the survey.
8. No, Brad cannot reply to the e-mail that asked him to take the survey.

Translation of E-mail Thread 2 (for Reference)

译文：

邮件 2-1

主题：客户服务请求
发件人：户外用品店客户服务
日期：2012 年 12 月 10 日
收件人：拉德·布拉德

亲爱的顾客，

我们接到了您需要把您已订购雪鞋更换成大一号的要求。我们客户服务中心的服务代理人员会就此事在四十八小时内用电子邮件与您联系。电子邮件的标题将包括如下信息：

客户服务中心服务序号 70989

若您在四十八小时内仍未见客户服务中心的答复电子邮件，请在垃圾电子邮件箱查找一下。因为不少时候，我们的答复邮件被错送到了那儿。我们的服务代理人员将向您提供退货许可号码。也会告知您所要更换的“雪鞋”是否有货存及如何将需退换物品寄回。

感谢您与户外用品店联系，我们期待着帮您解决问题。

此致，

顾客服务中心
户外用品店
888-555-0175
www.outdoorgear.com

邮件 2-2

主题：告诉我们您的想法
发件人：户外用品店客户服务民意调查
日期：2012 年 12 月 29 日
收件人：拉德・布拉德

我们重视您的评价。为了保证能够收到我们的邮件，请您将这个信箱地址加到你的电子邮件通信录中。

亲爱的户外用品顾客，

对我们来说您对我们服务的评价非常重要。作为优良服务的一部分，希望我们的回复满足您的需求。请花点时间完成我们的调查。若您能在一月十七日，星期二以前完成这个客户调查，您就能获得一顶带有户外用品公司标志的棒球帽。作这个客户调查，请连接下列网址。

www.outdoorgear.com/customerservicesurvey

谢谢您对户外用品店的关注。我们希望今后能再次为您服务！

顾客服务中心
户外用品店
888-555-0175
www.outdoorgear.com

请勿回复此邮件。这个网址不能接受任何电子邮件。

Lesson 6

E-banking
网上银行业务

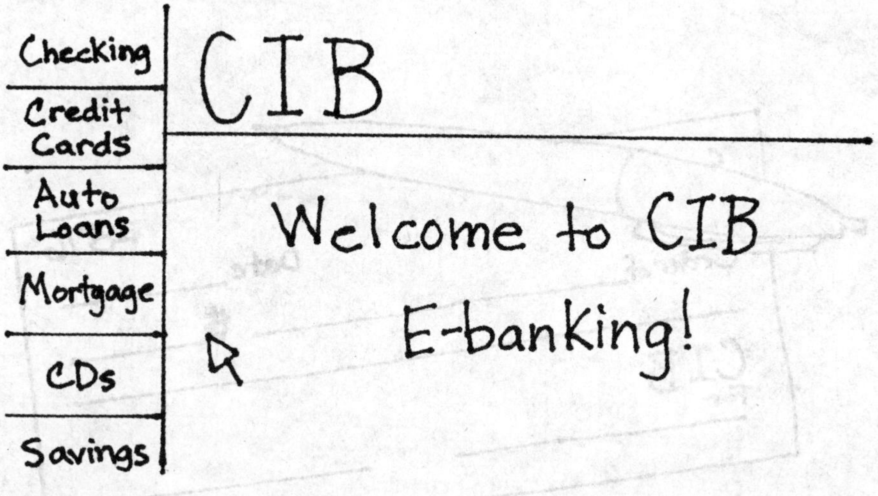

Learning Objectives

In this lesson, you will learn the following:

- How financial institutions market services to customers
  金融机构客户服务宣传
- How financial institutions e-mail financial statements
  金融机构的财务报表邮件
- How financial institutions confirm customers' electronic payments
  客户电子支付确认
- How financial institutions protect their customers' privacy
  客户隐私保护
- How financial institutions legally protect themselves
  金融机构合法自我防护

E-mail Thread 1

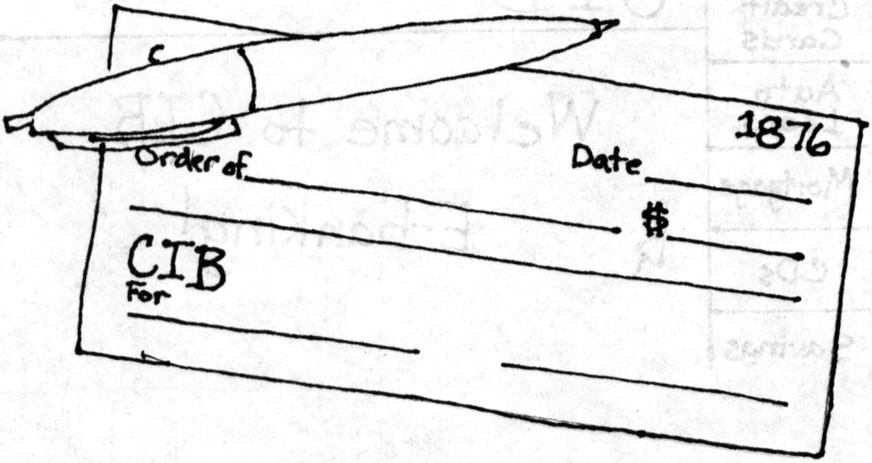

Subject: Are You Getting the Most Out of Your CIB Benefits?
From: CitizensIndustrialBank@cmail.com
Date: March 16, 2012
To: CourtneyWest@cmail.com

Courtney,

You are already receiving Preferred Checking Account Benefits from Citizens Industrial Bank (CIB). But did you know you could receive Preferred Checking Account Plus Benefits? You only have to do one of the following to receive them:

—use your CIB check card or CIB credit card to make everyday purchases or

—take out a loan.

Then you will receive Preferred Checking Account Plus Benefits such as

—our best interest rates on certificate of deposit accounts and

—discounts on vehicle loans for multiple cars.

Contact us at citizensindustrialbank@cmail.com to learn more about Preferred Checking Account Plus Benefits. It's easy!

Sincerely,

Citizens Industrial Bank
1-800-555-0185
www.citizensindustrialbank.com

For legal disclosures about our products and services, please visit our website at www.citizensindustrialbank.com/legaldisclosures.

Subject: Complimentary Home Mortgage Analysis
From: CitizensIndustrialBank@cmail.com
Date: April 16, 2012
To: CourtneyWest@cmail.com
Courtney, Citizens Industrial Bank (CIB) is committed to helping you meet your financial needs. Because you are a valued CIB customer, we are offering you a complimentary mortgage analysis. The analysis will determine whether your current mortgage still meets your needs. **Call us today at 1-800-555-0185.** We urge you to take advantage of your complimentary mortgage analysis. It's as easy as calling **1-800-555-0185**, our toll-free number that is only for CIB customers. We look forward to helping you explore your mortgage options. Sincerely, Citizens Industrial Bank 1-800-555-0185 www.citizensindustrialbank.com P.S. Call **1-800-555-0185** today. We are committed to helping you meet your mortgage needs. *For legal disclosures about our products and services, please visit our website at www.citizensindustrialbank.com/legaldisclosures.*

New Words 1

1. analysis [ə'næləsis] *n.* 分析；分析报告
2. benefit ['benifit] *n.* 好处；福利
3. confirm [kən'fəːm] *v.* 批准；确认

4. discount ['diskaunt] *n.* 折扣；打折扣
5. explore [iks'plɔː] *v.* 探索；探究
6. legally ['liːgəli] *adv.* 法律上；合法地
7. service ['səːvis] *n.* 服务
8. urge [əːdʒ] *v.* 极力主张；催促

Phrases and Expressions 1

1. certificate of deposit account 定期存单（CD）
2. check card 银行卡
3. credit card 信用卡
4. customers' privacy 客户隐私
5. electronic payment 电子支付
6. everyday purchase 日常消费
7. financial institutions 金融机构
8. financial statements 财务报表
9. legal disclosures 信息披露 （法律规定的）
10. mortgage analysis 按揭分析
11. mortgage options 按揭选择
12. multiple cars 多部汽车
13. to be committed to 责无旁贷地
14. to take advantage of 利用优势
15. to take out a loan 贷款；借贷
16. toll-free number 免费电话
17. valued customer 贵客
18. vehicle loans 车贷

Proper Names 1

1. Citizens Industrial Bank 公民产业银行
2. Complimentary Home Mortgage 免费房贷分析
3. Courtney West 科特妮·韦斯特
4. Plus Benefits 更佳优惠账户

5. Preferred Checking Account 优惠支票账户

Notes 1

1. *checking account benefits* (支票账户优惠): The more money a customer keeps in a checking account, the more benefits most US banking institutions give the customer. Benefits include free checks and discounts on service charges.
绝大多数美国银行都会向客户提供这样的优惠，即在银行支票账户的存款越多，福利越好。其中包括免费建立支票账户及在服务费的征收上获得百分之三到五不等的减免。服务费包括：使用 ATM 的月费；信誉分数查询费用等。

1.1. *preferred* 是形容词，意思是“首选的，最佳的”。

例：1) It is a preferred stock, not a common stock.
这是优先股，不是普通股。
2) It's preferred above all others.
在所有事物中首先要考虑这件事。

1.2. *preferable* 也是形容词，意思是“更可取的，更好的，更优越的”。

例：Poverty is preferable to poor health.
贫穷总比不健康好。

2. *everyday* 和 *every day* 有所不同。everyday 是形容词，常用作定语；而 every day 这一词组则用作状语。

例：1) Walking the dog is an everyday chore for Peter.
遛狗是彼得每天的差事。
2) Dennis has tennis practice every day this month.
这个月丹尼斯每天都有网球训练。

3. *to be committed to* 是一组固定词组，是“to devote”，“pledge”的意思。to 在这里是介词，因此后面的宾语只能是名词或动名词短语。

例：1) Big countries are committed to helping poor countries.
大国有义务帮助穷国。

2) Mr. Hopkins committed himself to raising money for the flood victims in Pakistan.
霍普金斯先生承诺要为巴基斯坦遭水灾的灾民募捐。

4.1. *urge* 是动词，意思是“催促，要求”。该词有两种常用用法。通常用法是：to urge somebody to do something

例：1) The weather was terrible in the mountains, so the park ranger urged us to leave right away.
山里的天气糟糕极了，护林员催促我们马上离开。

2) My friends urged me to apply for the intern job in California.
朋友们都力劝我申请那份加州的实习工作。

3) I urged them to visit Colorado instead of New York City this winter.
我极力主张他们冬天去科罗拉多看看，而不是纽约市。

4.2. 第二种用法有虚拟语气成分，该句型应当是 to urge that somebody (should) do something。类似词还有“suggest, propose, order, command”等。

例：The lawyer suggested that she should tell him everything.
律师建议她把一切告诉他。

5.1. *check card* (银行卡): When a customer purchases items with a check card (also called a “debit card”), the funds are withdrawn from the customer’s checking account.
当银行用户使用“个人扣账卡或称银行卡”消费时，所用金额将从用户的个人支票账户中扣除。若支票账户中无存款，客户将无法使用“个人扣账卡或称银行卡”消费。

5.2. *credit card* (信用卡): When a customer purchases items with a credit card (also called a “charge card”), the credit card company actually pays for the items, and the customer reimburses the credit card company about a month later. If the reimbursement is late, the company charges the customer interest until full payment is made.
“信用卡”也称“赊购卡”。当用户使用它购物时，实际上是信用卡公司先为用户付款。用户再在一个月后“归还”信用卡公司。若有拖欠信用卡公司会征收较高的利息直到全部还清为止。

6. *certificate of deposit* (又称 CD，定期存款单) is a type of savings account in which customers earn interest on the money in the account.

客户存入银行一笔钱款并以定期（三个月、半年、一年、两年不等）的形式获取利息。

7. *mortgage* (房贷): A mortgage is a type of loan for buying homes and property. The bank agrees to lend the customer money, and the customer agrees to give the bank the home or property if the customer cannot pay the loan.
一种用于房地产的贷款。银行借贷给客户，条件是若客户无力偿还房贷，其房产或地产将被银行没收。

8. *toll-free number* (免费电话): Organizations such as banks, telephone companies, and utilities companies set up toll-free numbers so that people can call them without charge; the organization pays for the cost of the call.
各种服务机构（例如：银行、电话公司、电力煤气公司等）均设有供消费者与其联系的免费电话号码，而服务机构则承担这些电话费用。

9. *legal disclosures* (信息披露): US law requires companies to disclose certain company policies that affect customers.
美国法律要求各公司颁布某些与消费者有关的公司条例。

Exercises 1

I. Answer the following questions.

1. Is Courtney West a customer of Citizens Industrial Bank?
2. What checking account benefits does Courtney currently receive?
3. Name one thing Courtney has to do to receive Preferred Checking Account Plus Benefits.
4. Name one Preferred Checking Account Plus Benefit Courtney would receive.
5. What is CIB committed to helping Courtney with?
6. Why doesn't Courtney have to pay for the mortgage analysis?
7. Who is CIB's toll-free number for?
8. Where are CIB's legal disclosures?

II. Write the key points of this e-mail thread.

III. Fill in the blanks.

1. The mortgage analysis ________ complimentary.
2. Please visit the bank's website for legal disclosures ________ the bank's products and services.
3. I get a discount ________ my vehicle loan because I have multiple cars.
4. I use my credit ________ to make everyday purchases.
5. Please take advantage ________ the complimentary mortgage analysis.
6. Does your bank have a toll-________ number?
7. Is that the best rate on a certificate ________ deposit account?
8. He urged me ________ take out a loan at his bank.

IV. Fill in the missing information.

Dear Customer Service Representative,

I am a customer of your bank and have a home mortgage with you. My wife and I have a new baby, and our financial needs have changed. Can you help me determine whether my mortgage still meets my needs?

Sincerely,

Sidney Ramos

Dear Sidney,

Thank you for contacting Citizens Industrial Bank. We are committed to helping you ________ your financial needs. Because you are a valued ________, we would like to offer you a complimentary mortgage analysis. To ________ advantage of the analysis, call our toll-free________. We will help you explore your mortgage options.

Sincerely,

Citizens Industrial Bank Customer Service

V. Choose the correct answer. Only one answer is correct.

1. Did you know you ________ receive Preferred Checking Account Plus Benefits?
   A. could B. must C. should have to D. had to
2. We ________ $10 left now.
   A. only have B. have only C. only had D. had only
3. I am ________ your visit next time.
   A. seeing B. waiting
   C. looking forward to D. hoping for
4. You ________ be tired, as you only started working a minute ago.
   A. shouldn't B. mustn't C. may not D. can't
5. The CIB credit card can be used to make ________ purchases.
   A. every day B. everyday C. usually D. seldom
6. Customer service is dedicated ________ its customers' needs.
   A. to meet B. to meeting
   C. for meeting D. for having met
7. They urged that the museum ________ open during the holiday.
   A. was kept B. were kept
   C. be kept D. will be kept.
8. It was decided that the search ________.
   A. was ended B. be ending
   C. had to be ended D. should be ended

VI. Translate the following from English into Chinese.

1. They would benefit by reducing their labor costs.
2. You can pay directly into my bank account.
3. The book I wanted was out on loan.
4. The unemployment rate is going up a lot these days.
5. The murder must have been committed around 11:00 p.m.

VII. Translate the following from Chinese into English.

1. 我真希望你能通过这次访问获得巨大收获。
2. 我在北京银行开了个账户。
3. 如果有必要我可以从银行贷款。

4. 你需要几张招待券？
5. 来得容易去得快。

Writing Tips

What to Capitalize	
Awards	Capitalize when using the specific award name (but not for general uses): Nobel Prize; Academy Award; state fair awards
Brand names, products, and programs	Capitalize: Buick; Nike shoes
Buildings and other structures	Capitalize (including "Building," "Tower," "Bridge," etc.): Empire State Building; Golden Gate Bridge
Geographical and political place names	Capitalize (including "River," "State," etc.): the Mississippi River; the Missouri and Mississippi Rivers; New York State, *but* the states of New York and New Jersey; North America; the Rocky Mountains; Chicago is the Windy City
Months and days of the week	Capitalize (but note that seasons are not capitalized): January, February; Saturday, Sunday; fall, spring
Nationalities of people; academic, business, government, military, religious, and royalty titles	Capitalize nationalities of people: Americans, African Americans, Asian Americans, Caucasians, native Americans Capitalize titles before a name, but not after: President Abraham Lincoln, *but* Abraham Lincoln was a president of the United States
Organizations, teams, businesses, institutions, government bodies, and political parties	Capitalize (except for articles and prepositions in the name): National Association for the Advancement of Colored People; Colorado Avalanche hockey team; Microsoft Corporation; Colorado College; United Nations General Assembly; the Democratic Party

Publication titles	Capitalize and italicize book, magazine, movie, newspaper, painting, and play titles: *The Adventures of Tom Sawyer*; *Newsweek*; *Shrek*; *New York Times*; *Starry Night*; *Romeo and Juliet* Capitalize and enclose in quotation marks chapter, magazine article, and poem titles: "Lesson 6: E-banking"; "10 Top Things"; "The Road Not Taken"
Religions, gods, and holidays	Capitalize: Buddhism, Mormonism; God, Zeus; the Fourth of July, Thanksgiving
Vehicles (ships, spacecraft, planes, and trains)	Capitalized and italicize when using specific names (but not for general uses): USS *Constitution*; *Air Force One*, Boeing 747; *Orient Express*; *Apollo 11*, space shuttle

E-mail Thread 2

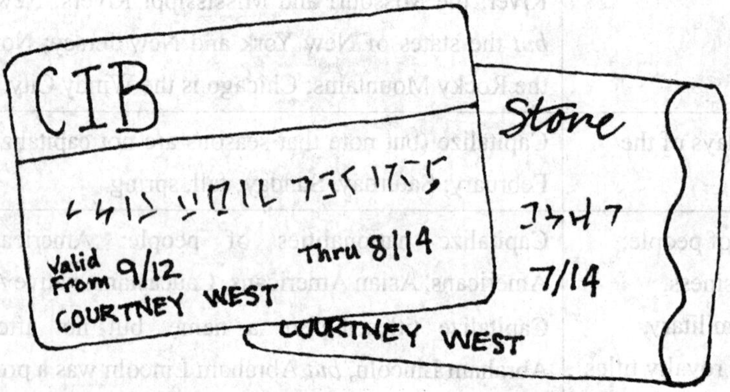

Subject: Credit Card Statement Is Ready
From: CitizensIndustrialBank@cmail.com
Date: May 31, 2012
To: CourtneyWest@cmail.com

Courtney, The monthly statement for your Citizens Industrial Bank credit card account ending in *xxxx* is available on our website. To view your statement, click the following link: www.citizensindustrialbank.com/mycreditcardaccount. Then enter your username and password. If you need assistance, please contact Customer Service. Agents are available 24/7. Sincerely, Citizens Industrial Bank 1-800-555-0185 www.citizensindustrialbank.com *If you are concerned about the authenticity of this message, please call the phone number on the back of your credit card.*

Subject: Thank You for Your Credit Card Payment
From: CitizensIndustrialBank@cmail.com
Date: June 15, 2012
To: CourtneyWest@cmail.com
Dear Courtney, Thank you for using our online payment service to schedule your credit card payment. Your payment of US$504.93 will be credited to your credit card account ending in *xxxx* on June 30, 2012. Do you know all the convenient ways that you can manage your account online? Log on to www.citizensindustrialbank.com/mycreditcardaccount and select the "Options" link to

access account management features such as
—viewing statements online and
—setting up monthly automatic payments.

If you have questions, please call Customer Service at 1-800-555-0185.

Thank you again for using online payments.

Sincerely,

Citizens Industrial Bank
1-800-555-0185
www.citizensindustrialbank.com

New Words 2

1.	authenticity	[ˌɔːθen'tisiti]	*n.*	真实性；可靠性
2.	feature	[fiːtʃə]	*n.*	特征；特色
3.	message	['mesidʒ]	*n.*	信息；消息
4.	access	['ækses]	*v.*	使用；取得
5.	enter	['entə]	*v.*	登录；将……输入
6.	select	[si'lekt]	*v.*	选择；挑选
7.	username	['juːzə neim]	*n.*	用户名

Phrases and Expressions 2

1.	account management feature	账户管理特色
2.	convenient way	便利的方式
3.	credit card account	信用卡账户
4.	credit card statement	信用卡结单
5.	customer service	客户服务
6.	monthly statement	每月结账单

7. online account 网上账户
8. online payment service 网上支付服务
9. to be concerned about 对……担心
10. to be credited to 转入；存入
11. to set up 建立

Proper Names 2

"Options" link "可选键" 连接

Notes 2

1. *24/7* means something is open or available 24 hours a day, seven days a week.
这是美国各公司服务行业常用的缩写。意思是一周七天，每天二十四小时营业或服务。

2. *username* (用户名): Username is a series of letters and numbers used to identify the user of an online account. It is also called an "account name," a "log-in name," and a "user ID."
用户名是由一组字母和数字组成的，其功能为"网上客户账户识别"。也可称为"账户名"、"登录名"或"用户名"。

3. *password* (密码): Password is a series of letters and numbers that allow the user to log on to a computer or account. The best passwords are long, unique phrases that use letters and numbers.
由用户设置的允许用户登录某电脑或账户的一组数字及字母。最好的密码是长、独特并包含字母和数字的短句。

4. *authenticity of this message* (信息的真实性): Thieves sometimes steal financial and personal information by sending fake e-mails that appear to come from banking institutions. Fake e-mails contain misspellings and other errors. Customers who believe an e-mail is fake can contact the institution to verify whether the e-mail is authentic.
为了盗取个人财产信息，网上行窃者通常假冒金融机构发送伪造电子邮件。这些邮件往往带有拼写错误及其他漏洞。若客户对此类邮件有疑惑，可与此机构联系辨别其电子邮件的真实性。

5. *credit card account ending in xxxx* (用卡以 *xxxx* 结束的账户): To protect the credit card account, companies often provide only the last four numbers of the account, which are unique to the account.
   为确保信用卡账户的安全，公司及金融机构通常仅提供此账户特有的最后四位账号号码。

Exercises 2

I. Answer the following questions.

1. How does Courtney West view her monthly credit card statement?
2. Who can Courtney contact if she needs assistance?
3. When are Customer Service agents available?
4. If Courtney is concerned about the authenticity of the message, what should she do?
5. What service did Courtney use to schedule her credit card payment?
6. How much is Courtney's credit card payment?
7. When will Courtney's payment be credited to her account?
8. What link can Courtney select to set up automatic payments?

II. Write an e-mail from a bank about a customer's credit card payment.

Key to E-mail Thread 1 Exercises (for Reference)

I. Answer the following questions.

1. Yes, Courtney West is a customer of Citizens Industrial Bank.
2. Courtney currently receives Preferred Checking Account Benefits.
3. To receive Preferred Checking Account Plus Benefits, Courtney can either 1) use her CIB check card or CIB credit card to make everyday purchases or 2) take out a loan.
4. Courtney would receive Preferred Checking Account Plus Benefits such as 1) CIB's best interest rates on certificate of deposit accounts and 2) discounts on vehicle loans for multiple cars.
5. CIB is committed to helping Courtney meet her financial needs.
6. Courtney does not have to pay for the mortgage analysis because it is complimentary.

7. CIB's toll-free number is only for customers.
8. CIB's legal disclosures are on its website.

II. Write the key points of this e-mail thread.

- Courtney West is a Citizens Industrial Bank (CIB) customer.
- Courtney receives Preferred Checking Account Benefits but would receive Preferred Checking Account Plus Benefits if she does one of the following: 1) uses her CIB check card or CIB credit card to make everyday purchases or 2) takes out a loan.
- Preferred Checking Account Plus Benefits include CIB's best interest rates on certificate of deposit accounts and discounts on vehicle loans for multiple cars.
- Courtney can visit CIB's website for legal disclosures about its products and services.
- CIB is committed to helping Courtney meet her financial needs.
- Because Courtney is a valued customer, CIB offered her a complimentary mortgage analysis. The analysis will determine whether her current mortgage still meets her financial needs.
- To take advantage of the analysis, Courtney needs to call the toll-free number that is only for CIB customers.

III. Fill in the blanks.

1. The mortgage analysis <u>was</u> complimentary.
2. Please visit the bank's website for legal disclosures <u>about</u> the bank's products and services.
3. I get a discount <u>on</u> my vehicle loan because I have multiple cars.
4. I use my credit <u>card</u> to make everyday purchases.
5. Please take advantage <u>of</u> the complimentary mortgage analysis.
6. Does your bank have a toll-<u>free</u> number?
7. Is that the best rate on a certificate <u>of</u> deposit account?
8. He urged me <u>to</u> take out a loan at his bank.

IV. Fill in the missing information.

Dear Sidney,

Thank you for contacting Citizens Industrial Bank. We are committed to helping you <u>meet</u>

your financial needs. Because you are a valued customer, we would like to offer you a complimentary mortgage analysis. To take advantage of the analysis, call our toll-free number. We will help you explore your mortgage options.

Sincerely,

Citizens Industrial Bank Customer Service

V. Choose the correct answer. Only one answer is correct.

1. A 2. B 3. C 4. D 5. B 6. B 7. C 8. D

VI. Translate the following from English into Chinese.

1. 他们通过降低劳动成本获得收益。
2. 你可以把钱直接打入我的账户。
3. 我想要的书借出去了。
4. 最近失业率正在大幅上升。
5. 凶杀肯定发生在晚上 11 点左右。

VII. Translate the following from Chinese into English.

1. I do hope that you will benefit greatly from the visit.
2. I've opened an account with Beijing Bank.
3. I can get a loan from the bank if necessary.
4. How many complimentary tickets do you need?
5. Easy come, easy go.

Translation of E-mail Thread 1 (for Reference)

译文：

邮件 1-1

主题：你得到 CIB 的最高福利待遇了吗？

发件人：公民产业银行
日期：2012 年 3 月 16 日
收件人：科特妮・韦斯特

科特妮，

你已经获得了 CIB 的优惠支票账户福利待遇。但你是否知道仅需参与如下服务之一，你就将获得最优支票账户福利待遇。

即：一使用你的 CIB 的银行卡或 CIB 的信用卡消费
　　一向 CIB 贷款

最优支票账户福利待遇包括
一定期存款将获得最高利率回报
一享受多部汽车贷款优惠

用此网址很容易与我们联系并请了解更多有关最优支票账户福利待遇的信息。

此致，

公民产业银行
电话号码：1-800-555-0185
网址：www.citizensindustrialbank.com

有关法律要求的信息披露及其他，请浏览我们的网页。

邮件 1-2

主题：免费房贷分析
发件人：公民产业银行
日期：2012 年 4 月 16 日
收件人：科特妮・韦斯特

科特妮，

CIB 致力于帮助你满足你的财务需求。

因为你是 CIB 贵客，我们将为你提供免费房贷分析，帮助你实现最佳经济投资的意愿。此房贷分析将确定你目前的房贷利率是否仍适合你的情况。

请今天就拨打这个电话：1-800-555-0185。

我们敦促你不要错过这个免费房贷分析的时机。其步骤非常简单，只要拨打这个仅为 CIB 客户使用的 **1-800-555-0185** 免费电话。我们期望能帮你探索出最佳房贷利率方案。

此致，

公民产业银行
电话号码：1-800-555-0185
网址：www.citizensindustrialbank.com
附言：请今天就打电话：1-800-555-0185。我们有义务帮助满足你的房贷需求。

有关法律要求的信息披露及其他，请浏览我们的网页。

Key to E-mail Thread 2 Exercises (for Reference)

I. Answer the following questions.

1. Courtney West views her monthly credit card statement by clicking on a link and entering her username and password.
2. Courtney can contact Customer Service if she needs assistance.
3. Customer Service agents are available 24/7.
4. If Courtney is concerned about the authenticity of the message, she should call the phone number on the back of her credit card.
5. Courtney used the online payment service to schedule her credit card payment.
6. Courtney's payment is US$504.93.

7. Courtney's payment will be credited to her account on June 30, 2012.
8. To set up automatic payments, Courtney can select the "Options" link.

Translation of E-mail Thread 2 (for Reference)

译文:

邮件 2-1

主题：信用卡每月结单已可查询
发件人：公民产业银行
日期：2012 年 5 月 31 日
收件人：科特妮·韦斯特

科特妮，

你现在可随时在我们网站查看你卡号以 *xxxx* 结束的 CIB 信用卡的每月结单。请点击以下网址输入你的用户名及密码。

网址：www.citizensindustrialbank.com/mycreditcardaccount

如果你需要协助，请随时与客户服务中心的代理联系。

此致，

公民产业银行
电话号码：1-800-555-0185
网址 www.citizensindustrialbank.com

若你担心此信息的真实性，请拨打你信用卡背面的电话号码核实。

邮件 2-2

主题：谢谢你的信用卡付款
发件人：公民产业银行
日期：2012 年 6 月 15 日
收件人：科特妮·韦斯特

亲爱的科特妮，

谢谢你使用网上支付信用卡账单业务。2012 年 6 月 30 日，你所支付的$504.93 将会被充入以 *xxxx* 结束的账户内。

你知道那些在网上管理你账户的便利方法吗？登陆此网址选择“可选项”连接到使用账户管理功能：
—查看每月结单；
—安排每月自动还款业务。

若有任何问题，请拨打客户服务中心免费电话：1-800-555-0185。

再次感谢使用网上支付业务。

此致，

公民产业银行
电话号码：1-800-555-0185
网址：www.citizensindustrialbank.com

Lesson 7

Office Communication
办公室内的沟通

Learning Objectives

In this lesson, you will learn the following:

- How work colleagues communicate informally through e-mail
  同事间非正式电子邮件交流
- How to notify colleagues of vacations and other absences
  告知同事休假和缺席
- How colleagues respond to a fellow colleague's personal events
  对同事私事的回应
- How Americans honor a person's memory
  美国人对已故人的纪念方式

E-mail Thread 1

Subject: Vacation

From: JCooper@acmeproductioncompany.com

Date: May 16, 2012

To: <Development Team>

All,

I will be on vacation next week, starting Monday, May 21, and returning Tuesday, May 29 (the day after Memorial Day). If you need assistance, please contact Hayley Martin, who will be filling in for me. Note that Acme Production Company will be closed on Memorial Day (Monday, May 28).

Jeremy

Jeremy Cooper
Product Development Coordinator
Acme Production Company
JCooper@acmeproductioncompany.com
555-555-0165, ext. 43

Subject: Out of Office Reply: Re: Schedule a Meeting

From: TJohnson@acmeproductioncompany.com

Date: May 22, 2012

To: JCooper@acmeproductioncompany.com

I will be out of the office until Tuesday, May 29, and will answer your e-mail upon my return. If you need to speak with someone before then, please contact Hayley Martin at HMartin@acmeproductioncompany.com or extension 48. Please note that Acme Production will be closed on Memorial Day (Monday, May 28).

Thank you,

Jeremy

Jeremy Cooper
Product Development Coordinator
Acme Production Company
JCooper@acmeproductioncompany.com
555-555-0165, ext. 43

—Original Message—
From: TJohnson@acmeproductioncompany.com
Sent: Tuesday, May 22, 2012, 11:10 a.m.
To: JCooper@acmeproductioncompany.com
Subject: Schedule a Meeting

Hi Jeremy,

I have some questions about the product development process, which I'm describing in the report I'm writing. Can we schedule some time this week for a one-hour meeting to go over the process?

Thanks,

Travis Johnson
Technical Writer
Acme Production Company
TJohnson@acmeproductioncompany.com
555-555-0165, ext. 67

New Words 1

1. extension [iks'tenʃən] *n.* 电话分机
2. note [nəut] *v.* 注；注释
3. process ['prəuses] *n.* 步骤；程序；工序；制作法
4. return [ri'təːn] *v.* 返回

5. vacation [vei'keiʃən] *n.* 休假

Phrases and Expressions 1

1. office communications 办公室内的沟通
2. product development coordinator 生产发展部主管
3. product development process 产品发展步骤
4. technical writer 技术撰稿人
5. to be closed 将关闭
6. to fill in 代替

Proper Names 1

1. Acme Production 艾克米产品公司
2. Hayley Martin 哈利·马丁
3. Jeremy Cooper 杰里米·库珀
4. Memorial Day （美国）阵亡将士纪念日
5. Travis Johnson 特拉维斯·约翰逊

Notes 1

1.1. *on Tuesday* 在时间前一般用介词“*on*，*in* 和 *at*”。但用法各不相同，也没有特定的规律。

1.1.1. *on* 表示“在具体的某一天”或“某一天的早上、中午、晚上”等。

例：1) John White was born on July 23, 1983.
约翰·怀特生于 1983 年 7 月 23 日。
2) They left home on a summer morning for their vacation.
他们是在一个夏天的早上离开家去度假的。

1.1.2. *on* 表示“星期几”或“在星期几的早上、中午、晚上”等。

例：1) We usually don't go to school on Saturday and Sunday
我们一般周六、周日都不用上学。

2) When do you get up on Sunday mornings?
你在周日早晨几点起床？

1.1.3. *on* 表示“在某一节日的那一天”。

例：I always receive his Christmas card on Christmas Eve.
我总是在圣诞节前夜收到了他的圣诞贺卡。

1.2.1. *in* 表示“在某年；年代；月；季节”。

例：1) Dr. Hughes came to this small city in the late ’80s.
休斯医生是 1980 年代末来到这个小城市的。
2) The weather here is cold and wet in the winter.
这里的冬天又湿又冷。

1.2.2. *in* 表示“在将来的时间”。

例：I will be leaving for the States in a week.
我一周后要去美国。

1.2.3. *in* 表示“在早、中、晚三个时间段”。

例：I will be back for dinner in the evening.
我晚上会回来吃晚饭。

1.3.1. *at* 表示“在某一具体时刻（即几点几分时）”。

例：I got up for a run at five o’clock this morning.
我今天早上五点钟就起床跑步了。

1.3.2. *at* 表示“在中午或夜晚”。

例：1) I usually eat a light lunch at noon so I don’t get tired in the afternoon.
我通常中午吃的很少，所以下午不会困。
2) You shouldn’t drive around at night; you could easily get lost.
晚上你就别开车转悠了，很容易迷路。

1.3.3. *at* 表示“在周末，节假日”。

例：What do Chinese people celebrate at the Spring Festival?

中国人如何过春节？

2.1. *need* 可用实义动词（full verb）和情态动词（model verb），用作情态动词时，意思是“有必要”或“需要”，其后接动词原形，通常只用于否定句或疑问句以及“if”或“whether”之后，一般不用于肯定句。

例：1) She's lazy and stubborn. Need I say more?
她懒散、固执，还需要我讲下去吗？
2) Den's tennis shoes wore out. He needs a new pair of tennis shoes again.
丹的网球鞋磨坏了，又需要给他买新的了。

2.2. *need* 用于实意动词的结构是“somebody needs to do something”。

例：1) We need to tell him the truth.
我们有必要告诉他真相。

3.1. *to be closed* 译为打烊，在这里 *closed* 是形容词。同样 *close* 在这种情况下，也可用于动词：“The store closes at 6 p.m.”商店下午六点关门。但是，*close* 作为及物动词时，意思则是永久性的关闭。

例：The company has decided to close down its two branches.
该公司已决定关闭它的两个分公司。

3.1.1. 另外，*close* 本身也是形容词。它的主要意思是“近；亲密”。

例：1) His house is close to the company he works at.
他的家靠近他上班的公司。
2) Sally and Bob have been close friends since high school.
从上高中开始莎莉和鲍勃就是挚友。
3) Your car is not parked close enough to the curb. You might get a parking ticket.
你的车停得离街边不够近，你可能会得到罚单。

4. *Memorial Day* (阵亡将士纪念日) is a national holiday commemorating everyone who died serving the United States during war. It is observed on the last Monday in May, and many businesses are closed. Traditional celebrations include parades, cleaning and decorating the graves of fallen military members, and flying the US flag.
阵亡将士纪念日是一个全国性假日，用来纪念在战争中为美国捐躯的将士。它被定在五月的最后的那个星期一。很多商家、企业在那天也不对外开放。传统的纪念活动有游行、打扫、装饰军队烈士陵园和挂美国国旗。

5. *signature* (署名): Many e-mail programs allow the user to automatically include contact information in every e-mail being sent.
很多电子邮件程序都允许用户在每一送出的邮件中自动包括你的联系信息。

6. *out of office reply* (不在办公室的自动回复): Many e-mail programs allow the user to set up automatic replies to incoming e-mails to indicate that the user is on vacation, traveling, or not in the office.
当电子邮件用户休假、旅行或者不在办公室的时候，很多电子邮件程序都能为使用者提供自动回复邮件。

Exercises 1

I. Answer the following questions.

1. When does Jeremy Cooper's vacation start?
2. When will Jeremy return?
3. Who will fill in for Jeremy?
4. Why is Acme Production closed on Monday, May 28?
5. When did Travis Johnson e-mail Jeremy?
6. What does Travis have questions about?
7. What is Travis writing?
8. When will Jeremy answer Travis's e-mail?

II. Write the key points of this e-mail thread.

III. Fill in the blanks.

1. She will be ________ vacation next week.
2. Please contact Jean Black at ________ 75.
3. He will answer e-mails upon ________ return.
4. Do you know who will fill ________ for her when she's out of the office?

5. The office ________ be closed on Memorial Day.
6. Please note ________ I will be on vacation next week.
7. The technical ________ is writing the report.
8. Can we schedule a one-hour meeting to go ________ the process?

IV. Fill in the missing information.

Dear Martha,

I would like to schedule a meeting with you and Dennis to discuss the product development process. Are you available on Friday morning?

Thanks,

Vicki

Vicki,

I will be on vacation, starting Friday and ________ Tuesday. Steve will ________ in for me. You can ________ him at extension 47.

Martha

V. Choose the correct answer. Only one answer is correct.

1. ________ Sunday morning
   A. on B. at C. in
2. ________ lunchtime
   A. on B. at C. in
3. ________ the morning of the 15th
   A. on B. at C. in
4. ________ night
   A. on B. at C. in
5. ________ May Day
   A. on B. at C. in

6. ________ half past eight

A. on B. at C. in

7. ________ a winter afternoon

A. on B. at C. in

8. ________ noon

A. on B. at C. in

VI. Translate the following from English into Chinese.

1. How much vacation do you get a year at your new job?
2. The air was filled with the sound of children's laughter.
3. I'm sorry to say that the vacancy has already been filled.
4. The new government called for a return to democracy in this area.
5. I don't mind where we go on vacation as long as it's close to a beach.

VII. Translate the following from Chinese into English.

1. 从现在到五月三十一日，星期二，我都不在办公室。
2. 回来上班后，我将立即回复你的邮件。
3. 我从明天开始度假。
4. 她听到身后的门关上了。
5. 很难形容我现在的感受。

Writing Tips

Common Tools of E-mail Programs	
Get mail, write, reply, forward, delete	Used to prepare, send, and manage e-mails
Attach	Used to attach various types of files to the e-mail
Folders	Used to store e-mails by category
Signature	Used to automatically include contact information

Address book	Used to store recipients' e-mail addresses and other contact information
Filters	Used to sort and file incoming e-mail by criteria that the user determines

E-mail Thread 2

Subject: Out the Rest of the Week	
From: DNelson@acmeproductioncompany.com	
Date: September 12, 2012	
To: HSmart@acmeproductioncompany.com	

Hilary,

I wanted to let you know that I will be out the rest of the week. My daughter passed away unexpectedly last night, and I will leave for Houston this afternoon to arrange the funeral. I

plan to take off the next three days, in accordance with Acme's bereavement policy. Nicole Anderson has graciously offered to fill in for me while I am gone. She can be reached at NAnderson@acmeproductioncompany.com or extension 109. Thank you for your understanding. Best, David David Nelson Director of Marketing Acme Production Company DNelson@acmeproductioncompany.com 555-555-0165, ext. 103

Subject: David Nelson's Daughter Alexis
From: HSmart@acmeproductioncompany.com
Date: September 13, 2012
To: <AllHands>
All, As you know, David Nelson's 28-year-old daughter Alexis passed away unexpectedly Tuesday night. David's family asks that, in lieu of flowers, donations be made to the local chapter of the Cystic Fibrosis Association, which helps people with this chronic genetic disease. Because David and his wife, Gloria, were active volunteers, the local association would like to do something special and permanent to honor Alexis—something like an Alexis Nelson memorial playground, library, picnic area, or garden. If you have an idea for a great memorial, please e-mail me. The Human Resources Department is coordinating donations for the memorial. We have

already received some donations from the marketing team. Please make your donation payable to the Cystic Fibrosis Association and send it to the Human Resources Department. Group donations (that is, donations from an entire department) will also be accepted.

Thank you in advance for your generosity!

Hilary Smart
Head of Human Resources
Acme Production Company
HSmart@acmeproductioncompany.com
555-555-0165, ext. 103

New Words 2

1.	coordinate	[kəu'ɔːdneit]	*v.*	协调
2.	donation	[dəu'neiʃən]	*n.*	捐款；捐献；捐赠
3.	funeral	[‘fjuːnərəl]	*n.*	葬礼
4.	generosity	[ˌdʒenə'rɔsiti]	*n.*	慷慨行为
5.	graciously	[‘greiʃəsli]	*adv.*	亲切地；仁慈地
6.	honor	[‘ɔnə]	*v.*	给……以荣誉
7.	library	[‘laibrəri]	*n.*	图书馆；图书室
8.	memorial	[mi'mɔːriəl]	*n.*	纪念活动
9.	offer	[‘ɔːfə]	*v.*	给予；提供
10.	payable	[‘peiəbl]	*adj.*	应支付的
11.	permanent	[‘pəːmənənt]	*a.*	永久的；常在的
12.	unexpectedly	[‘ʌnik'spektidli]	*adv.*	未料到地；意外地

Phrases and Expressions 2

1.	active volunteer	积极的志愿者
2.	all hands	同事们
3.	bereavement policy	丧亡政策

4. chronic genetic disease 慢性遗传疾病
5. director of marketing 营销部主任
6. group donation 集体捐款
7. Human Resources Department 人力资源部
8. in accordance with 符合；遵照
9. in lieu of flowers 除了鲜花以外
10. local association 地方协会
11. local chapter 地方分会
12. memorial playground 纪念游乐场
13. picnic area 野餐区
14. to be reached 与……取得联系
15. to pass away 去世；死亡
16. to take off 离开

Proper Names 2

1. Alexis Nelson 亚历克西斯·尼尔森
2. Cystic Fibrosis Association 纤维性囊肿协会
3. David Nelson 大卫·尼尔森
4. Gloria 葛罗瑞亚
5. Hilary Smart 希拉里·斯玛特
6. Houston (Texas; TX) 休斯顿（得克萨斯州）
7. Nicole Anderson 尼可·安德森

Notes 2

1. *I plan to take off the next three days*（我打算从明日起，休假三日）：在这里 *off* 是副词，它的作用是进一步补充、完成 *take* 的意思。这句话也可说成："I plan to take the next three days off." 在平时生活中，另外一种句型也很常用："We will have three days off at Tomb Sweeping." 清明节我们休息三天。

2. *while I am gone*：这句话不是被动语态。gone 是形容词，在这里做表语，表示一种状态。

因此应译为“在我不在期间”。

3. *group donations* 是“集体捐赠品”的意思。group 一词可当名词也可当动词用。近期在中国有一词很流行，是 groupon，译为团购。它起源于美国，是一种多方共赢（消费者、商家）消费的模式。

4. *cystic fibrosis* (纤维性囊肿): Cystic fibrosis is a genetic disease that affects 30 000–40 000 Americans. The disease affects the lungs and digestive system. Improvements in treatments have increased the median life expectancy for a patient in the United States to 37 years old.
三四万美国人患有纤维性囊肿。这是一种遗传病，它影响人的肺和消化系统。即使在美国采用最先进的药物和治疗手段，病人预期的寿命也仅有三十七年。

5. *Human Resources Department* (人力资源部): Many companies have a Human Resources Department that hires new employees; trains all employees; and oversees company policies and employee benefits such as health insurance and wage increases.
很多公司都有自己的人力资源部门。承担员工雇用及培训，监督公司政策，员工福利待遇。员工福利待遇包括健康保险、加薪等等。

6. *bereavement policy* (丧亡政策): Many large companies in the United States allow employees to take time off for making funeral arrangements and attending the visitation, funeral, and burial of a family member. Usually employees are allowed to take off three days, with or without pay, depending on the company.
许多美国大公司给予员工处理家人丧葬事物的假期。各公司视经济情况而定，通常给予员工带薪或不带薪的假期三天。

Exercises 2

I. Answer the following questions.

1. Why will David Nelson out of the office for the rest of the week?
2. When will David leave for Houston?
3. How many days does David plan to take off?

4. Who will fill in for David while he is gone?
5. What can employees give in lieu of flowers?
6. What would the local association like to do to honor Alexis?
7. Who is coordinating donations?
8. Who do employees make their donations payable to?

II. Write an e-mail that explains why you will be out of the office.

Key to E-mail Thread 1 Exercises (for Reference)

I. Answer the following questions.

1. Jeremy Cooper's vacation starts on Monday, May 21.
2. Jeremy will return on Tuesday, May 29 (the day after Memorial Day).
3. Hayley Martin will fill in for Jeremy.
4. Acme Production will be closed on Monday, May 28, because it is Memorial Day.
5. Travis Johnson e-mailed Jeremy on Tuesday, May 22.
6. Travis has questions about the product development process.
7. Travis is writing a report.
8. Jeremy will answer Travis's e-mail upon Jeremy's return.

II. Write the key points of this e-mail thread.

- Jeremy Cooper sent an e-mail to the development team to tell them that he would be on vacation next week.
- Jeremy's vacation starts on Monday, May 21. He will return on Tuesday, May 29 (the day after Memorial Day).
- Jeremy's company, Acme Production, will be closed on Memorial Day (Monday, May 28).
- Hayley Martin will be filling in for Jeremy.
- Travis Johnson tried to schedule a meeting with Jeremy when Jeremy will be on vacation.
- Travis received an "out-of-office reply" from Jeremy.

III. Fill in the blanks.

1. She will be <u>on</u> vacation next week.

2. Please contact Jean Black at extension 75.
3. He will answer e-mails upon his return.
4. Do you know who will fill in for her when she's out of the office?
5. The office will be closed on Memorial Day.
6. Please note that I will be on vacation next week.
7. The technical writer is writing the report.
8. Can we schedule a one-hour meeting to go over the process?

IV. Fill in the missing information.

Vicki,

I will be on vacation, starting Friday and returning Tuesday. Steve will fill in for me. You can contact him at extension 47.

Martha

V. Choose the correct answer. Only one answer is correct.

1. A 2. B 3. A 4. B 5. A 6. B 7. A 8. B

VI. Translate the following from English into Chinese.

1. 你的新工作每年能休几天假？
2. 到处都充满了孩子们的笑声。
3. 对不起这个工作已有人做了。
4. 新政府要求这一地区恢复民主。
5. 我不在意去哪里度假，只要离海边近就行。

VII. Translate the following from Chinese into English.

1. I will be out of the office until Tuesday, May 31.
2. I will answer your e-mail upon my return.
3. I'm going on vacation tomorrow.
4. She heard the door close behind her.
5. It's difficult to describe how I feel.

Translation of E-mail Thread 1 (for Reference)

译文：

邮件 1-1

主题：休假
发件人：J. 库珀
日期：2012 年 5 月 16 日
收件人：发展部

同事们，

从下个星期一（五月二十一号）开始，我将休假。五月二十九日“阵亡将士纪念日”后回来上班。若你需要任何帮助，请与海莉·马丁联系，她将代我处理事宜。注意，五月二十八日艾克米公司将休息一天。

杰里米

杰里米·库珀
生产发展部主管
艾克米公司
电邮地址：JCooper@acmeproductioncompany.com
电话号码：555-555-0165，分机：43

邮件 1-2

主题：不在办公室自动回复/安排会面
发件人：T. 约翰逊
日期：2012 年 5 月 22 日
收件人：J. 库珀

从现在到五月二十九日，星期二，我都不在办公室。回来上班后，我将立即回复你的邮件。若你在此之前需要与代表谈话，请用这个网址或 48 分机与海莉·马丁联系。请注意，五月二十八日艾克米公司将休息一天。

杰里米·库珀
生产开发部主管
艾克米公司
电邮地址：JCooper@acmeproductioncompany.com
电话号码：555-555-0165，分机：43

原件：
主题：安排会面
发件人：T. 约翰逊
日期：2012 年 5 月 22 日
收件人：J. 库珀

杰里米，你好，

在我撰写的报告中，提出几个关于产品开发步骤的问题。我们能否在本周安排一个小时的会面，探讨一下？

谢谢，

特拉维斯·约翰逊
技术撰稿人
艾克米公司
电邮地址：TJohnson@acmeproductioncompany.com
电话号码：555-555-0165，分机：67

Key to E-mail Thread 2 Exercises (for Reference)

I. Answer the following questions.

1. David Nelson is out of the office for the rest of the week because his daughter Alexis died.

2. David is leaving for Houston this afternoon.
3. David plans to take off three days.
4. Nicole Anderson will fill in for David while he is gone.
5. Employees can give donations to the local chapter of the Cystic Fibrosis Association in lieu of flowers.
6. The local association would like to honor Alexis with a memorial playground, library, picnic area, or garden.
7. The Human Resources Department is coordinating donations.
8. Employees make their donations payable to the Cystic Fibrosis Association.

Translation of E-mail Thread 2 (for Reference)

译文：

邮件 2-1

主题：本周后几日我需请假
发件人：D. 尼森
日期：2012 年 9 月 12 日
收件人：H. 斯玛特

希拉里，

我想告诉你本周后几天我就不来了。我女儿昨天夜里突然过世了，我今天下午就要启程去休斯顿筹备葬礼。遵照艾克米公司的丧亡政策，我打算休假三天。尼可·安德森慷慨地提出在我不在的那几天承担我的工作。用此邮件地址或 109 分机能与她取得联系。

感谢你的理解。

祝好，

大卫

大卫·尼尔森
营销部主任
艾克米公司
电邮地址：DNelson@acmeproductioncompany.com
电话号码：555-555-0165，分机：103

邮件 2-2

主题：大卫的女儿亚里克西斯
发件人：H. 斯玛特
日期：2012 年 9 月 13 日
收件人：<同事们>

同事们，

大家一定都听说了，大卫·尼尔森的二十八岁的女儿亚里克西斯·尼尔森星期二夜里突然去世了。大卫一家人恳求大家除了鲜花以外，可向帮助纤维性囊肿患者的地方分会捐款。由于大卫和他太太葛罗瑞亚都是此会积极的志愿者，因而纤维性囊肿地方分会非常愿意建造“亚里克西斯·尼尔森纪念游乐场；图书室；野餐区或公园”，以这种特别形式来永久纪念她。要是你有任何更好的“纪念”想法，请给我发电子邮件。

我们人力资源部正在为这项纪念活动组织募捐，我们已经收到了销售部的部分捐款。请将抬头为纤维性囊肿协会的支票寄到人力资源部。我们也接受以整个部门为名义的集体捐款。

感谢你的慷慨解囊。

希拉里·斯玛特
人力资源部主管
艾克米公司
电邮地址：HSmart@acmeproductioncompany.com
电话号码：555-555-0165，分机：103

Lesson 8

Leaving the Workplace
离职

Learning Objectives

In this lesson, you will learn the following:

- How to send a personal announcement about leaving a workplace
  个人离职通知
- How to reply to a personal announcement
  回复个人通知
- What responsibilities the leaving employee has
  离职雇员离职前的职责
- How a company announces layoffs
  公司解雇通告

E-mail Thread 1

Subject: Regretfully, I Am Leaving the University
From: KWhite@su.com
Date: April 11, 2012
To: <American Studies Department>
All, I am sorry to say that I will be leaving the university at the end of the month. My husband and I will be moving to Chicago, Illinois, where he has accepted a new job. I do not have a job lined up yet, and I don't know what my future holds careerwise. : - (I've really enjoyed my nine years as a librarian at the university's library, and I will miss working with everyone in the American Studies Department. One of the other librarians will be taking over my responsibilities and will contact you soon. If you would like to meet with me before my departure, please let me know. I will be available through April 30 during my regular office hours (9:00 a.m.-12:00 p.m., 1:00-4:30 p.m., Monday through Friday). If you need to contact me after my university e-mail expires, please use this address: KWhite@cmail.com. Best, Krystal Krystal White Interdisciplinary Programs Librarian State University 555-555-0130, ext. 231

Subject: Re: Regretfully, I Am Leaving the University
From: LReed@su.com
Date: April 11, 2012
To: KWhite@su.com

Dear Krystal,

Thank you so much for your expertise and your help with the American Studies students and faculty. Many student and faculty researchers would have missed the resources and helpful links that you pointed us to, and our work would have been incomplete without your help. When the university's limited finances required changes in library management, you encouraged the faculty to read research-related journals online and you told us the importance of doing so.

I hope you will find a swimming team in Chicago and can continue to compete in an adult league. Perhaps we will see you if you return to the local competitions that you frequently participated in while you lived here. I have visited Chicago several times for academic conventions, and it is a very nice city with many cultural and sports activities and some fascinating museums.

Everyone will miss you very much, and we send our very best wishes to you and your family in your new home.

With good wishes,

Linda

Linda Reed
Professor, American Studies
State University
555-555-0130, ext. 348

New Words 1

1.	accept	[ək'sept]	*v.*	接受
2.	available	[ə'veiləbl]	*adj.*	有空的；可用的
3.	careerwise	[kə'riəwaiz]	*adv.*	从事业上来说
4.	departure	[di'pɑːtʃə]	*n.*	启程；离开；出发
5.	employee	[ˌemplɔi'iː]	*n.*	雇员；员工
6.	encourage	[in'kʌridʒ]	*v.*	鼓励；激发
7.	expertise	[ˌekspəː'tiːz]	*n.*	专门技能；专门知识
8.	expire	[iks'paiə]	*v.*	终止；期满；无效
9.	faculty	['fækəlti]	*n.*	大学全体教师
10.	fascinating	['fæsineitiŋ]	*adj.*	迷人的；醉人的
11.	frequently	['friːkwəntli]	*adv.*	频繁地；经常
12.	help	[help]	*n.*	帮助；协助
13.	incomplete	[ˌinkəm'pliːt]	*adj.*	不完善的；不完整的
14.	layoff	['leiɔːf]	*n.*	解雇
15.	librarian	[lai'brɛəriən]	*n.*	图书馆员
16.	museum	[mjuː'ziəm]	*n.*	博物馆；展览馆
17.	participate	[pɑː'tisipeit]	*v.*	参与；分担
18.	regretfully	[ri'gretfəli]	*adv.*	遗憾地；抱歉地
19.	related	[ri'leitid]	*adj.*	有关的
20.	research	[ri'səːtʃ]	*n.*	研究
21.	responsibility	[riˌspɔnsə'biliti]	*n.*	职责；义务

Phrases and Expressions 1

1.	academic convention	学术会议
2.	adult league	成人社团；成人俱乐部
3.	faculty researcher	大学研究者
4.	helpful links	有用网址
5.	interdisciplinary program	跨学科项目

6. library management 图书馆管理
7. personal announcement 个人通知
8. regular office hours 平常办公时间
9. required changes 必要的改变
10. state university 州立大学
11. to line up 安排妥当
12. to move to 搬到
13. to point us to 给我们指出

Proper Names 1

1. American Studies Department 美洲研究学系
2. Chicago, Illinois (IL) 伊利诺依州芝加哥
3. Krystal White 克里斯托·怀特
4. Linda Reed 琳达·瑞德

Notes 1

1. *emoticons* (情绪脸谱): Emoticons are combinations of letters and punctuation that create a facial expression when viewed sideways. Writers use them in informal e-mails to indicate their mood. 由“emotion”（情绪）和“icon”（图像，图标）拼缀而成，笑面谱，情绪脸谱横向显示。（由标点符号组成用以表达情感的符号，通常出现在电子邮件或网络聊天中，用以营造轻松友好的气氛）。: - (表示悲伤或生气的脸。

2.1. American Studies Department 在美国学校三级管理单位和领导分别是：

1) university 大学 president 校长
2) school 学院 dean 院长
3) department 学系 chair 系主任

2.2. *study* 在这里意思是 “研究”，该词通常用复数，指各方面的研究。*American studies* 译为美国研究。

例： He is a well-known professor of African American studies.

他是著名的美国黑人研究教授。

3. *ext.* 是 *extension* 的缩写词，意思是分机。

4. *our work would have been incomplete without your help* (要是没有你的协助，我们的工作就不能顺利完成)：这是一种虚拟语气的用法。用来表示说话人的主观愿望或假想，而不表示客观存在的事实，所说的是一个条件，不一定是事实，或与事实相反。*without your help* 相当于 "if it were not for your help"，如果没有你的帮助，前面的情况不可能成为现实。虚拟语气是动词的一种特殊形式，表示与事实相反的假设或主观假设，它通过谓语动词的特殊形式来表示。动词语气一般有三种：陈述语气、祈使语气和虚拟语气。

4.1.1. 真实条件状语从句与非真实条件状语从句：

例：If you don't hurry up and leave right now, you will be late for your first period class.
如果你现在不快点儿走，你第一节课肯定会迟到。(真实条件状语)

4.2.1. 表示与现在事实相反的情况：

例：1) If I knew how to contact her, I would have told you by now.
如果我知道怎么与她联系，我早就会告诉你。

2) If my brother were here, everything would be all right.
要是我哥哥在这儿，一切都没问题了。

3) If tomorrow were Sunday, then I would go see my grandmother.
如果明天是星期天，我就会去看望我奶奶。

4.2.2. 表示与过去事实相反的情况：

例：1) If Tommy had taken my advice not to drink that day, he would not have had a such terrible car accident.
如果那天汤姆听我的劝告不喝酒的话，就不会出这样可怕的车祸了。

2) If you had taken my advice, you wouldn't have failed the exam.
如果你按照我的建议去做，你一定不会考试不及格。

4.3. 表示对将来情况的主观推测：

例：1) If there were a big snowstorm again this weekend, we would not go skiing.
如果这个周末再下大雪，我们就不能去滑雪了。

2) If it were to snow this evening, then they wouldn't go out.
如果今晚下雪，他们将不出去了。

Exercises 1

I. Answer the following questions.

1. What is Krystal White's job?
2. Why is Krystal leaving her job?
3. Does Krystal have a job in Chicago yet?
4. How long did Krystal work at the university?
5. When is Krystal's last day at work?
6. Who did Krystal help at work?
7. What sport does Krystal compete in?
8. What is Chicago like?

II. Write the key points of this e-mail thread.

III. Fill in the blanks.

1. I am ________ during my regular office hours.
2. The new librarian is taking ________ her job responsibilities.
3. She is leaving because her husband has ________ a new job in Massachusetts.
4. The librarian pointed me to helpful ________ for reading online journals.
5. I just lined ________ a new job in Chicago.
6. He hopes he can continue to participate ________ local swimming competitions.
7. How can I contact you after your state university e-mail ________?
8. American Studies faculty frequently read ________-related journals.

IV. Fill in the missing information.

Dear Richard,

Regretfully, I am leaving the company on March 3. (I have accepted a job in New York City.) I will be available through March 17 to answer any questions you may have.

Best regards,

Christopher

Christopher,

I am sorry to hear that you will be ________. Thank you ________ your expertise and your help with our research.

I lived in New York for a year, and I'm sure you ________ enjoy its many cultural activities and fascinating museums.

Best wishes,

Richard

V. Choose the correct answer. Only one answer is correct.

1. I'd like to line ________ a job before we move to New York City.
   A. up B. on C. in D. over
2. Did her husband ________ the job?
   A. apply B. change to C. accept D. ask
3. Who will be taking ________ her responsibilities?
   A. under B. over C. from D. above
4. Professor Reed can't teach next semester, so one of ________ faculty will be teaching her classes.
   A. another B. the others
   C. the other D. every other
5. Excuse me, would you ________ me to the library's reference desk?
   A. tell B. talk
   C. point out D. point
6. Does my free e-mail account ________ at the end of the month?
   A. end up B. expire
   C. exist D. register

7. If you miss any resources, then your research will be ________.

A. incomplete B. a lot

C. a incomplete D. the incomplete

8. I thought the museum ________, but she thought it wasn't.

A. was fascinated B. is fascinating

C. was fascinating D. is interesting

VI. Translate the following from English into Chinese.

1. I am sorry to say that I will be leaving the university at the end of the month.
2. The street was lined with small shops.
3. Do you want a king size or regular bed?
4. The trees were planted at regular intervals on both sides of the street.
5. For elderly people, TV is a vital link with the outside world.

VII. Translate the following from Chinese into English.

1. 请接受这个小礼品。
2. 这是你的牛排，祝你吃好！
3. 我们还没有得到我们项目的启动资金。
4. 你能帮助我挑选一些新衣服吗？
5. 这是与吸烟有关的疾病。

Writing Tips

Popular Emoticons	
: -) or : ^ D	Used to indicate a smile or happiness
: - (	Used to indicate a frown or displeasure
; -)	Used to indicate a wink or irony
: - O	Used to indicate surprise

E-mail Thread 2

Subject: My Last Day at *Health + Lifestyle* Magazine
From: BPope@HLM.com
Date: November 2, 2012
To: JOwens@HLM.com; TRamirez@HLM.com; REsposito@HLM.com; MKim@HLM.com
Jim, Tina, Rachel, and Michael, I wanted to let you know that I gave my notice this morning and will leave *Health + Lifestyle* magazine in two weeks. The rumors of layoffs at the magazine worried me. Rather than wait for the layoffs, I decided to find another job because I have two kids in college. It was a difficult decision. I will start working at *Solar Power* magazine on November 19. I've enjoyed working with all of you and hope we can work together again. (If any positions

open up at *Solar Power* magazine, I will let you know—I will highly recommend each of you.) Please keep in touch.

Best,

Brian

Brian Pope
Production Editor
Health + Lifestyle Magazine
555-555-0159

Subject: Streamlining Operations at *Health + Lifestyle* Magazine

From: VWang@HLM.com

Date: November 27, 2012

To: <All Employees>

On November 26, 2012, the board of directors of *Health + Lifestyle* magazine decided to discontinue the print version of the magazine. The reasons are that the market for print publications is weak and it is difficult to sell advertising space. The December 2012 issue will be the last to appear on newsstands.

We will continue to publish our other products. These include an online version of *Health + Lifestyle* magazine, our weekly e-newsletter, and our consumer product guides.

Be assured that *Health + Lifestyle* is alive and well, despite the reduction in staff needed to streamline our products. While we're sad to discontinue the print version, we're happy about our new online publishing opportunities. We will continue to provide our readers with great health and lifestyle resources.

We would like to acknowledge and thank the *Health + Lifestyle* staff for their hard work.

Sincerely,

Victoria Wang
Vice President
Health + Lifestyle Magazine
555-555-0155

New Words 2

1.	acknowledge	[tuːək'nɔlidʒ]	*v.*	对……打招呼
2.	consumer	[kən'sjuːmə]	*n.*	消费者；顾客
3.	despite	[di'spait]	*prep.*	尽管；不论
4.	issue	['iʃjuː]	*n.*	问题；争议
5.	position	[pə'ziʃən]	*n.*	位置；立场
6.	publish	['pʌbliʃ]	*v.*	出版；发行
7.	rumor	['ruːmə]	*n.*	谣传；传闻
8.	sincerely	[sin'siəli]	*adv.*	真诚地；诚恳地
9.	streamline	['striːmlain]	*v.*	精简机构；提高效率

Phrases and Expressions 2

1.	advertising space	广告版面
2.	alive and well	强有力的
3.	board of directors	董事会
4.	consumer product guides	消费者指南
5.	difficult decision	艰难的决定
6.	health and lifestyle resources	健康与生活信息
7.	market for (something) is weak	对……较弱的市场
8.	on newsstands	在书报亭
9.	online version	网上电子版
10.	print publication	印刷版发行

11. print version 印刷版
12. production editor 作品编辑
13. rather than 情愿……而不；与其……，不如……
14. *Solar Power* magazine 太阳能杂志
15. streamlining operations 机构精简行动
16. to open up 建立；开创
17. weekly e-newsletter 电子版每周通讯

Proper Names 2

1. Brian Pope 布莱恩·波普
2. *Health + Lifestyle* magazine 《健康与生活》杂志
3. Jim 吉姆
4. Michael 麦克尔
5. Rachel 雷切尔
6. Tina 蒂娜
7. Victoria Wang 维多利亚·王

Notes 2

1. *I have two kids in college* is a common expression indicating that the parent needs a job to pay for the children's high college tuition.
"我有两个正在上大学的孩子"是很常用的词汇，表明家长需要工作用于支付孩子们昂贵的大学学费。

2. *advertising space* (广告版面): Magazines and newspapers make most of their income from selling advertising space in their publications. Other companies buy the space and print advertisements in it. Publications also generate income by selling subscriptions. Currently, American companies prefer to buy advertising space in online publications and websites rather than in printed publications, and many print publishers are struggling to stay in business.
杂志和报纸的主要收入是印刷刊登其他公司的广告。而其他的公司用购买的版面，印刷出示他们的广告。出版商也会从普通订阅中获得一些利润。和印刷版面相比，近来美国的一些公司更愿意投资电子或网上广告版面。因而不少印刷出版商的生存面临着严峻考验。

3. *layoffs* and *streamlining* (裁员和精简机构): During layoffs, companies reduce the size of their workforce by dismissing some of their employees. Because the term "layoff" has a negative connotation, some companies use more-positive-sounding terms, such as "streamlining," "rightsizing," and "downsizing."
在裁员期间，很多公司要减少他们的员工数量。因为"裁员"意味着消极的含义，因而有些公司用"精简机构"、"重组"和"压缩规模"这些积极向上的词语。

4. *to give one's notice* means "to make somebody know about something before it happens." *notice* here means "announcement."
由于在工作和商务活动中人们的法律意识越来越强了，因此 *to give one's notice* 这一词组也变得越来越常用了。

例：1) Do I have to give notice if I want to move?
如果我想搬出去需要提前通知你吗？
2) You have to give me three weeks' notice before you move.
你在搬家三个星期之前需通知我。
3) You must give advance notice of changes in the arrangements.
你要改变计划时必须事先通知大家。

5. *vice president* 在大学里是副校长，在公司里则是副总裁。在美国公司里有一些高层管理职务的常用英文词。

例：1) president 总裁
2) chairman 董事长
3) chief executive officer (CEO) 行政主管，行政总裁，总裁，首席执行官
4) chief financial officer (CFO) 财务总监；财务主管
5) chief operating officer (COO) 运营主管，项目总监
6) chief technology officer (CTO) 技术总监；技术主管
7) executive （英国）总经理

6. *rather than* (与其……不如……) is used with the infinitive form of a verb to indicate negation that is contrary to a choice or wish.

6.1 *rather than* 用于不定式，暗示相反的选择和愿望。

例：1) Rather than continue the argument, he angrily walked away.
他不愿继续争论下去而生气地走了。

2) Why don't you just finish one thing rather than have so many unfinished things?
与其什么都做不完，你不如就做完一件有用的事。

6.2 *rather than* 还有"and not"，而不是的意思。

例：1) Jessica chooses to play piano rather than sing at school.
杰西卡在学校选择弹钢琴而不是唱歌。

2) He feels very happy rather than sad.
他觉得很高兴而不是伤心。

Exercises 2

I. Answer the following questions.

1. When did Brian Pope give notice?
2. When will Brian leave *Health + Lifestyle* magazine?
3. What rumors did Brian hear?
4. Why did Brian decide to find another job?
5. What magazine will Brian start working for?
6. Who decided to discontinue publishing the print version of *Health + Lifestyle* magazine?
7. Which issue will be the last issue to appear on newsstands?
8. Will the company continue to publish other products?

II. Write an e-mail that explains when and why you are leaving your company.

Key to E-mail Thread 1 Exercises (for Reference)

I. Answer the following questions.

1. Krystal White is a librarian.
2. Krystal is leaving her job because her husband accepted a job in Chicago, Illinois.

3. No, Krystal does not have a job in Chicago yet.
4. Krystal worked at the university for nine years.
5. Krystal's last day at work is April 30.
6. Krystal helped students and faculty in the American Studies Department.
7. Krystal competes in adult swimming.
8. Chicago is a very nice city with many cultural and sports activities and some fascinating museums.

II. Write the key points of this e-mail thread.

- Krystal White is leaving her job because her husband accepted a job in Chicago, Illinois.
- Krystal does not have a job lined up yet.
- Krystal enjoyed being a librarian and working with the American Studies Department.
- Krystal worked at the university for nine years.
- Another librarian is taking over Krystal's responsibilities.
- Krystal will be available to help faculty and students through April 30.
- Linda Reed thanked Krystal for her expertise and for her help with students and faculty.
- Linda hopes Krystal will be able to join an adult swimming league in Chicago and continue competing.
- Linda says Chicago is a nice city with many cultural and sports activities.
- Everyone in the American Studies Department wishes Krystal and her family well.

III. Fill in the blanks.

1. I am available during my regular office hours.
2. The new librarian is taking over her job responsibilities.
3. She is leaving because her husband has accepted a new job in Massachusetts.
4. The librarian pointed me to helpful links for reading online journals.
5. I just lined up a new job in Chicago.
6. He hopes he can continue to participate in local swimming competitions.
7. How can I contact you after your state university e-mail expires?
8. American Studies faculty frequently read research-related journals.

IV. Fill in the missing information:

Dear Richard,

Regretfully, I am leaving the company on March 3. (I have accepted a job in New York City.) I will be available through March 17 to answer any questions you may have.

Best regards,

Christopher

Christopher,

I am sorry to hear that you will be leaving. Thank you for your expertise and your help with our research.

I lived in New York for a year, and I'm sure you will enjoy its many cultural activities and fascinating museums.

Best wishes,

Richard

V. Choose the correct answer. Only one answer is correct.

1. A 2. C 3. B 4. C 5. D 6. B 7. A 8. C

VI. Translate the following from English into Chinese.

1. 我很抱歉地告诉你们，这个月末我就离开这个大学了。
2. 街道两旁都是小商店。
3. 你想要一个超大床还是标准床？
4. 大树按固定间隔种在街道两边。
5. 对于老年人来讲电视是他们了解外界的重要渠道。

VII. Translate the following from Chinese into English.

1. Please accept this small gift.
2. Here's your steak, enjoy!
3. Money is not yet available for us to start our project.
4. Would you help me choose some new clothes?
5. It is a smoking-related disease.

Translation of E-mail Thread 1 (for Reference)

译文：

邮件 1-1

主题：抱歉，我将离开大学
发件人：克里斯托·怀特
日期：2012 年 4 月 11 日
收件人：<美洲研究系>

大家好，

我很抱歉地告诉你们，这个月末我就离开这个大学了。我和我丈夫要搬到伊利诺依州的芝加哥。他在那儿接受了一个新工作。我目前还没有工作，还不知道我的事业前景。: - (

我非常喜爱这九年的大学图书馆馆员的工作。我会想念与美洲研究系各位同事一起工作的日子。另一位图书馆馆员将接替我的工作，并会马上与你们联系。

若你想在我离开前见个面的话，请告诉我。从现在到四月三十号，我还是平常时间办公，(周一到周五上午九点至十二点；下午一点到四点半办公)。

若你想在我大学电邮信箱无效后与我联系，请用这个邮件地址：KWhite@cmail.com.

祝好，

克里斯托

克里斯托·怀特
跨科目学科图书馆员
州立大学
电话号码：555-555-0130，分机：231

邮件 1-2

主题：回复：抱歉，我将离开大学
发件人：琳达·瑞德
日期：2012年4月11日
收件人：克里斯托·怀特

亲爱的克里斯托，

非常感谢你高超的专业知识及对我们美洲研究系师生的协助。若没有你为学生和教授提供查找线索，不少学生和教授会在他们的研究中错过有价值的资料和网上资源。更进一步说，没有你的帮助，我们的研究工作也不会顺利完成。当学校经费缩减，图书馆的管理必须有所变更时，你鼓励我们定期在网上阅读与研究有关期刊，还告诉大家这样做的重要性。

我希望你能在芝加哥找到一个游泳队，而且能继续参加成人队的比赛。你住这儿的时候不是经常参加比赛吗？也许我们能在你回来参赛时见到你。我因学术会议去过几次芝加哥。这座美好的城市常有许多文化和体育活动，还有迷人的博物馆。大家都会非常想念你的。请把我们的祝福带到你的新家。

祝福你，

琳达·瑞德
美洲研究系教授
州立大学
电话号码 555-555-0130，分机：348

Key to E-mail Thread 2 Exercises (for Reference)

I. Answer the following questions.

1. Brian Pope gave a notice this morning.
2. Brian will leave *Health + Lifestyle* magazine in two weeks.
3. Brian heard rumors of layoffs.
4. Brian decided to find another job because he is worried about layoffs and he has two kids in college.
5. Brian will start working for *Solar Power* magazine.
6. *Health + Lifestyle*'s board of directors decided to discontinue publishing the print version of the magazine.
7. The December 2012 issue will be the last issue to appear on newsstands.
8. Yes, the company will continue to publish other products, including an online version of *Health + Lifestyle* magazine, a weekly e-newsletter, and consumer product guides.

Translation of E-mail Thread 2 (for Reference)

译文：

邮件 2-1

主题：我在《健康与生活》杂志的最后一天
发件人：布莱恩·波普
日期：2012 年 11 月 2 日
收件人：吉姆，蒂娜，雷切尔，麦克尔

我今天早上要告知你们，我两个星期后将离开《健康与生活》杂志社。杂志社裁员的传闻让我很担心，与其等着被裁，还不如找别的工作，而且也因为我有两个正在读大学的孩子。这是一个艰难的决定。11 月 19 日起我会开始在《太阳能》杂志上班。

我们一起工作很愉快，我也希望能再次一起工作。（要是《太阳能》杂志有空缺职位，我将告诉你们，并极力推荐你们每一位。）

保持联系。

祝好，

布莱恩
布莱恩·波普
作品编辑
《健康与生活》杂志
电话号码：555-555-0159

邮件 2-2

主题：《健康与生活》的机构精简
发件人：维多利亚·王
日期：2012 年 11 月 27 日
收件人：<全体员工>

2012 年 11 月 26 号，董事会决定停止《健康与生活》印刷版的出版发行。原因是印刷版市场需求较弱，广告版面销售困难。2012 年 12 月刊将为书报亭出售最后一期。

我们还将继续出版其他版本，如在线电子版的《健康与生活》、《每周通讯》和《消费者指南》。

为了能使《健康与生活》越办越好，我们将精简人员，提高效率。在我们难过地终止印刷版的同时，我们很高兴地看到发行新的在线电子版机会。我们的《健康与生活》仍将为读者们提供最佳的健康与生活信息来源。

我们要向大家宣布和感谢《健康与生活》的员工对这个杂志所作出的贡献。

真诚的，

维多利亚·王
《健康与生活》副总经理
《健康与生活》杂志
电话号码：555-555-0155

Lesson 9

Job Search
找工作

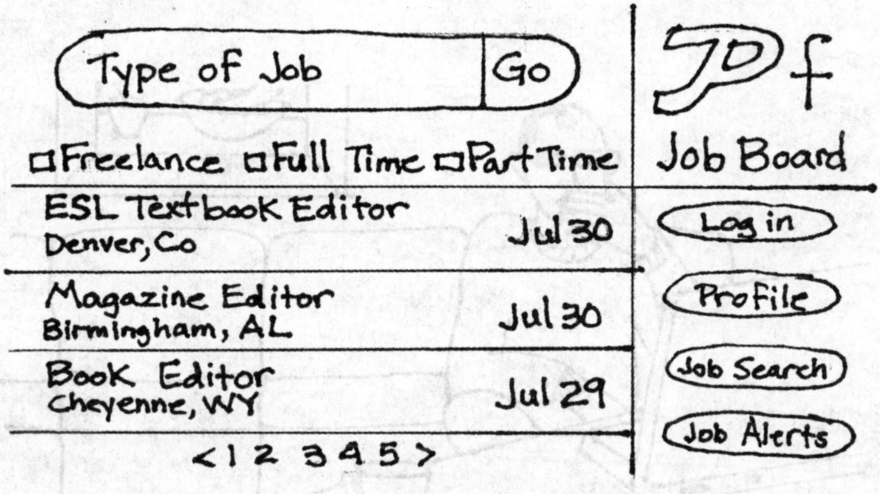

Learning Objectives

In this lesson, you will learn the following:

- How to casually inquire about work opportunities
  非正式地了解就业机会
- How to sign up for a job board
  登录工作网
- What services a job board provides
  工作网站的服务项目
- What a job posting looks like
  公开招聘细节
- How to reply to a job posting
  应聘

E-mail Thread 1

Subject: Re: Editing work?
From: Ryan@cmail.com
Date: July 9, 2012
To: Lindsey@cmail.com

Hi Lindsey,

I'm a freelancer, so I work for a variety of companies. (Most of my current clients publish textbooks.) I'll let you know if any opportunities come up, but my business has been very slow.

You might want to sign up at a job board so you can receive job postings. (I joined the Publishing Freelancer job board.) You can find job boards by searching the World Wide Web with the keywords "freelance editing job board." You can also check the websites of some of the big publishers—they sometimes have a "careers" link with information about applying for freelance or offsite positions.

Best wishes in your search,

Ryan

—Original Message—
From: Lindsey
To: Ryan
Sent: July 9, 2012, 8:38 a.m.
Subject: Editing Work?

Lindsey wrote:

Hi Ryan,

I've been looking for part-time, flexible work. I remember that you are an editor and seem to have a flexible schedule. Does the company you work for have any work available? I would greatly appreciate your referring me, because I need to increase my income to pay for upcoming dental work. I have 35 years of experience as an office manager and have worked on all kinds of written communications. I'm also detail oriented. I've been reading (and editing) since about age three, which is a long time!

Thanks, Ryan.

Lindsey

Subject: Your Job Board Enrollment
From: enrollment@publishingfreelancer.com
Date: July 12, 2012
To: Lindsey@cmail.com

Lindsey Martinez:

Thank you for creating an account with Publishing Freelancer. We have billed the annual fee of $75 to your credit card account ending in *xxxx*.

First, you need to set up your profile by listing the details of your résumé. After you set up your profile, you will automatically receive job postings. You will also receive job offers from employers who view your profile. Click here to create your profile:

www.publishingfreelancer.com/myprofile.

Second, you can track your job search by storing cover letters, job openings, communications with employers, and notes in your account. Click here to access your account:

www.publishingfreelancer.com/myaccount.

Finally, you can create job alerts that e-mail you job postings matching your pay rate and expertise. Click here to set up job alerts:

www.publishingfreelancer.com/myjobalerts.

Our goal is to provide you with the best freelance job opportunities in the publishing world. Please let us know if you have any questions about our comprehensive services.

Sincerely,

Publishing Freelancer
www.publishingfreelancer.com

For information about our privacy policy, please click on www.publishingfreelancer.com/privacy.

New Words 1

1.	appreciate	[ə'pri:ʃieit]	*v.*	感谢；感激
2.	bill	[bil]	*v.*	付账，付款
3.	casually	['kæʒjuəli]	*adv.*	非正式地；漫无目的地
4.	enrollment	[in'rəulmənt]	*n.*	注册人数；招生
5.	expertise	[ˌekspə:'ti:z]	*n.*	专门技术；专门知识
6.	freelance	['fri:'lɑ:ns]	*adj.*	自由的；独立的
7.	freelancer	['fri:lænsə]	*n.*	自由职业者
8.	keyword	[ki:wə:d]	*n.*	关键词，关键字
9.	profile	['prəufail]	*n.*	个人情况；个人信息
10.	publisher	['pʌbliʃə]	*n.*	出版商；出版公司
11.	résumé	[ri'zju:m]	*n.*	个人简历
12.	search	[sə:tʃ]	*v.*	找；查找
13.	store	[stɔ:]	*v.*	保管；容纳

14. upcoming	['ʌpˌkʌmiŋ]	*adj.*	即将来临的
15. view	[vjuː]	*v.*	查看；观看

Phrases and Expressions 1

1. annual fee 年费
2. comprehensive service 综合服务
3. cover letter 求职扉页；说明信
4. current clients 目前客户
5. dental work 治疗牙齿
6. detail oriented 关注细节
7. editing work 编辑工作
8. flexible schedule 弹性时间安排
9. flexible work 弹性工作
10. job alert 工作机会通知
11. job board 工作网站
12. job offer 工作录用通知
13. job opening 工作机会
14. job posting 聘用发贴
15. job search 寻求工作
16. offsite position 公司的异地工作岗位
17. pay rate 工资标准
18. privacy policy 隐私政策
29. to come up 发生；出现
20. to inquire about 咨询有关……
21. to set up 创立；建立
22. to sign up 登记；注册
23. work opportunity 工作机会
24. written communications 文字交流

Proper Names 1

1. Lindsey Martinez 林赛·马丁尼兹

2. Ryan Weber 瑞恩·韦伯
3. World Wide Web 全球资讯网

Notes 1

1. *freelancer* (自由职业者): Freelancer is someone with a particular skill who contracts with many companies to perform the skill. Freelancers are self-employed. The word "freelancer" comes from the Middle Ages term for "mercenary solider." To freelance means "to work as a freelancer."
自由职业者是具有某种特别才能的人。他们与很多公司都签有合同，并用他们的才能为公司服务。自由职业者是个体经营者。freelancer 这个词是用来称呼中世纪受雇佣的士兵。To freelance 可用作动词，是指自由职业的工作方式。

2. *job board* (工作网站) 和 *job postings* (聘用发贴): A job board is a website where companies post job openings and list the jobs' requirements. Job boards help a company find qualified candidates. Some job boards list all kinds of jobs, and some list jobs in a particular industry, profession, or region. Some job boards are free, and some charge a fee. A job posting lists a specific job opening, its requirements, and information for contacting the company posting the job.
工作网站是一个网页。许多公司都在上边发贴，告知工作机会和要求。工作网站帮助公司搜寻合格的人选。有些工作网站刊登各种不同类型的工作机会，有些仅登某种行业、某种职业、某个地区的工作机会。有些工作网站是免费的，而有些则需付一定的费用。job postings（聘用发贴）列出具体的工作机会，要求和相关信息及如何与公司联系的方式。

3. *offsite positions* (其他地理位置): Many companies allow employees to work "offsite," or from home or even from a different city. Offsite employees use technologies such as the Internet, the telephone, texting, e-mail, and instant messaging to interact with colleagues and perform their duties. This is called "telecommuting."
很多公司允许员工在"异地"而不是在公司，如"在家"，"甚至在别的城市"工作。异地工作员工利用网络、电话、短信、电子邮件、QQ 等与同事们沟通，完成他们的职责。这就叫"异地办公"。

4. *job alert* (工作机会通知): Job alert is a notification that a job posting website sends when a job matching the subscriber's criteria becomes available. It alerts (i.e., notifies by e-mail, SMS, or other means) the subscriber to look at the job posting and determine whether to apply for it.
工作网站发出的工作机会通知，告知此工作机会与你所要寻找的工作条件相符。工作机会通知通过电子邮件，发短信或其他手段，提醒你看一下这个工作机会并是否要申请。

5. *client* (客户)：一般提供专业咨询或服务的个人或团体的客户使用*client*，如律师、会计师和医生等。而*customer*通常译为顾客，它同 client 的区别在于 customer 接受的通常是普通服务，例如在商店和饭店的顾客通常用 customer 一词。在公司两个词都可用，公司客户既可以用 client, 也可用 customer。

例：1) Attorney Smith drew up a will for her client.
史密斯律师为她的客户起草了一份遗嘱。
2) My local grocery store thinks of me as a regular customer because I shop there at least once a week.
我们当地的食品杂货店觉得我是老顾客，因为我每周至少在那儿采购一次。

6. *to apply for* 的宾语在内容上应当是希望获得的事物，例如工作、奖金、贷款等。而 *apply to* 的宾语在内容上则应当是对之作出申请的个人或机构。

例：1) Josie applied for a part-time summer job at the nearby grocery store.
乔希在附近的食品杂货店申请了夏季打零工。
2) How many top-10 universities have you applied to?
你向几所前十名的大学提出了申请？
3) The law against drinking while driving applies to all drivers.
严禁酒后开车的法律适用于所有的司机。

7. *written communications* (笔头交流): *communication* 是抽象名词，抽象名词是表示状态、品质、情感等没有实物的名词，如“love, law”等。用抽象名词时，一般它的前面不加冠词，后面没有复数形式。但在很多情况下，有许多抽象名词可以具体化。具体化的名词前面可加冠词，也可变成可数名词。

例：1) Science books tell us about the law of gravity.
自然科学书籍告诉我们“万有引力定律”。
2) Last year, I had an unusual travel experience.
去年我有过一次不同寻常的旅行经历。

3) China is doing its best to achieve the four modernizations.
中国正在努力实现四个现代化。

8. *cover letter*：从广义上来说，是指在正式文件之前的一封简短说明信。它与其他文件一起发送并进行简明说明同时提供资料清单。另外在一些情况下，cover letter 也有附信的意思。目前在职场中，cover letter 通常理解为求职信的扉页，是简历的一部分。一般在信中你要简要介绍自己的情况，以及你要申请的职位和你的最大的优势。

Exercises 1

I. Answer the following questions.

1. What kind of work has Lindsey Martinez been looking for?
2. What did Lindsey ask Ryan Weber?
3. What would Lindsey appreciate Ryan doing for her?
4. Does Ryan work for more than one company?
5. What did Ryan tell Lindsey to do?
6. What is the annual fee for the Publishing Freelancer job board?
7. What must Lindsey set up first?
8. What things can Lindsey store in her account?

II. Write the key points of this e-mail thread.

III. Fill in the blanks.

1. You can't view my résumé until I set ________ my profile.
2. The job board has ________ the annual fee of $100 to your credit card account.
3. He is a ________, so he works for a variety of companies.
4. She searched the World Wide Web with the ________ "freelance editing job board."
5. I would greatly ________ your referring me for work at your company.
6. Can I ________ cover letters and communications with employers in my job board account?
7. College students need jobs that have a part-time, ________ schedule.
8. I signed ________ at a job board so I can receive job postings.

IV. Fill in the missing information.

Dear Mina,

My business has been slow, and I'm looking for more freelance jobs. I remember that you belong to a job board. I would appreciate your telling which job board you joined.

Thanks,

Ben

Hi Ben,

I belong to the Publishing Freelancer job ________. I like the comprehensive services that it provides. For example, I set up a ________ that lists the details of my résumé. Then I created job ________ that e-mail me job postings matching my pay rate and expertise. I can also store my ________ letters in my account.

Regards,

Mina

V. Choose the correct answer. Only one answer is correct.

1. She had to get a second job to ________ her income.
   A. decrease B. increase C. rise D. reduce
2. Do you have a/an ________ with the Publishing Freelancer job board?
   A. record B. work C. count D. account
3. I've never received any job postings from that job ________.
   A. board B. company C. office D. room
4. You have to pay me ________ the money you owe me.
   A. for B. to C. X D. with
5. Unfortunately, that job board doesn't let you ________ your notes in your account.
   A. store B. send C. to send D. to store
6. I have to look after my baby in the morning, so my plan is to get ________.

A. a part-time work B. full-time work

C. a part-time job D. a full-time job

7. For further information, apply ________ the secretary of the company.

A. for B. at C. with D. to

8. How do I ________ for the job board?

A. sign over B. sign on C. sign up D. sign in

VI. Translate the following from English into Chinese.

1. You will also receive job offers from employers who view your profile.
2. He is freelancing for several companies at home.
3. I'm thinking of signing up for a yoga course.
4. Sometimes you have to keep a low profile.
5. I'm not an expert, but I appreciate fine works of art.

VII. Translate the following from Chinese into English.

1. 在使用之前不要忘了签字。
2. 毕业后他在美国申请了三个工作。
3. 怀孕后她想做兼职工作。
4. 我的工作计划比较灵活。
5. 在给你我们最后的书面计划之前，我需要同你核实几件事。

Writing Tips

	Writing Styles for E-mails
Personal	Used to communicate with close friends, colleagues, and relatives; this style often expresses emotions and ideas, including thanks, invitations, and regret and condolences; uses informal writing style, slang, and abbreviations
Social	Used to communicate with close friends, close colleagues, and social acquaintances; may express appreciation; often provides

	information about certain events; uses informal or formal writing style, depending on the event
Business	Used for communication between individuals and companies or organizations; may ask for information about products, services, or job opportunities; may complain about products or services; or may explain or advertise products and services; uses formal writing style and does not use slang and abbreviations

E-mail Thread 2

Subject: Job Alert: Textbook Editor
From: jobpostings@publishingfreelancer.com
Date: July 30, 2012
To: RWeber@rweberediting.com
Job Description:
Seeking freelance editors for ongoing work during 2012-2013. Expertise in English as a

second language or educational publishing is a huge plus. Must be detail oriented and able to work quickly and efficiently using word processing software. Freelancers will be hired on a project-by-project basis.

Pay rate: $20-$25 per hour, DOE

Contact Information:
Contact Name: Human Resources Department
Contact Method: Contact by E-mail
E-mail: HR@ESLbooks.com
www.ESLbooks.com

Subject: Freelance Textbook Editor Positions
From: RWeber@rweberediting.com
Date: July 31, 2012
To: HR@ESLbooks.com
Attachments: RyanWeberResume.pdf

Dear Sir or Madam,

I am responding to your job posting for textbook editors, which was listed on the Publishing Freelancer job board. I reviewed your website and am very impressed with the quality of your textbooks.

I have nearly 20 years of experience editing educational materials, including 15 textbooks for teaching English as a second language. Moreover, I have experience with learning a second language, because I have been studying Mandarin for 10 years. As a result, I understand how foreign language textbooks are designed.

In addition to my expertise, I am able to edit in word processing and PDF software. I can also e-mail files and download and upload files on websites. I am detail oriented and work quickly and efficiently, even under deadline.

My résumé is attached for your review. Please contact me if you have questions or need further information. I look forward to hearing from you.

Sincerely,

Ryan Weber
53 Open Sky Dr.
Fort Collins, CO 80521
555-555-0189
RWeber@rweberediting.com

New Words 2

1.	attachment	[ə'tætʃmənt]	*n.*	附件
2.	deadline	['dedlain]	*n.*	截止日期
3.	efficiently	[i'fiʃəntli]	*adv.*	效率高地
4.	electronically	[ilek'trɔnikəli]	*adv.*	电子地
5.	Mandarin	['mændərin]	*n.*	汉语；普通话
6.	quality	['kwɔliti]	*n.*	质量
7.	attach	[ə'tætʃ]	*v.*	附加
8.	design	[di'zain]	*v.*	设计；构思；绘制
9.	hire	['haiə]	*v.*	雇用；聘用
10.	impress	[im'pres]	*v.*	留下印象；印象
11.	list	[list]	*v.*	列表；列在
12.	review	[ri'vjuː]	*v.*	复习；浏览

Phrases and Expressions 2

1.	DOE (depending on experience)	根据经验而定
2.	editor position	编辑职位
3.	educational material	教育方面的资料
4.	ESL (English as a second language)	英语为第二语言

6. freelance editor 自由职业的编辑
7. FTP site 资料传送站
8. huge plus 格外的益处；优先
9. job description 工作性质描述
10. ongoing work 目前进行的工作
11. PDF software 可移植文档格式的文件编辑软件
12. project-by-project basis 以逐一项目为原则
13. to respond to 回复
14. to upload a file 在网络上传送文件
15. word processing 文字处理

Notes 2

1. *ongoing work* (正在进行的工作): *ongoing* 是形容词，“being actually in process”表示一种状态。这里译为“在此期间的工作”。

例： There is an *ongoing* debate over the issue of raising property taxes.
是否提高房地产税的话题还在辩论着。

2.1. *ESL* (English as a second language) refers to the use or study of English by people who speak a different native language. Various terms, including “ESL” and “English for speakers of other languages (ESOL),” are used in different countries to describe this situation. Usually these terms refer to teaching and learning English, but they may also refer to demographic groups of people.
ESL 和 ESOL 是指英语为第二语言的学生学习，使用英文。课程的目标在于增进学生的英语技能。在不同的国家，这些术语都指教授和学习英语技能，它们也可指这个特定群体。

2.2 *teaching English as a second language* 简称为 TESL，译为“作为二外的英语教学”。在语言教学中，还有一个术语是 *teaching English as a foreign language*，简称为 TEFL，译为“作为外语的英语教学”。二外教学与学习和外语教学与学习是有区别的。从表面上来讲，你在中国学习英语，你就是一个外语学习者，而你去了美国学习英语，你就是一个二外学习者。在中国，外语学习多从语法和翻译入手，没有语言环境的支持，理论学习多于实践。在美国学习外语就容易多了，上课学习语言，下课使用语言，能体会语言中的文化，从而加深对语言的理解，因此两者的学习和教学方法都不一样。

3.1. *Mandarin* 原指北京话或北方方言，现在多指普通话。方言一词英语为 dialect。The English word *Mandarin* comes from the Malaysian word for *counselor* that sixteenth-century Portuguese traders used to address Asian officials. 英文中的 *Mandarin* 是马来西亚语，意思是专员。在 16 世纪葡萄牙商人用来称呼亚洲官员。

例： Shanghai dialect
上海话

3.2. 鸳鸯在汉英字典中被译为“Mandarin duck”，而实际上“love duck”才是鸳鸯。

Exercises 2

I. Answer the following questions.

1. What expertise does the company desire?
2. What must freelance editors be able to do?
3. On what basis will freelancers be hired?
4. What is the pay rate?
5. How many years of editing experience does Ryan Weber have?
6. What software is Ryan able to edit in?
7. Can Ryan download and upload files on websites?
8. Is Ryan detail oriented?

II. Write an e-mail that responds to a job posting.

Key to E-mail Thread 1 Exercises (for Reference)

I. Answer the following questions.

1. Lindsey Martinez has been looking for part-time, flexible work.

2. Lindsey asked Ryan Weber whether the company he worked for had any work available.
3. Lindsey would greatly appreciate Ryan referring her for any work at his company.
4. Yes, Ryan works for a variety of companies.
5. Ryan told Lindsay to sign up at a job board and to check the websites of some of the big publishers.
6. The annual fee for the Publishing Freelancer job board is $75.
7. Lindsey must set up her profile first.
8. Lindsey can store cover letters, job openings, communications with employers, and notes in her account.

II. Write the key points of this e-mail thread.

- Lindsey Martinez is looking for part-time, flexible work and asks Ryan Weber to refer her for any work that is available at his company.
- Because Ryan is a freelancer and his business is slow, he cannot refer her to a company.
- Ryan tells Lindsey to search the World Wide Web for job boards and sign up with one. He also tells her to check the websites of publishing companies for freelance and offsite jobs.
- Lindsey signs up with the Publishing Freelancer job board.
- Publishing Freelancer billed the annual fee of $75 to Lindsey's credit card.
- Lindsey needs to create a profile so that she can receive job postings and job offers.
- Lindsey can use her account to track her job search progress and create job alerts.

III. Fill in the blanks.

1. You can't view my résumé until I set up my profile.
2. The job board has billed the annual fee of $100 to your credit card account.
3. He is a freelancer, so he works for a variety of companies.
4. She searched the World Wide Web with the keywords "freelance editing job board."
5. I would greatly appreciate your referring me for work at your company.
6. Can I store cover letters and communications with employers in my job board account?
7. College students need jobs that have a part-time, flexible schedule.
8. I signed up at a job board so I can receive job postings.

IV. Fill in the missing information.

Hi Ben,

I belong to the Publishing Freelancer job board. I like the comprehensive services that it provides. For example, I set up a profile that lists the details of my résumé. Then I created job alerts that e-mail me job postings matching my pay rate and expertise. I can also store my cover letters in my account.

Regards,

Mina

V. Choose the correct answer. Only one answer is correct.

1. B　2. D　3. A　4. C　5. A　6. C　7. D　8. C

VI. Translate the following from English into Chinese.

1. 你会收到看过你个人信息的雇主所发出的工作录用通知。
2. 作为自由职业者他在家同时为几家公司工作。
3. 我正在考虑报一个瑜伽班。
4. 有时你需要保持低调。
5. 我不是一个专家，但是我赏识好的艺术作品。

VII. Translate the following from Chinese into English.

1. Don't forget to sign it before using it.
2. After graduation, He applied for three jobs in the United States.
3. She wants to work part-time after having baby.
4. My work schedule is fairly flexible.
5. I have to check a few things with you before sending you our final written plan.

Translation of E-mail Thread 1 (for Reference)

译文：

邮件 1-1

主题：回复：编辑工作?
发件人：Ryan@cmail.com
日期：2012 年 7 月 9 日
收件人：Lindsey@cmail.com

你好林赛，

我是自由职业者，因而为很多不同的公司工作。（我目前绝大多数的客户出版教科书）。若有工作机会我会告知你，不过最近业务不多。你也可以在工作网站注册，这样你可以收到聘用发贴。（我就加入了出版业的自由职业者工作网站。）在全球资讯网输入关键字“独立编辑工作网站”，你就能找到工作网站。你也可以搜寻一下那些大出版商的网站，有时侯“职业”一栏也会为自由职业者提供申请工作和某公司异地工作信息。

祝你好运，

瑞恩

—邮件原件—
主题：编辑工作
发件人：林赛
日期：2012 年 7 月 9 日上午 8:38
收件人：瑞恩

林赛写到：

你好瑞恩，

我一直在寻找时间灵活的兼职工作。我记得你是编辑，而且可以灵活地安排工作时间。你工作的公司需要人吗？若你能推荐我，我会非常感谢。因为我马上要有治牙的花销，需要增加收入。我有三十五年做办公室主任的经验，对各种文字交流都非常熟悉。我还是一个非常细致的人。从三岁起就开始读书（编辑）了，可算得上是有年头了吧。

谢谢你，瑞恩。

林赛

邮件 1-2

主题：你的求职登记
发件人：enrollment@publishingfreelancer.com
日期：2012 年 7 月 12 日
收件人：Lindsey@cmail.com

林赛・马丁尼兹，

谢谢你在出版界自由职业者上建立了账户。你交付 75 美元的年费已从你以 *xxxx* 结束的信用卡账户扣除。首先你得创建一个详细的个人概况网页，然后就会自动收到聘用发贴。你也会收到看过你个人概况网页的雇主所发出的工作录用通知。点击此网址建立个人概况网页：

www.publishingfreelancer.com/myprofile.

第二，你可以在个人网页中，通过求职扉页和工作机会、与雇主的电子邮件交流及个人笔记分类了解你找工作的情况。点击此网址进入你的账户：

www.publishingfreelancer.com/myaccount.

最后，你还可以建立工作机会通知。如果聘用发贴与你的专长和你希望的薪资相符时，它会用电子邮件通知你。点击此网址建立工作机会通知：

www.publishingfreelancer.com/myjobalerts

我们的目的是为你提供最好的出版界自由职业者的工作机会。若你对我们的综合服务有任何疑问，请告知。

此致，

出版自由职业者
www.publishingfreelancer.com

有关我们的保密制度，请点击
www.publishingfreelancer.com/privacy

Key to E-mail Thread 2 Exercises (for Reference)

I. Answer the following questions.

1. The company desires expertise in English as a second language or in educational publishing.
2. The freelance editors must be able to work quickly and efficiently using word processing software.
3. Freelancers will be hired on a project-by-project basis.
4. The pay rate is \$20–\$25 per hour, depending on experience.
5. Ryan Weber has 20 years of editing experience.
6. Ryan is able to edit in word processing and PDF software.
7. Yes, Ryan can download and upload files on websites.
8. Yes, Ryan is detail oriented.

Translation of E-mail Thread 2 (for Reference)

译文：

邮件 2-1

主题：工作机会通知：教科书编辑
发件人：jobpostings@publishingfreelancer.com
日期：2012 年 7 月 30 日
收件人：瑞恩・韦伯

工作职责说明：

为 2012-2013 年度的工作项目寻找自由职业的编辑。优先考虑申请人的英语为第二语言及教育出版专业知识。工作要求注重细节，快速高效地使用电脑文字处理软件。自由职业者的聘用将根据项目而定。

酬金：每小时 20-25 美元，根据经验而定。

联系信息：
联系人：人力资源部
联系方式：电子邮件
网址：HR@ESLbooks.com
www.ESLbooks.com

邮件 2-2

主题：自由职业教科书编辑位置
发件人：R・韦伯
日期：2012 年 7 月 31 日
收件人：HR@ESLbooks.com

附件：瑞恩·韦伯个人简历

亲爱的先生/女士，

我回应出版社自由职业工作网站上有关教科书编辑的聘用发贴。我浏览了你们的网页，你们高质量的教科书给我留下了很深刻的印象。

我有近二十年编辑教育资料的经验，其中包括十五本英语为第二语言的课本。再有，我还有学习第二语言的经验。因为我学汉语学了十年了，所以了解外语教科书是如何构思的。

除了我的专长以外，我还能用电脑进行文字处理和 PDF 软件。我也能用电子邮件发送文件并能在网站下载和上传文件。尽管有时间限制，我能做到认真细致，快速高效。

附上我的个人简历便您过目。若有任何问题或需更多信息请与我联系。我期待着您的回音。

此致，

瑞恩·韦伯
通天路 53 号
科罗拉多州柯林斯堡，邮编 80521
电话：555-555-0189
RWeber@rweberediting.com

Lesson 10

Travel Arrangements

旅行安排

Learning Objectives

In this lesson, you will learn the following:

- How to combine a business trip with a personal visit
  出差与个人拜访相结合
- How to forward travel information to someone
  发送旅行信息
- What information an electronic airline itinerary contains
  旅行社电子行程表内容
- What information a hotel reservation contains
  旅馆预订信息
- What information an rental car reservation contains
  预订租车信息

E-mail Thread 1

Subject: New York Trip	
From: ShawnSuzuki@businessassociates.com	
Date: January 12, 2012	
To: TheGuptas@cmail.com	

Hey Derek and Jasmine,

Greetings from Wyoming! I wanted to drop you a line about my trip to New York for an upcoming convention. I will arrive on Friday, March 9, and will head home on Wednesday, March 14. If you have some free time while I'm in New York, I would love to see you. I'll even treat you to dinner at your favorite brewpub!

Hope all is well in New York!

Cheers,

Shawn

Shawn Suzuki, Director of Marketing
Business Associates
www.businessassociates.com
ShawnSuzuki@businessassociates.com
1-800-555-0184

P.S. I will send you my airline itinerary for your reference.

Subject: Fwd: Airline Confirmation for New York Trip	
From: ShawnSuzuki@businessassociates.com	
Date: January 14, 2012	
To: TheGuptas@cmail.com	

Hi again,

I'm glad we'll be able to get together for dinner, and I'm looking forward to seeing you!

Here is my itinerary. I will be staying at Hotel New York. Since I will be renting a car, I can pick you up at your place and drive to the brewpub.

I'll be in touch before I leave for New York.

Best,

Shawn

-------- Original Message --------
Subject: Airline Confirmation for New York Trip
Date: Tuesday, January 10, 2012, 9:45 a.m.
From: <OnlineTravel>
To: ShawnSuzuki@businessassociates.com

Online Travel wrote:

Dear Shawn,

Thank you for reserving your flight through Online Travel!

This is an e-ticket, so you will not receive a paper ticket. Your e-ticket confirmation number is 7797749412. The following itinerary is also available in your Online Travel account.

Itinerary (Times are given in local time.)
Cheyenne, WY (CYS) to New York-John F. Kennedy International Airport (JFK), New York City, NY
Flight 5410

Fri., Mar. 9	06:15 a.m.	Cheyenne, WY (CYS) to
	02:03 p.m.	New York-John F. Kennedy International Airport (JFK)

Nonstop
Requested Seat: 03D
Total Travel Time: 5 hr 48 min

New York-John F. Kennedy International Airport (JFK) to Cheyenne, WY (CYS)
Flight 4970
Wed., Mar. 14 09:46 a.m. New York-John F. Kennedy International Airport (JFK) to
12:00 p.m. Cincinnati, OH (CVG)
2 hr 14 min
Requested Seat: Please check in at the ticket counter for seat assignments.

Stop—Change Planes in Cincinnati, OH (CVG)
Connection Time: 0 hr 55 min
Flight 5363
Wed., Mar 14 12:55 p.m. Cincinnati, OH (CVG) to
01:56 p.m. Cheyenne, WY (CYS)
3 hr 1 min
Total Travel Time: 6 hr 10 min

Passenger Information
Passenger Name*: Shawn Suzuki
Ticket Number: 003409146
Frequent Flyer Number: 124408456

*You must have a government-issued photo ID (such as a driver's license or passport) to board the airplane. The passenger name on the reservation must match your ID.

Complete your travel plans! Click on the following links to
Reserve a Hotel Room
Check In Online
Check for Airport Delays
Check Flight Status

Billing Information
Total Airline Charges (Includes Taxes & Fees): US$610.70
Total Online Travel Fees: US$10.00
Total Amount Charged to Credit Card Ending in *xxxx*: US$625.70
Your ticket is nonrefundable.

To cancel or change your trip, call Customer Service:
In the US: 1-800-555-0112
Outside the US: (1)-555-555-0113

New Words 1

1.	account	[ə'kaunt]	*n.*	账单；账户
2.	board	[bɔːd]	*v.*	登（车；船；飞机）
3.	cheers	[tʃiəs]	*n.*	祝贺；干杯
4.	confirmation	[ˌkɔnfə'meiʃən]	*n.*	确认；认可
5.	contain	[tkən'tein]	*v.*	包含；容纳；装有
6.	fee	[fiː]	*n.*	费用
7.	forward	['fɔːwəd]	*v.*	发送；递送
8.	head	['hed]	*v.*	出发（向某个方向）
9.	nonrefundable	[nʌnri'fʌndəbl]	*adj.*	不退还的
10.	nonstop	[nɔn'stɔp]	*adj.*	直达的；不停的
11.	passport	['pɑːsˌpɔːt]	*n.*	护照
12.	reserve	[ri'zəːv]	*v.*	预约；预订
13.	tax	[tæks]	*n.*	税；税金

Phrases and Expressions 1

1. airport delay 机场延误
2. billing information 账单信息
3. Business Associates 商业伙伴
4. driver's license 驾车执照

5.	electronic airline itinerary	电子航空行程表
6.	e-ticket	电子票
7.	favorite brewpub	最喜欢的售餐酒吧
8.	flight status	飞机飞行情况
9.	Frequent Flyer	常飞旅客
10.	government-issued photo ID	由政府颁发带有照片的身份证
11.	hotel reservation	旅馆预订
12.	local time	当地时间
13.	paper ticket	纸质票
14.	passenger information	旅客信息
15.	rental car reservation	租车预订
16.	requested seat	特别要求的座位
17.	seat assignment	座位安排
18.	ticket counter	票证柜台
19.	to check for	检查
20.	to check in	办理登记；登机手续
21.	to drop a line	留言；留信息
22.	total airline charges	机票总额
23.	upcoming convention	即将召开的会议

Proper Names 1

1.	Cheyenne	夏延
2.	Cincinnati	辛辛那提市（俄亥俄州）
3.	Derek	德里克
4.	Guptas	格塔司
5.	Hawaii (HI)	夏威夷
6.	Jasmine	贾斯敏
7.	John F. Kennedy International Airport	肯尼迪国际机场
8.	New York	纽约
9.	Ohio (OH)	俄亥俄州
10.	Online Travel account	网上旅行预订账户
11.	Shawn Suzuki	肖恩·铃木
12.	Wyoming (WY)	怀俄明州

Notes 1

1. *US time zones* (美国的不同时间区域): The United States has six time zones: Eastern, Central, Mountain, Pacific, Alaska, and Hawaii-Aleutian. In addition, most states follow Daylight Savings Time by moving clocks forward one hour at 2:00 a.m. on the second Sunday in March. This makes summer days longer by "moving" one hour of daylight from the morning to the evening. Clocks move back one hour on the first Sunday in November. Travel itineraries use the local time zone.
美国有六个不同的时间区：它们是东部、中部、山脉地区、太平洋区、阿拉斯加和夏威夷。每年三月第二个周日把时钟从凌晨两点调为三点。沿用夏季白天多一小时的节能时间。而在每年十一月的第一个周日将凌晨三点再调回为两点。旅行行程表使用当地时间区的时间。

2. *brewpub* (售餐酒吧) is a popular type of restaurant. The atmosphere is casual, and the beer is brewed at the restaurant. The menu includes hamburgers and English-style "pub food" such as "bangers and mash" (sausage and mashed potatoes) and shepherd's pie (a baked dish of meat, mashed potatoes, and vegetables).
售餐酒吧是一种很流行的餐馆。它有休闲的环境及自家酿造的啤酒。其菜单包括汉堡和英式酒吧食品，诸如腊肠、土豆泥和牧羊人肉饼、土豆泥、蔬菜。

3. *John F. Kennedy* (约翰逊・肯尼迪) was the 35th US president. He was assassinated in 1963, and New York City's Idlewild Airport was renamed to John F. Kennedy International Airport (JFK) in his honor. Itineraries specify "JFK" to distinguish it from New York City's other major airport, La Guardia Airport. (This airport is named after New York mayor Fiorello La Guardia.)
约翰逊・肯尼迪是美国第三十五届总统。在他 1963 年被刺杀后，为纪念约翰逊・肯尼迪，纽约市的 Idlewild 机场更名为"肯尼迪国际机场（JFK）"。行程表标明（JFK）即有别于另一个纽约市的以市长"拉瓜迪亚"命名的主要机场。

4. *to drop somebody a line* 在过去是给某人写封信。现在随着通信方式增多，这组动词短语的意思也增加了一些。它本身有留言的意思，所以在生活中可以是写信，发电子邮件或者发手机短信。

5. *to treat somebody to dinner* 意思是邀请某人吃晚饭。*to treat somebody* (*with something*)是用什么来款待某人。两个句型的意思接近，但有时用法不同。

例：1) I will treat you to Ben & Jerry's ice cream after the game.
比赛以后我请你吃“本和杰瑞”冰淇淋。

2) I'll treat you with an ice cream.
我用冰淇淋来招待你。

3) I'll treat myself to a sunbath.
我要好好地享受一次日光浴。
但在这种情况下，用 *to treat myself with a sunbath* 这一句型就不是很恰当。

6.1. *to head home*（回家）在这里 *head* 是不及物动词，意思是“朝某个方向走”。head 后面常跟介词“for。”

例：Then we headed for the small town. 后来我们向那个小镇方向走去。

6.2. *home* 是副词，同不及物动词连用时不用加介词。

例：Let's go home. 我们回家吧。

7. *Fwd*: 在电子邮件的 subject 后面有时会有 *Fwd*:，它是“forward”一词的缩写，在此处有“转递或转交”这个意思。这说明这封信是别人转发给你的或者主要内容来自于别人。

8. *to be (get) in touch* 是固定动词短语，意思是保持联系。这是在电话中、信中和会谈中的结束用语。如同某人保持联系， 需加介词“with”。

例：I asked her to get in touch with Henry as soon as possible.
我要求她尽快与亨利联系。

9. *e-ticket* 是电子机票。在许多地方它已代替了传统的纸质机票（paper ticket）。在机场，你只需出示你的身份证，航空公司就可以调出你的姓名、航班等信息并为你办理相关登机手续。

10.1. *hotel room:* 出差时，我们会根据自己的情况在饭店预订各种不同的房间。

例：1) twin room　标准间

2) double room　双人间

3) single room　单人间

4) suite　套房

10.2. 在美国，预订单人间时会注明所需床的大小及尺寸。Queen-sized bed 是 1.5 米宽的床，最大的是 king-sized bed，接近 2 米宽。

10.3. *check in* 和 *check out* 是动词，意思是办理入住和办理退房手续。另外 check in 还有办理登记手续的意思。*check-in* 和 *check-out* 是名词，它还可以做定语修饰名词。

例：check-in desk 入住办理处。

Exercises 1

I. Answer the following questions.

1. Who did Shawn Suzuki drop a line to?
2. Why is Shawn coming to New York?
3. What will Shawn send the Guptas for their reference?
4. Did Shawn receive an e-ticket or a paper ticket?
5. What city does Shawn leave from on March 9?
6. Does Shawn have seat assignments for his March 14 flights from New York to Cheyenne?
7. Where does Shawn stop and change planes on March 14?
8. What kind of ID does Shawn need to board the airplanes?

II. Write the key points of this e-mail thread.

III. Fill in the blanks.

1. I haven't seen her in a while, so I will __________ her a line.
2. Total airline charges include taxes and __________.
3. I don't know when she arrives because she didn't forward her airline __________ to me.
4. Do you have to change planes in Cincinnati, or do you have a __________ flight?
5. Do I have to check __________ at the ticket counter for my seat assignment?
6. They can't get their money back because their tickets are__________.
7. What is the confirmation number __________ your e-ticket?

8. All passengers must have a __________-issued photo ID to board the plane.

IV. Fill in the missing information.

Dear Aunt Grace,

I'll be in San Francisco during the week of May 8 and would love to see you. Do you have any free time that week? I would love to treat you to dinner.

Love,

Robin

Dear Robin,

I'm glad we'll be able to get together! Yes, I have free time _____ May 8, 9, and 10. Send me your _____, and I will pick you up at the airport. What hotel will you be staying _____ ?

Love,

Aunt Grace

V. Choose the correct answer. Only one answer is correct.

1. He has some more places to visit ________ his itinerary.

   A. at B. with C. for D. on

2. They are looking forward ________.

   A. to our visit B. for our visit C. to visit us D. to visit them

3. I used ________ there every day.

   A. for go B. to going C. to go D. for going

4. I am used ________ early now.

   A. to get up B. to getting up C. for get up D. for getting up

5. With his mother's help, he ________ leave China before the war broke out.

   A. could B. might C. would D. was able to

6. I will be in touch before I ________ New York.

A. leave for B. leave to C. left for D. left to

7. Since I will be renting a car, I can ________ at your place.

A. pick up you B. pick for you C. pick you up D. pick you for

8. Could you ________ dinner?

A. treat to me B. treat me to C. treat me for D. treat me on.

VI. Translate the following from English into Chinese.

1. I just dropped you a line to let you know that I won't be able to come.
2. Leave your itinerary so we can reach you in case of emergency.
3. Do you want a one-way or round-trip ticket?
4. She gave up her berth ticket to her friend.
5. She picked up Chinese very quickly.

VII. Translate the following from Chinese into English.

1. 我在三月九日周五到达，并在三月十四日周三回家。
2. 他不大可能是坏人。
3. 你可以打电话给他询问一下即将召开的会议。
4. 可以结账了吗？
5. 他们已预订了旅馆房间。

Writing Tips

Forming Plural Nouns*	
Add an *s*: 1. reservation+*s*=reservations 2. Wednesday+*s*=Wednesdays 3. photo+*s*=photos 4. sister-in-law+*s*=sisters-in-law; eight- year-old=eight-year-olds 5. 100+*s*=100s; A+*s*=As; CEO+*s*= CEOs	1. Used to form most plural nouns 2. Used to form the plural of nouns ending in a vowel + *y* 3. Used to form the plural of many nouns ending in *o* 4. Used to form the plural of compound nouns 5. Used to form the plural of numbers, capital letters, and acronyms

Add *es*: 1. tax + *es* = taxes 2. potato + *es* = potatoes	1. Used to form the plural of nouns ending in *s*, *x*, *z*, *ch*, and *sh*, including proper nouns 2. Used to form the plural of some nouns ending in *o*
Change *y* to *i* and add *es*: itinerary + *i*/*es*: itineraries	Used to form the plural of nouns ending in a consonant + *y*
Change *f* or *fe* to *v* and add *es*: knife + *v*/*es* = knives	Used to form the plural of some nouns ending in *f* or *fe*
No change: 1. deer = deer 2. sheep = sheep	Used when the singular and plural form are the same
Irregular plurals: 1. man = men 2. woman = women 3. child = children 4. foot = feet	Used for irregular nouns

*When in doubt, check the dictionary.

E-mail Thread 2

Subject: Hotel Confirmation

From: <OnlineTravel>

Date: January 10, 2012

To: ShawnSuzuki@businessassociates.com

Dear Shawn,

Thank you for using Online Travel to reserve your hotel room for your New York trip!

Reservation Information

Hotel New York

828 15th Ave.

New York, NY 10274

1-800-555-0101

1 Adult, 0 Children / 5 Nights

Check in on Friday, March 9 (check-in time: 3:00 p.m.)

Check out on Wednesday, March 14 (check-out time: 12:00 p.m.)

Rate: $150.00 per night

Name	**Confirmation Number**	**Room Preference**
Shawn Suzuki	81308066	Nonsmoking/Queen-Size Bed

Billing Information

Total Hotel Charges (Includes Taxes & Fees):	US$ 660.00
Total Online Travel Fees:	US$ 10.00
Total Amount Charged to Credit Card Ending in *xxxx*:	US$ 670.00

To cancel or modify your trip, call Customer Service:

In the US: 1-800-555-0112

Outside the US: (1)-555-555-0113

Subject: Car Rental Reservation Confirmation
From: <CheapRentalCars.com>
Date: January 10, 2012
To: ShawnSuzuki@businessassociates.com
Hello Shawn Suzuki, Thank you for choosing Cheap Rental Cars. Your car rental information is listed below. Please do not reply to this e-mail. Please print a copy for your reference. Confirmation Number: B408302F1 Traveler: Shawn Suzuki Pick-Up: Rental car counter, New York-John F. Kennedy International Airport Fri., Mar. 9, 2:45 p.m. Car Type: Economy Size, 2 Door, Air-Conditioning Return: Rental car counter, New York-John F. Kennedy International Airport Wed., Mar. 14, 7:00 a.m. Daily Rate: $75.00, Unlimited Mileage Tax: 19.62% Airport Fee: $7.64 Insurance: Optional; ask the rental car agent about insurance. Additional charges for taxes, insurance, extra days, airport surcharges, additional drivers, and gasoline may apply. You must have a valid photo driver's license. At check-in, you must present a major credit

card with your name on it. You must be at least 25 years old.

For questions or additional help, please call toll-free 1-800-555-0197.

New Words 2

1. modify ['mɔdifai] *v.* 更改；修改
2. optional ['ɔpʃənəl] *adj.* 可选的；非必需的
3. rate [reit] *n.* 价格；比率
4. valid ['vælid] *adj.* 合法的；有效的

Phrases and Expressions 2

1. airport surcharges 机场费
2. billing information 账单信息
3. check-in time 登记入住时间
4. check-out time 结账离开时间
5. confirmation number 确认号码
6. customer service 客户服务
7. economy size 经济型
8. major credit card 主要信用卡
9. pick-up 取；提取
10. room preference 首选房间
11. toll-free 免费电话
12. unlimited mileage 无里程限定

Proper Names 2

1. Cheap Rental Cars 经济实惠租车
2. Online Travel 网上旅行

Notes 2

1. *modify* 和 *change* 都有同样的意思“改变”，但它们的区别主要是程度上的区别。modify 的定义是“to improve or to make small changes in order to make something better”。

例：The feedback from the students can be used to modify your course for next semester.
学生的意见可用来改进你下学期的课程。

2. *rate* 同 *change, fee* 在 e-mails 中，都可以译为“价格和费用”。“daily rate”的定义是 a charge or fee that is set according to a standard scale for a day。

例：Some hotels offer special rates for children.
有些宾馆对孩子提供特别价格。

3. *valid photo* 在这里 valid 的意思是“有效的，大家都可以接受的” valid 一词通常用来修饰 ticket, document, agreement or credit card。

例：Your plane ticket is valid for three months.
你的飞机票三个月内有效。

4. *unlimited mileage* (无里程限制) means there is no extra charge for the number of miles driven by the person renting the car.
在驾车里程上不向租车人征收额外费用。

Exercises 2

I. Answer the following questions.

1. What hotel will Shawn Suzuki stay at?
2. How many adults and how many children will stay in his room?
3. What is the hotel's check-in time?
4. What is Shawn's room preference?
5. Where will Shawn pick up his rental car?

6. What type of car did Shawn reserve?
7. Does Shawn have to buy insurance for the rental car?
8. What kind of ID does Shawn need to rent the car?

II. Write an e-mail in which you tell a friend that you will be visiting his city and would like to see him.

Key to E-mail Thread 1 Exercises (for Reference)

I. Answer the following questions.

1. Shawn dropped a line to Derek and Jasmine Guptas.
2. Shawn is coming to New York for a convention.
3. Shawn will send the Guptas his airline itinerary for their reference.
4. Shawn received an e-ticket.
5. Shawn leaves from Cheyenne, Wyoming, on March 9.
6. No, Shawn does not have seat assignments for his March 14 flights from New York to Cheyenne.
7. Shawn stops and changes planes in Cincinnati, Ohio, on March 14.
8. Shawn needs a government-issued photo ID (such as a driver's license or a passport).

II. Write the key points of this e-mail thread.

- Shawn is going to New York for a convention.
- Shawn will be in New York from Friday, March 9, to Wednesday, March 14.
- Shawn would like to see Derek and Jasmine Guptas while he is there. He would like to treat them to dinner at their favorite brewpub.
- Shawn will stay at the Hotel New York.
- Shawn will rent a car. He will pick up the Guptas and drive them to the brewpub.
- Shawn sent the Guptas his itinerary.
- On March 14, Shawn will leave New York City, stop in Cincinnati, Ohio, and arrive in Cheyenne, Wyoming.
- Shawn needs a government-issued photo ID to board the plane.

III. Fill in the blanks.

1. I haven't seen her in a while, so I will drop her a line.
2. Total airline charges include taxes and fees.
3. I don't know when she arrives because she didn't forward her airline itinerary to me.
4. Do you have to change planes in Cincinnati, or do you have a nonstop flight?
5. Do I have to check in at the ticket counter for my seat assignment?
6. They can't get their money back because their tickets are nonrefundable.
7. What is the confirmation number for your e-ticket?
8. All passengers must have a government-issued photo ID to board the plane.

IV. Fill in the missing information.

Dear Robin,

I'm glad we'll be able to get together! Yes, I have free time on May 8, 9, and 10. Send me your itinerary, and I will pick you up at the airport. What hotel will you be staying at?

Love,

Aunt Grace

V. Choose the correct answer. Only one answer is correct.

1. D 2. A 3. C 4. B 5. D 6. A 7. C 8. B

VI. Translate the following sentences from English into Chinese.

1. 我刚给你留了言，只想告诉你我来不了了。
2. 请把你的旅行计划留下来，以便在遇到急事时我们和你取得联系。
3. 你想买单程票还是往返票？
4. 她把卧铺票让给了她的朋友。
5. 她学习中文进步很快。

VII. Translate the following sentences from Chinese into English.

1. I will arrive on Friday, March 9, and will head home on Wednesday, March 14.
2. He couldn't be a bad man.

3. You can call him about the upcoming meeting.
4. Can I have the bill?
5. They have reserved rooms at a hotel.

Translation of E-mail Thread 1 (for Reference)

译文：

邮件 1-1

主题：纽约之行
发件人：肖恩・铃木
日期：2012 年 1 月 12 日
收件人：TheGuptas@cmail.com

你们好，德里克，贾斯敏，

从怀俄明州向你们问好。我只想简单向你们通报一下我将去纽约参加一个会议。我三月十九日周五到纽约，三月十四日周三返回。要是你们在我在纽约的那段时间有空，我非常希望能与你们一聚。我甚至可以在你们喜爱的酒吧请你们吃晚餐。

万事如意，

祝好，

肖恩

肖恩・铃木，市场总监
商业伙伴
www.businessassociates.com
ShawnSuzuki@businessassociates.com
电话：1-800-555-0184

附言：我将把行程安排发给你参考。

邮件 1-2

主题：转发：航空公司确认纽约之行
发件人：肖恩·铃木
日期：2012 年 1 月 14 日
收件人：TheGuptas@cmail.com

你好,

我很高兴我们能一起共进晚餐，我期待着与你的相会。这是我的行程安排，我将下榻纽约的酒店。到时我会租辆车，可以去那儿接你，我们再一起到售餐酒吧。离开纽约前我会和你联系。

最好的，

肖恩

原始邮件
主题：航空公司确认纽约之行
发件人：网上旅行预订
日期：2012 年 1 月 10 日星期二 上午 9:45
收件人：ShawnSuzuki@businessassociates.com

网上旅行预订写到：

亲爱的肖恩，

感谢你在“网上旅行预订”订购你的机票。因为这是电子机票，所以你不会收到传统印刷出来的机票。你电子机票的确认号码为：7797749412。你也可在你网上旅行账户看到下面的行程。

行程安排（时间为当地时间）

怀俄明州 夏延到纽约州纽约市—肯尼迪国际机场

航班号：5410
3 月 9 日星期五
上午 6:15　　怀俄明州　夏延　到
下午 2:03　　纽约—肯尼迪国际机场
无停留
要求座位：03D
总行程时间为：5 小时 48 分钟

纽约州纽约市—肯尼迪国际机场到怀俄明州 夏延纽约
航班号：4970
3 月 14 日星期三
上午 9:46　纽约—约翰肯尼迪国际机场到
下午 12:00　（美国俄亥俄州）辛辛那提市
2 小时 14 分钟
要求座位：请在服务台前选择座位
在辛辛那提市停留并转机
换机时间：　55 分钟
航班号：　5363
3 月 14 日星期三
下午 12:00　（美国俄亥俄州）辛辛那提市
下午1:56　怀俄明州　夏延
3 小时 1 分钟
总行程时间为：6 小时 10 分钟

旅客信息：
旅客姓名：肖恩·铃木
机票号码：003409146
常飞旅客号码：124408456

*登机前，你必须出示由政府签发带有照片的有效证件，如：驾驶执照或护照。确认书上旅客姓名必须与有效证件上的姓名一致。

完成你的旅行计划，可点击以下网页：

预订酒店房间

网上办理

查询飞机是否准时

查询飞机的位置

账单信息：

航空公司收费总额：（含税及杂费）610.70 美元

网上旅行预订收费：10 美元

信用卡收费总额：625.70 美元

你的机票是不可退换的。

取消或更改行程，请致电客户服务：

（在美国国内）（1-800-555-0112）

（在其他国家）（1）-555-555-0113

Key to E-mail Thread 2 Exercises (for Reference)

I. Answer the following questions.

1. Shawn will stay at Hotel New York.
2. One adult and no children will stay in his room.
3. The hotel's check-in time is 3:00 p.m.
4. Shawn's room preference is a nonsmoking room with a queen-size bed.
5. Shawn will pick up his rental car at the rental car counter at New York—John F. Kennedy International Airport.
6. Shawn reserved an economy-size car with two doors and air-conditioning.
7. No, Shawn does not have to buy insurance for the rental car because it is optional.

8. Shawn needs a valid photo driver's license to rent the car.

Translation of E-mail Thread 2 (for Reference)

译文：

邮件 2-1

主题：旅馆确认
发件人："网上旅行"
日期：2012 年 1 月 10 日
收件人：肖恩・铃木

亲爱的肖恩，

感谢你用 "网上旅行" 为你的纽约之行预订旅馆房间。

预订信息如下：
纽约市 15 街 282 号纽约旅馆
免费电话 1-800-555-0101

一位成人；五夜
入住时间：周五 三月九日 （登记入住时间：下午 3:00）

结账时间：周三 三月十四日 （结账时间：中午 12:00）
价格：每晚 150 美元

姓名	确认号码	首选房间
肖恩・铃木	81308066	无烟/双人床

账单信息：
共计旅馆费 (含税及费用)： 660.00 美元

网上旅行预订费：　　　　　　10.00 美元
总额 670.00 美元由信用卡尾号 *xxxx* 支付

若取消或更该你的行程，请电话联系“顾客服务中心”：
美国国内：1-800-555-0112
美国国外：(1)-555-555-0113

邮件 2-2

主题：租车预订确认
发件人：“经济实惠租车”
日期：2012 年 1 月 10 日
收件人：肖恩·铃木

你好，肖恩·铃木，

感谢你选择经济实惠租车公司。
你的租车信息如下。请不要回复此邮件，打印出此件供你参阅。

确认号码：B408302F1

旅客姓名：肖恩·铃木

取车信息：

租车柜台：纽约—肯尼迪国际机场
周五 三月九日，下午　2:45

车型：经济型，两门，带空调

还车信息：
租车柜台：纽约—肯尼迪国际机场
周三、三月十四日，上午 7:00

日价：75.00 美元，无里程限定
税金：19.62%
机场费：7.64 美元
保险：任选；请向租车公司代理询问有关保险事宜。

其他费用如：税、保险金、额外天数、机场费、其他驾驶人、汽油费可能被征收。

你必须持有有效的驾驶执照。登记时必须提供在你名下的主要信用卡。你必须满二十五周岁。

若有问题或需帮助，请打此免费电话 1-800-555-0197。

Lesson 11

Weather

天气

Learning Objectives

In this lesson, you will learn the following:

- How to write about different weather conditions
  天气描述
- What the four seasons are
  一年四季
- What the four directions are
  四个方向
- What technologies Americans use to check on weather conditions
  查询天气状况的技术
- How weather affects work and travel plans
  天气对工作和旅行的影响

E-mail Thread 1

Subject: Leaving for Our Trip
From: Beth@cmail.com
Date: April 20, 2012
To: Steve@cmail.com
Hi Steve, Just a quick note, because I am busy packing for our trip to Birmingham, Alabama, to visit Mom and Dad. Rob, the kids, and I will stay with them until April 27. We will leave Buffalo, New York, the first thing in the morning. We will drive south through Ohio, Kentucky, and Tennessee. The drive should take two days if the weather is good. Unfortunately, the weather report says there will be a big thunderstorm tomorrow. We hope to stay ahead of the rain. The weather in Alabama is humid and hot, with temperatures in the 90s. I am glad Mom and Dad's house has air-conditioning! I'm sorry we won't see you at Mom and Dad's this spring. Maybe we can all get together back east this summer. Love, Beth

Subject: Re: Leaving for Our Trip
From: Steve@cmail.com
Date: April 20, 2012
To: Beth@cmail.com
Hi Beth, Mom and Dad are excited about your visit. Too bad you are not driving west to visit me in California. The weather is very comfortable, with warm, sunny days and cool nights. Maybe I'll be able to visit you in the fall.

Have a safe trip!
Take care,
Steve

New Words 1

1. affect [ə'fekt] *v.* 对……影响；改变
2. direction [di'rekʃən] *n.* 方向；方位
3. fall [fɔːl] *n.* 秋天
4. note [nəut] *n* 笔记；便条；注释
5. season ['siːzn] *n.* 季；季节
6. technology [tek'nɔlədʒi] *n.* 技术
7. temperature ['tempritʃə] *n.* 温度；气温
8. thunderstorm ['θʌndəˌstɔːm] *n.* 雷暴；大雷雨
9. unfortunately [ʌn'fɔːtʃənitli] *adv.* 遗憾地；可惜地

Phrases and Expressions 1

1. air-conditioning 空调；冷气
2. the first thing in the morning 上午要做的第一件事情
3. to leave for 动身去
4. to pack for 为……收拾
5. to stay ahead 保持领先
6. to take care 照顾；保重
7. travel plan 旅行计划
8. weather condition 天气状况
9. weather report 天气预报

Proper Names 1

1. Alabama (AL) 亚拉巴马州
2. Beth 贝丝

3. Birmingham 伯明翰
4. Buffalo 布法罗
5. California (CA) 加利福尼亚州
6. Kentucky (KY) 肯塔基州
7. New York (NY) 纽约州
8. Ohio (OH) 俄亥俄州
9. Tennessee (TN) 田纳西州

Notes 1

1. *temperature measurements* (温度测量单位): Americans use the Fahrenheit scale to measure temperatures. On that scale, water freezes at 32 degrees Fahrenheit (32ºF), or 0 degrees Celsius (0℃). Water boils at 212ºF, or 100℃. To convert Fahrenheit to Celsius, subtract 32 from the Fahrenheit temperature, then divide the result by 1.8. To convert Celsius to Fahrenheit, multiply the Celsius temperature by 1.8, then add 32 to the result.
美国人使用华氏温度制，其冰点为32ºF或0℃。水的沸点为212ºF或100℃。华氏与摄氏互换公式为y℃= (x ºF – 32)/1.8；yºF = x℃×1.8 + 32。

2. *Just a quick note, . . .* 在这里just a quick note，是一个常用短语，它省掉了主语"it"及动词"is"。另外，*quick*在这里应理解为"仓促，简短"。
例：1) Can I ask just one quick question?
能问你一个着急的问题吗？
2) Could I just make a quick phone call?
能马上打个简短的电话吗？
3) Do I have time for a quick shower before we go out?
我们走之前我能迅速洗个澡吗？

3. *the first thing in the morning* 这个常用短语是由一个名词词组*the first thing*加上一个介词词组in the morning组成。the first thing是状语，表示要做的第一件事情。此外，还可以讲"the last thing at night"（晚上做的最后一件事）。

4. *at Mom and Dad's* 在这里是指"爸妈的房子"。在大家都清楚名词所有格后面修饰的是什么词时，它往往被省略。

例：John's bike is better than Mike's.
约翰的自行车比迈克的好。

4.1. 另外，当名词所有格后面表示几个人共有一样东西，只需在最后一个人的名字后加'ｓ。如表示各自所有，则需在各个名字后加'ｓ。如：

例：1) This is Tom and Jason's room.
这是汤姆和杰森共有的房间。
2) These are Tom's and Jason's rooms.
这些是汤姆和杰森各自的房间。

5. *take care* 译为"保重"，但实际上这个词组常用于告别时或者信的结尾，相当于"再见"。在口语中，人们通常讲："Take care and see you."
另外 *Take care* 还有小心的意思。

例：Take care that your money is safe.
注意看好你的钱。

Exercises 1

I. Answer the following questions.

1. Who is going to Birmingham, Alabama?
2. What city and state will they leave from?
3. What states will they drive through?
4. What direction will they drive?
5. How long should the drive take?
6. What does tomorrow's weather report say?
7. What is the weather like in Alabama?
8. What is the weather like in California?

II. Write the key points of this e-mail thread.

III. Fill in the blanks.

1. Just a quick note, because I am busy packing ________ my trip.

2. The weather in New York is hot, with _________ in the 90s.
3. We will leave New York the_________ thing in the morning.
4. We hope to stay _________ of the rain.
5. The _________report says it will rain tomorrow.
6. Take _________ and have a safe trip.
7. We will stay _________ Mom and Dad.
8. They plan to visit you _________ the fall.

IV. Fill in the missing information.

Brandon,

I am busy packing for my trip to Tennessee. Didn't you live there? What is the weather like in the spring? Is it hot? Do I need a raincoat?

Thanks,

Ryan

Ryan,

Yes, I lived in Tennessee. The weather in the spring is very comfortable. The temperatures are ________ the 80s, but most buildings have air-________. There are big ________, so you should bring a raincoat.

Brandon

V. Choose the correct answer. Only one answer is correct.

1. "I'm terribly sorry that I spilled the coffee all over the table." The best response to the dialogue is _________.

   A. Don't mention it. B. Forget it. It really doesn't matter.

   C. Too bad! There isn't any left. D. Never mind, I'll clean it up soon.

2. "I want to thank you very much for all your help in this matter." The best response to the dialogue is _________.

A. Not at all, it was a pleasure. B. It doesn't matter.
C. That's all right. D. I don't mind helping.

3. The weather forecast ________ it would fine all day.
A. told B. said C. speaks D. All are correct.

4. "Then you must buy a good umbrella. It rains a lot here." The best response to the dialogue is ________.
A. Must I? B. Do they? C. Really? D. Will it?

5. I always watch the ________ after the news.
A. weather B. climate C. temperature D. All are correct.

6. I've always wanted ________ speak Japanese.
A. that I will B. that I should C. to be able to D. that I can

7. "You don't mind if I smoke, do you?" The best response to the dialogue is ________.
A. Yes, I do mind. B. Sorry, I don't have any cigarettes.
C. No, thanks, I don't. D. Well, I'd rather you didn't, actually.

8. "Does John look like his brother?" The best response to the dialogue is ________.
A. He looks quite well. B. He is a big man with curly hair.
C. No, he is much taller. D. Yes, he likes him very much.

VI. Translate the following from English into Chinese.

1. There are homeless people sleeping on the streets in all weathers.
2. The temperature in Colorado dropped to minus 20 degrees last night.
3. It's too bad that you couldn't come to the party last night.
4. I hope we get some warm weather soon.
5. Snow was falling heavily as we drove to school.

VII. Translate the following from Chinese into English.

1. 今天美国天气怎么样？
2. 尽管昨天阳光明媚，但温度是零度以下。
3. 你最好收拾一下你的行装，我们一个小时后出发。
4. 我们提前半小时完成了任务。
5. 这个房间有空调吗？

Writing Tips

Texting Abbreviations and More Emoticons	
^^	Used to indicate being happy
>.>	Used to mean, "I'm avoiding or not looking at (something)"
?_?	Used to ask, "What?"
X_X	Used to mean "dead"
o_0	Used to mean "crazy" or "unable to understand"
o_o	Used to indicate a blank stare
-_-	Used to indicate, "Really . . ."
<3	Used to draw a heart
---}---@	Used to draw a rose
oxxxx}::::::::::::>	Used to draw a sword
d(^_^)b	Used to draw a person wearing headphones

E-mail Thread 2

Subject: Snowstorm!
From: Jared.Jefferson@InternationalSoftwareDevelopment.com
Date: February 23, 2012
To: Home@cmail.com
Rita, What is the weather like at home? It's snowing like crazy at work. There's much more snow as you go north. Some of my colleagues who are working at home are getting dumped on. (Spencer has a foot of snow at his house.) I heard on the radio while driving to work that a lot of schools are closed. Check out the view on the city park's webcam—www.citywebcam.com. It sure looks like winter! Jared Jared Jefferson Software Engineer International Software Development Jared.Jefferson@InternationalSoftwareDevelopment.com 1-800-555-0101, ext. 5043

Subject: Re: Snowstorm!
From: Home@cmail.com
Date: February 23, 2012
To: Jared.Jefferson@InternationalSoftwareDevelopment.com
Jared, We only have 5 or 6 inches of snow at home. But it's very windy and cold. The weather reports on the Internet forecast another 6-12 inches of snow in the next 24 hours! All the schools are closed. I saw a special report on TV that said the northbound highway is

also closed, because of icy roads. The side streets are icy, too. (You can check the road conditions on the traffic cams—www.citytrafficcam.com.)

You should leave work early!!

Rita

New Words 2

1.	snowstorm	['snəustɔːm]	*n.*	暴风雪
2.	view	[vjuː]	*n.*	景色；视野

Phrases and Expressions 2

1.	a foot of snow	一英尺厚的雪
2.	at work	在工作时
3.	like crazy	太大了（表示程度）
4.	northbound highway	北行线高速公路
5.	side street	小巷；辅路
6.	to check out	退房
7.	to get dumped on	下了大量的（雪）

Proper Names 2

1.	International Software Development	国际软件开发公司
2.	Jared Jefferson	贾里德·杰弗逊
3.	Rita	丽塔
4.	Spencer	斯宾塞

Notes 2

1.1.1. *Spencer has a foot of snow at his house*: *a foot* 是量词。在英语中量词和名词常常是固定搭配的。

例：1) a tub of skin cream
2) a jar of jam
3) a bottle of cooking oil
4) a can of soda
5) a bag of milk powder
6) a packet of biscuits
7) a sack of rice

1.1.2. 当数词是单数时，量词和名词都是单数。

例： piece of paper

当数词为复数时，若名词为不可数名词，那么量词是复数，但名词为单数。

例： two pieces of paper

若名词为可数名词，那么量词和名词都是复数。

例： two pairs of shoes

2. *It sure looks like winter!* 在这里 *sure* 是副词，在口语中 sure 常用于副词，相当于“indeed”或“certainly”。

例： 1) He will come, sure enough.
他必来无疑。
2) It sure was a cold night.
这的确是个寒冷的夜晚。

3. *Side street* is smaller than a main street, but is often connected to it. A “sidewalk” is a paved path at the side of a street for people to walk on, and it is the term used in the United States. British people use “pavement.”
与主要街道相连的小巷要比主要街道窄小。在美国“sidewalk”是在街道两侧专为行人走路用的小道，英国人则称之为“pavement”。

4. W*ebcam* and *traffic cam* are abbreviations for “web camera” and “traffic camera.”
摄像头(w*ebcam*)及交通监视头(*traffic cam*)是“web camera”和“traffic camera”的缩写。
Some webcams are mounted near a computer and used for videoconferencing. Some are mounted outside to capture time-lapse digital photos or streaming videos of a location. A traffic cam is a type of web cam that takes pictures of the traffic on major roads and displays

them on a website.
有的摄像头嵌在电脑里可以用来做视频会议。有的则架设在某处抓拍延时数码照片或在某地连续播放影像资料。交通监视摄像头被用于在主要街道拍摄交通情况照片并在网站显示。

5. *working from home* (在家工作): Many US companies allow employees who work with computers or telephones to work from home, or telecommute. Employees may telecommute occasionally or on a regular basis. Employees' reasons for telecommuting vary: they don't live near the company, they want to concentrate on a project without distractions, they are working overtime, or the weather is bad and they don't want to drive to the office. A home office is a common room in many American homes.
很多美国公司允许用电脑或电话的员工在家里远距离办公。公司可接受员工偶尔或定期的远距离办公。其原因有：住的地方离公司较远；不受干扰地集中精力完成项目；加班；不想在天气不好的情况下开车上班。很多美国家庭都用一间普通的房间当家庭办公室。

6. *5 or 6 和 6–11*: Using "or" between numbers, as in *5 or 6*, means that the quantity is approximate. Using an en dash (-) or dash (—) indicates a range of numbers. Ranges can also be written with the words "from/to" and "between/and."
用"or"（或者）5 或 6，为大致估计。而用半方破折号（-）或破折号（—）则表明一个数字范围。数字范围也可用"from"（从），"to"（到），"between"（之间），"and"（和）表示。

例：1) The recipe uses two or three cloves of garlic.
菜谱建议用两三瓣蒜。

2) Most classes have 25–30 students.
大多班级有 20 到 30 个学生。

3) I lived in Tennessee from 2001 to 2003.
从 2001 到 2003 年我住在田纳西州。

4) A house in that neighborhood costs between $300 000 and $475 000.
那个邻近地区的房价在 30 万和 47.5 万美元之间。

Exercises 2

I. Answer the following questions.

1. Where is Jared Jefferson?

2. Is it snowing where Jared is?
3. Where are some of Jared's colleagues?
4. How much snow is at Spencer's house?
5. What did Jared hear on the radio?
6. Where did Rita Jefferson find the weather reports?
7. What did Rita see on TV?
8. How can Jared check the road conditions?

II. Write an e-mail asking about the weather conditions for a trip you will take.

Key to E-mail Thread 1 Exercises (for Reference)

I. Answer the following questions.

1. Beth, her husband Rob, and their kids are going to Birmingham, Alabama.
2. They will leave from Buffalo, New York.
3. They will drive through Ohio, Kentucky, and Tennessee.
4. They will drive south.
5. The drive should take two days, if the weather is good.
6. Tomorrow's weather report says there will be a big thunderstorm.
7. The weather in Alabama is humid and hot, with temperatures in the 90s.
8. The weather in California is very comfortable, with warm, sunny days and cool nights.

II. Write the key points of this e-mail thread.

- Beth wrote a quick note to Steve to tell him about her family's trip to Birmingham, Alabama.
- Beth, her husband, Rob, and their kids will visit Beth and Steve's mother and father. Beth's family will stay until April 27.
- The family will drive south to Alabama. They will drive through Ohio, Kentucky, and Tennessee.
- Tomorrow's weather report says there will be a big thunderstorm. Beth and her family

hope to stay ahead of the rain.

- The weather in Alabama is hot and humid, with temperatures in the 90s. The weather in California is comfortable, with warm, sunny days and cool nights.
- Beth's parents' house has air-conditioning.
- Beth is sorry she won't see Steve this spring. Steve says he might be able to visit her this fall.

III. Fill in the blanks.

1. Just a quick note, because I am busy packing <u>for</u> my trip.
2. The weather in New York is hot, with <u>temperatures</u> in the 90s.
3. We will leave New York the <u>first</u> thing in the morning.
4. We hope to stay <u>ahead</u> of the rain.
5. The <u>weather</u> report says it will rain tomorrow.
6. Take <u>care</u> and have a safe trip.
7. We will stay <u>with</u> Mom and Dad.
8. They plan to visit you <u>in</u> the fall.

IV. Fill in the missing information.

Ryan,

Yes, I lived in Tennessee. The weather in the spring is very comfortable. The temperatures are <u>in</u> the 80s, but most buildings have air-<u>conditioning</u>. There are big <u>thunderstorms</u>, so you should bring a raincoat.

Brandon

V. Choose the correct answer. Only one answer is correct.

1. D 2. A 3. B 4. C 5. A 6. C 7. D 8. C

VI. Translate the following from English into Chinese.

1. 无论是刮风或是下雨，都有无家可归的人露宿街头。
2. 昨晚美国科罗拉多州的气温降至零下 20 摄氏度。
3. 你昨天没来参加晚会太遗憾了。
4. 我希望天气很快就暖和了。

5. 当我们开车上学时雪下得很大了。

VII. Translate the following from Chinese into English.

1. What's the weather like today in the United States?
2. It was sunny yesterday, but the temperature was well below zero.
3. You'd better pack your bags. We're leaving in an hour.
4. We finished it half an hour ahead of schedule.
5. Is this room air-conditioned?

Translation of E-mail Thread 1 (for Reference)

译文：

邮件 1-1

主题：为旅行作准备
发件人：贝丝
日期：2012 年 4 月 20 日
收件人：史蒂夫

你好，史蒂夫，

只是想通知你，我正忙着收拾行装并将前往亚拉巴马州伯明翰市看望爸妈。我、罗布和孩子们同他们住到 4 月 27 日。

我们明天一早就离开纽约州布法罗。我们将驱车向南穿过俄亥俄、肯塔基和田纳西州。如果天气好，需要开车两天。遗憾的是，天气预报说，明天将会有大雷雨。但愿能避开雷雨。

亚拉巴马州的天气又热又湿，温度在 90 华氏度左右。我很高兴爸妈的房子里有空调！

我很遗憾，这个春天我们不能在爸妈那里见面。也许这个夏天我们都能在东部相会。

爱你的，

贝丝

邮件 1-2

主题：回复：为旅行作准备
发件人：史蒂夫
日期：2012 年 4 月 20 日
收件人：贝丝

你好，贝丝，

爸妈对你的来访感到兴奋。可惜你不能开车到西部经加州来看我。

这儿天气舒服极了，温暖、明媚、夜晚凉爽。或许我能在今秋去看你。

祝你一路平安，保重！

史蒂夫

Key to E-mail Thread 2 Exercises (for Reference)

I. Answer the following questions.

1. Jared Jefferson is at work.
2. Yes, it is snowing like crazy at Jared's work.
3. Some of Jared's colleagues are working at home.
4. There is about a foot of snow at Spencer's house.
5. Jared heard on the radio that a lot of the schools were closed.
6. Rita Jefferson found the weather reports on the Internet.
7. Rita saw a special report on TV that said the northbound highway was closed because of icy roads and that the side streets were icy, too.

8. Jared can check on the road conditions by looking at the traffic cams.

Translation of E-mail Thread 2 (for Reference)

译文：

邮件 2-1

主题：暴风雪
发件人：Jared.Jefferson@InternationalSoftwareDevelopment.com
日期：2012 年 2 月 23 日
收件人：Home@cmail.com

丽塔，

咱家附近的天气如何？我公司这里的雪下得太大了，而且越往北雪越大。我的那些在家工作的同事们所居住地区都下了大雪。斯宾塞家附近一下子下了一英尺厚的雪。我在上班路上听广播说，许多学校都停课了。

你查看一下 www.citywebcam.com，城市街心公园一定看起来是一幅冬天的景色了！

贾里德

贾里德·杰弗逊
软件工程师
国际软件发展
Jared.Jefferson@InternationalSoftwareDevelopment.com
电话：1-800-555-0101，分机：5043

邮件 2-2

主题：回复：暴风雪
发件人：Home@cmail.com

日期：2012 年 2 月 23 日
收件人：Jared.Jefferson@InternationalSoftwareDevelopment.com

贾里德，

我们家附近只有五六英寸的雪。不过很冷，风也很大。网上的天气预报说，24 小时内还会有六到十二英寸的雪。所有学校都停课了。我看到电视里特别预报说，由于路面结冰的缘故，北行线高速公路已经关闭了。辅路上也有很多冰雪。（你可用城市交通网查看路况）。

你应该早点下班回家！

丽塔

Lesson 12

International Visitors

国际访问者

Learning Objectives

In this lesson, you will learn the following:

- How American organizations host an international visitor
  美国机构招待国际访问者
- How some organizations coordinate the agenda for a visitor
  机构对来访者的活动日程安排
- How to discuss local sites and cultural events
  谈论当地文化风情
- What an agenda looks like
  活动日程安排表

E-mail Thread 1

Subject: Upcoming Visit from a Chinese Professor
From: IrinaPetrova@su.com
Date: February 23, 2012
To: <Education Department Faculty and Staff>
Hello everyone, From March 20 to March 25, Dr. Liu Huiying, a professor of education from Peking University, will be visiting our university to participate in our upcoming International Education Conference. As you know, the conference focuses on developing international cooperation to improve the quality of education worldwide. Because our Education Department is hoping to establish an exchange program with a Chinese university, I would like each faculty and staff member to meet with Dr. Liu before the conference. We will spend March 20 with her. Faculty members will present their research and its relationship to US educational policies. Department staff will assist with a tour of the department's facilities and join us for lunch. Faculty, please let me know when you can meet with the professor that day so that I can create an agenda. We are honored to have such a prominent professor visit our school. I appreciate your efforts to make Dr. Liu feel welcome. Thank you, Irina Petrova, PhD Chair, Education Department State University 555-555-0145, ext. 104

Subject: Re: Upcoming Visit from a Chinese Professor
From: SimonWellington@su.com
Date: February 23, 2012
To: IrinaPetrova@su.com
Irina, I'm looking forward to meeting Dr. Liu. This is a great opportunity for us to develop an exchange program as well as international research projects. I will be available to present on March 20 from 10:30 a.m. to 12:00 p.m. and from 3:30 to 5:30 p.m. May I suggest that we take Dr. Liu out to dinner that night? It would also be nice to take her sightseeing and to some cultural events. Simon Wellington, PhD Professor, Education Department State University 555-555-0145, ext. 109

New Words 1

1.	chair	[tʃεə]	*n.*	系主任；会议主持人
2.	coordinate	[kəu'ɔːdneit]	*v.*	协调；调节
3.	faculty	['fækəlti]	*n.*	（大学的）全体教职员
4.	present	['preznt]	*v.*	提交；出席
5.	prominent	['prɔminənt]	*adj.*	显著的；重要的
6.	sightseeing	['saitˌsiːiŋ]	*n.*	观光；游览

Phrases and Expressions 1

1. cultural events 文化活动

2. exchange program 交流项目
3. local sites 本地景点
4. PhD 博士学位
5. research project 科研项目
6. to be available 有空，可被利用的
7. to be honored 荣幸的
8. to create an agenda 制定时间表
9. to focus on 重点在于
10. to participate in 参加

Proper Names 1

1. Edith 伊蒂丝
2. Irina Petrova 伊琳娜·佩特洛娃
3. Simon Wellington 西蒙·惠灵顿
4. State University 州立大学

Notes 1

1. *Professor, Dr.,* and *PhD* indicate a person's education level and occupation.
教授和博士表示受教育程度和职业。

1.1. *Professor* is a both an occupation and a social title and is used in written and spoken English. It is the highest academic level at a university or college. When used as an occupation, it is lowercased. When used as a social title, it is capitalized and appears before the name.
在英文书面语和口语里，“教授”可被用于职业和社会头衔。它是高等院校中的最高头衔。当“教授”用于职业称呼时，第一个字母应该小写。而当“教授”作为社会头衔使用时，第一个字母应该大写并放在姓名之前。

例：1) Who is your favorite professor?
谁是你最喜爱的教授？
2) Professor Wellington teaches at State University.

惠灵顿教授在州立大学执教。

1.2. *Dr.* is the abbreviation for "doctor." It is a social title for people with doctoral degrees. It is used in written and spoken English and appears before a full or shortened name.

*Dr.*是"doctor"医生或博士的缩写，是博士学位获得者的社会头衔。"Dr."适用于英文书面及口语并应放于全名或姓之前。

例：1) Dr. Bob and his wife, Edith, are coming to dinner.
鲍勃博士和他太太伊蒂丝会来参加晚宴。

2) Dr. Lee said I have a cavity in my tooth.
李医生说，我有一个龋齿。

3) Dr. Simon Wellington teaches at State University.
西蒙·惠灵顿博士在州立大学执教。

1.3. *PhD* is the abbreviation for "doctor of philosophy." It is an advanced academic degree awarded by universities. PhD indicates a person's education level and is not a social title. It is used in written English and appears after a person's name. It is set off with one comma when the name stands alone and with two commas when the name appears in the middle of a sentence. Sometimes it is used as a noun.

PhD 是哲学博士学位。PhD 显示某人所受教育程度，不是社会头衔。被用于口语和书面英语中，书写时应放在全名或姓之前。书写规则为全名加一个逗号加 PhD。若全名在句中应有两个逗号将 PhD 隔开。有时 PhD 被用作名词。

例：1) The list of attendees includes Simon Wellington, PhD.
参会者名单包括西蒙·惠灵顿博士。

2) Simon Wellington, PhD, teaches at State University.
西蒙·惠灵顿博士在州立大学执教。

3) She's a PhD, so there are many profound words in her papers.
她有博士学位，所以在她的文章里很多深奥的词汇。

2. *faculty and staff* 都是不可数名词，分别代表学院的全体教职员和职工。同时 *faculty* 也有大学里的分支学术机构的意思。

例：1) the law school faculty
法学院教职人员

2) Both faculty and students oppose the measures.
教师和学生都反对这些措施。

3) Our school has a staff of seven.
我们学院有七名职工。

3. *to make Dr. Liu feel welcome* 也可以讲"to make (somebody) welcome"，意思是让某人感到他很受欢迎，大家很喜欢他的到来。与此意思相关的另一个词组是"to make (somebody) feel at home"。

例：1) We try to make the new students feel welcome.
我们尽量使新生感到很受欢迎。
2) I didn't feel welcome in the club.
我在俱乐部不受欢迎。
3) We'd like to make our customers feel at home.
我们想让我们的客户感到很自在。

4.1. *I suggest that we take* . . .: "To suggest that (somebody) do (something)"是一个固定句型。*suggest* 后面可以跟一个宾语从句组成一个虚拟语气的句子：句中通常省掉情态动词"should"，跟动词原型。

例：They suggested that she (should) come again.
他们建议她改天再来。

4.2. 与 suggest 相同用法的动词还有："recommend, order, insist, propose, demand"等。

例：I recommend that you (should) get some advice from her.
我认为你最好从她那里得到一些建议。

Exercises 1

I. Answer the following questions.

1. What will Dr. Liu Huiying participate in?
2. What does the conference focus on?
3. What is the Education Department hoping to establish?
4. What will faculty members do with Dr. Liu?
5. What will department staff do with Dr. Liu?
6. What did Irina Petrova ask the Education Department faculty and staff to let her know?

7. When is Simon Wellington available on March 20?
8. What did Simon suggest?

II. Write the key points of this e-mail thread.

III. Fill in the blanks.

1. Please let me know what time you are ________ to present on December 10.
2. Our university is honored to have such a ________ professor speak at our conference.
3. Faculty members will ________ their research at the conference.
4. Many high school students travel to foreign countries to participate ________ programs.
5. Our department wants to develop an international research ________.
6. I would like to take him ________ and to some cultural events.
7. Does the conference focus ________ education or international cooperation?
8. I can't ________ an agenda until you let me know when we can meet.

IV. Fill in the missing information.

Hello faculty,

Dr. Nigel Smith, a professor of education from England, is coming to our university on June 9. This is a great opportunity for our department to develop an exchange program. I would like faculty members to present their research and its relationship to Dr. Smith's research. Please let me know when you are available that day.

Thank you,

Joe Taylor
Chair

Joe,

I am honored to have such a prominent professor visit us. I will be available _____ 10:30 a.m. to 2:30 p.m.

I suggest that we take Dr. Smith on a ________ of the department's facilities. If he has not been to America before, we also could take him sightseeing and to some cultural ________.

Nancy Reed

Professor

V. Choose the correct answer. Only one answer is correct.

1. He is so interested in his career that felt he needed to focus ________ it.
   A. less on B. more on C. less in D. more in
2. An agenda is ________to be discussed at a meeting.
   A. a list of the subjects B. a list of places
   C. a list of papers D. a list of people
3. We ________that caring for children is an important job.
   A. accept B. take C. appreciate D. are happy
4. I'm having some flowers ________ for her birthday.
   A. transporting B. transported C. delivering D. delivered
5. ________, the country needs a change of government.
   A. In my view B. In my point C. In my thought D. In my criticism
6. The quality of Chinese wines can sometimes ________the wines from France.
   A. compared to B. be compared to C. compare to D. be comparing with
7. We'll be back with more after ________.
   A. short break B. a short holiday C. a short break D. short holiday
8. Why don't you ________for a drink one evening?
   A. drop off B. drop on C. drop at D. drop in

VI. Translate the following from English into Chinese.

1. Students need to have time for relaxation and cultural activities on campus.
2. The mall's rule is not to allow returns or exchanges.
3. He thinks he needs to focus more on his career
4. I can let you have another $10, but no more.
5. The police had to let him go due to lack of evidence.

VII. Translate the following from Chinese into English.

1. 被选进该队我感到很荣幸。
2. 你今天有哪些工作要做?
3. 上百人要来参加开业典礼。
4. 全体教师和学生都反对这些措施。
5. 我爸爸不让我晚上出门。

Writing Tips

Indefinite and Definite Articles	
A, an	Use these indefinite articles to refer generally to an object that is not distinguished from other similar objects. The object can be any of the following: 1. Singular: a professor 2. Uncountable: a group 3. Generalized: a conference (i.e., any conference); a suggestion The object can never be plural—wrong: a professors) Use *a* or *an* depending on the sound of the word that follows it: 1. Use *a* before words starting with a consonant sound, including /y/, /h/, and /w/ sounds: a car; a year; a history of America; a wall. 2. Use *an* before words starting with a vowel sound: an article; an hour; an X-ray.
The	Use this definite article to refer to an object that the speakers are familiar with. That is, use *the* when the object is any of the following: 1. Familiar: the conference (i.e., our upcoming conference) 2. About to be described: the Lake Café 3. Important: the research projects The object can be singular or plural.

E-mail Thread 2

Subject: Re: Volunteers for Dr. Liu's Visit	
From: TomGerber@su.com	
Date: February 24, 2012	
To: IrinaPetrova@su.com	

Irina,

I would like to take Dr. Liu out on the evening of March 20. I always take visitors to City Park, which has a great view of the downtown area and the lake. The art museum is open late that night, so we could stop into see the exhibits. The Lake Cafe is nearby, and it features regional American cuisine as well as live music.

Tom Gerber
Technology Specialist, Education Department

State University
555-555-0145, ext. 110

——Original Message——
From: IrinaPetrova@su.com
Sent: Friday, February 24, 2012, 8:35 a.m.
To: <Education Department Faculty and Staff>
Subject: Volunteers for Dr. Liu's Visit

Irina Petrova wrote:

Hello everyone,

Simon had a wonderful suggestion: we take Dr. Liu out for sightseeing, dinner, and perhaps cultural activities. The department will pay all entertainment expenses.

Please let me know if you are available to spend the evening of March 20 with her. Also let me know if you have ideas for places to take her.

Thank you,

Irina Petrova, PhD
Chair, Education Department
State University
555-555-0145, ext. 104

Subject: Final Agenda for Dr. Liu's Visit
From: IrinaPetrova@su.com
Date: March 16, 2012
To: <Education Department Faculty and Staff>

Hello everyone,

Thank you for your suggestions and help with our International Education Conference and Dr. Liu's visit. I am looking forward to an exciting week. Our agenda for the professor's visit on March 20 follows:

8:00-8:15 a.m.: Welcome and introductions by Dr. Irina Petrova; Education Department Conference Room

8:15-9:30 a.m.: Tour of the Education Department, including the Educational Technology Center, by Tom Gerber, Brittany Hunt, and Angela Yazzie

9:30-9:45 a.m.: Break

9:45-10:45 a.m.: Presentation: "US Policies for Elementary and Middle School Education" by Dr. Margaret Gray; Education Department Conference Room

10:45-11:45 a.m.: Presentation: "Secondary Education: A Comparison of US and International Education Policies" by Dr. Simon Wellington; Education Department Conference Room

11:45 a.m.- 12:00 p.m.: Break

12:00-1:30 p.m.: Lunch (to be delivered by New York State Deli) with all faculty and staff; University Dining Room

1:30-2:30 p.m.: Presentation: "Postsecondary Education: Worldwide Trends" by Dr. Irina Petrova; Education Department Conference Room

2:30-2:45 pm.: Break

2:45-3:45 p.m.: Presentation: "New Research on Special Education in the United States" by

Dr. Marcus Howard; Education Department Conference Room

3:45-4:45 p.m.: Presentation: "Exchange Programs for Teachers" by Dr. Anita Viejo; Education Department Conference Room

4:45 p.m.: Adjourn; Dr. Irina Petrova takes Dr. Liu to University Park Hotel, 45 High St.

5:30 p.m.: Sightseeing; Tom Gerber picks up Dr. Liu at University Park Hotel and drives through City Park

6:00 p.m.: Visit to the art museum (500 Central Ave.) with faculty and staff who are dining with Dr. Liu

7:00 p.m.: Dinner at the Lake Cafe (713 Central Ave.; table reserved under Gerber) with faculty and staff who are dining with Dr. Liu

9:00 p.m.: Adjourn; Tom Gerber drops off Dr. Liu at University Park Hotel

Irina Petrova, PhD
Chair, Education Department
State University
555-555-0145, ext. 104

New Words 2

1.	adjourn	[ə'dʒəːn]	*v.*	休会；闭会；中止活动
2.	cuisine	[kwi'ziːn]	*n.*	菜肴
3.	exhibit	[ig'zibit]	*n.*	展品
4.	feature	[fiːtʃə]	*v.*	有……的特征/特色
5.	regional	['riːdʒənəl]	*adj.*	地方的；区域的
6.	under	['ʌndə]	*prep.*	在……下面，在……下方

7. volunteer [ˌvɔlən'tiə] *n.* 志愿者

Phrases and Expressions 2

1. a great view 令人难忘的风景
2. art museum 艺术博物馆
3. downtown area 城市中心区
4. drops off 留下；放下
5. Education Department 教育系
6. entertainment expense 娱乐活动花销
7. live music 现场音乐会；露天音乐会
8. secondary education 中学教育；中等教育
9. special education 特别教育
10. stop in 短暂停留；停止于
11. technology specialist 技术专家；技术顾问；技术员
12. to be available 有空闲；可行的
13. worldwide trends 国际趋势；国际走向

Proper Names 2

1. Angela Yazzie 安吉拉·亚杰
2. Anita Viejo 安尼塔·威究
3. Brittany Hunt 布兰妮·亨特
4. City Park 市区公园
5. International Education Conference 国际教育会议
6. Lake Café 湖滨餐馆
7. Marcus Howard 马可思·霍华德
8. Margaret Gray 玛格丽特·格雷
9. Tom Gerber 汤姆·格伯

Notes 2

1. *Surnames in America*: America's history of immigration from around the world has given it a diverse population. This is reflected in the wide variety of surnames. Some of the

immigrants' surnames are spelled as they were in their native countries. But others were simplified, romanized, translated into the English word for the name's meaning, or "Americanized" to help the immigrants assimilate into US society.

姓氏在美国：美国来自世界各地的移民历史给美国带来了背景各异的人口。这些体现在各种各样的姓氏。有些移民的姓氏的拼写，是按照在他们的祖国的拼写方式。但也有些被简化了，罗马拼音化了，或将名字的意思译成英文单词，或称"美国化"，以便帮助外来的移民融入美国社会。

Most Native American tribes did not use surnames until they came into contact with Westerners. Modern Native American surnames may indicate a clan affiliation, or they may have been assigned by missionaries or created when an ancestor registered with the government. African Americans who are descended from slaves have a similar history of obtaining a surname. Many slaves did not have a last name, partly because many African cultures did not use them and partly because, as slaves, they did not have rights and did not "need" a legal name. After being freed, some slaves took the plantation owner's surname, while others chose to use the names of famous Americans, geographic locations, and concepts such as "Freeman." The civil rights movement of the mid-twentieth century spurred some African Americans to adopt African or Islamic names to better reflect their heritage or culture.

很多美国本土印地安人在与西方人接触前是不用姓氏的。近代的美国本土印地安人的姓氏，表明氏族隶属关系，或可能由传教士赐于或当祖先在政府注册时所建立的。非裔美国人的奴隶后裔获得姓氏也具有相似的历史。不少奴隶没有姓氏，一部分原因是非洲文化不用姓氏，一部分原因是作为奴隶没有权利拥有姓氏和合法的姓名和不需要姓名。当奴隶获得解放后，一些人选用了种植园主的姓氏，而另一些人则选择美国名人，区域和概念如自由人作为他们的姓氏。二十世纪中叶的民权运动促使了非裔采用非洲或伊斯兰的名字，以更好地反映他们的遗产或文化。

2. *Deli* is short for *delicatessen*. Delis are shops or small restaurants that sell sandwiches, soups, and cold salads. They also sell sliced sandwich meat and cheeses for people to take home to make their own sandwiches. Delis are very popular in the northeastern United States, particularly in New York, but can be found throughout the country.

deli 是熟食店简称。熟食店商店或小餐馆出售的三明治、汤和冷沙拉。它们也卖切片夹心肉和奶酪给那些想回家自己做三明治的人。在美国东北部地区，熟食店很流行也很受欢迎，特别是在纽约地区，但在美国全国各地也都有。

3. *late that night* 意思是那天晚上博物馆关门很晚。此外，类似的词组搭配还有“late last night”昨天深夜，“late into the night”到深夜，“late at night”每天深夜。

例：1) I went to bed late last night, and that is why I got up late today.
我昨晚睡的很晚，因此起床也很晚。
2) I don't like working late into the night.
我不喜欢工作到很晚。
3) Going to bed late at night is not good for your health.
晚睡对你的身体有害。

4. *stop in* 是固定动词词组，在这里 *in* 是副词。stop in 意思是短暂停留，顺便去一下。

例：1) I'll stop in and see you on my way home.
在回家的路上我想顺道看你一下。
2) I need to stop in at the library.
我得去趟图书馆。

4.1. 在口语中另外一个常用动词词组是“drop in”。意思也是短暂停留，顺便去一下，但同 *stop in* 的区别在于，drop in 不用事先安排。

例：Why don't you drop in for a drink one evening?
如某天晚上有空，到家里来玩。

5.1. *to take (somebody) out for* 是固定动词词组，意思是“to take (someone) as a guest to a restaurant, cinema, or club or to take them to do (something)”。

例：1) We will take him out for a meal next week.
下周，我们想带他去餐馆吃顿饭。
2) Let's take her out for a walk.
让我们带她散散步吧。

5.2. *to take (something) out* 也常用于口语种，通常有两种意思。

例：1) How much would you like to take out? (to get money from a bank account)
你想取多少钱？
2) You can take out three books at a time. (to borrow books from a library)
你一次只能借三本书。

6. *Lunch will be delivered by* 意思是由谁负责出钱安排午餐，*delivered* 在这里是过去分词，相当于动词“given”。类似的用法还有“to deliver a speech”。

例：The CEO delivered a televised speech yesterday.
昨天公司总裁官发表了电视讲话。

7. *To drop off (somebody) at (a place)* means to take a person by car to a place and leave the person there, especially when the driver is on the way to another place.

例：1) Just drop me here—I can walk home.
把我放在这里吧，我可以走回家。
2) She dropped me at the school yesterday.
昨天她开车顺便把我送到了学校。

Exercises 2

I. Answer the following questions.

1. Who volunteered to take Dr. Liu out on March 20?
2. Where does he always take visitors?
3. What view does that place have?
4. What does the Lake Café feature?
5. Who will pay all the entertainment expenses?
6. What is New York State Deli doing?
7. Who will take Dr. Liu to University Park Hotel at 4:45 p.m.?
8. What will Dr. Liu do at 6:00 p.m.?

II. Write an e-mail that explains how you would welcome a visitor from another country.

Key to E-mail Thread 1 Exercises (for Reference)

I. Answer the following questions.

1. Dr. Liu Hui Ying will participate in the Education Department's upcoming International

Education Conference.

2. The conference focuses on developing international cooperation to improve the quality of education worldwide.
3. The Education Department is hoping to establish an exchange program with a Chinese university.
4. Faculty members will present their research and its relationship to US educational policies.
5. Department staff will assist with a tour of the department's facilities and join the faculty and Dr. Liu for lunch.
6. Irina Petrova asked the Education Department faculty and staff to let her know when they could meet with Dr. Liu on March 20.
7. Simon Wellington is available from 10:30 a.m. to 12:00 p.m. and from 3:30 to 5:30 p.m. on March 20.
8. Simon suggested that the department take Dr. Liu out to dinner as well as take her sightseeing and to some cultural events.

II. Write the key points of this e-mail thread.

- Education Department Chair Irina Petrova wrote an e-mail to department faculty and staff. She told them that Dr. Liu Hui Ying, a professor of education in Beijing, will be visiting the university to participate in the department's upcoming International Education Conference.
- The conference focuses on developing international cooperation to improve the quality of education worldwide.
- Because the Education Department is hoping to establish an exchange program with a Chinese university, Irina would like each faculty and staff member to meet with Dr. Liu on March 20.
- Faculty members will present their research and its relationship to US educational policies to Dr. Liu. Department staff will assist with a tour of the department's facilities and join the faculty and professor for lunch.
- Irina asked faculty to let her know when they could meet with the professor on March 20 so that she could create an agenda.
- Dr. Simon Wellington replied that meeting with Dr. Liu was a great opportunity.
- Simon will be available on March 20 from 10:30 a.m. to 12:00 p.m. and from 3:30 to

5:30 p.m.

- Simon suggested that the Education Department faculty and staff take Dr. Liu out to dinner as well as sightseeing and to some cultural events.

III. Fill in the blanks.

1. Please let me know what time you are available to present on December 10.
2. Our university is honored to have such a prominent professor speak at our conference.
3. Faculty members will present their research at the conference.
4. Many high school students travel to foreign countries to participate exchange programs.
5. Our department wants to develop an international research project.
6. I would like to take him out and to some cultural events.
7. Does the conference focus on education or international cooperation?
8. I can't create an agenda until you let me know when we can meet.

IV. Fill in the missing information.

Joe,

I am honored to have such a prominent professor visit us. I will be available from 10:30 a.m. to 2:30 p.m.

I suggest that we take Dr. Smith on a tour of the department's facilities. If he has not been to America before, we also could take him sightseeing and to some cultural events.

Nancy Reed

Professor

V. Choose the correct answer. Only one answer is correct.

1. B 2. A 3. B 4. D 5. A 6. B 7. C 8. D

VI. Translate the following from English into Chinese.

1. 在校园里，学生要有娱乐和文化活动的时间。
2. 购物中心的规定是不准退货、换货。
3. 他认为他须更注重他的事业。

4. 我只能再给你 10 美元了。
5. 由于证据不足，警察只好把他放了。

VII. Translate the following from Chinese into English.

1. I felt honored to be included in the team.
2. What's on your agenda today?
3. Hundreds of people will participate in the opening ceremony?
4. Both faculty and students oppose the measures.
5. My dad won't let me come out at night.

Translation of E-mail Thread 1 (for Reference)

译文：

邮件 1-1

主题：中国教授即将来访
发件人：伊琳娜・佩特洛娃
日期：2012 年 2 月 23 日
收件人：〈教育系全体教职工〉

大家好，

北京大学教育学教授刘惠英将于三月二十号到二十五号参加在我校召开的国际教育学术会议。正如大家所了解的，这个学术会议着重于如何发展国际合作，以提高教育水平。

由于我们教育系希望建立与中国的大学相互交流的项目，我想请每位教学及教辅人员都能在会议前认识一下刘教授。我们会在三月二十日接待她，系教学人员将介绍他们的研究成果及其与美国教育政策的关系。系文秘人员将协助参观我系的设施并共进午餐。我想了解一下教学人员在二十日什么时间能与刘教授见面，以便我制订一个日程表。

我们非常荣幸有这样著名的教授来访我校。我也对大家热情接待刘博士的工作表示感谢。

谢谢，

伊琳娜·佩特洛娃，博士
教育系系主任
州立大学
电话：555-555-0145，分机：104

邮件 1-2

主题：回复：中国教授即将来访
发件人：西蒙·惠灵顿
日期：2012 年 2 月 23 日
收件人：伊琳娜·佩特洛娃

伊琳娜，

我期待着认识刘博士。这对我们开展交流活动及开发国际研究项目都是一个极好的机会。

我在三月二十日上午十点半到十二点和下午三点半到五点半这两个时间段有空作报告。

我建议我们当天晚上邀请刘博士吃晚饭。最好能安排她参加一些观光和文化活动。

西蒙·惠灵顿，博士
教育系教授
州立大学
电话：555-555-0145，分机：109

Key to E-mail Thread 2 Exercises (for Reference)

I. Answer the following questions.

1. Tom Gerber, the Education Department's technology specialist, volunteered to take Dr. Liu Huiying out on March 20.

2. Tom always takes visitors to City Park.
3. City Park has a view of the downtown area and the lake.
4. The Lake Café features regional American cuisine and live music.
5. The Education Department will pay all the entertainment expenses.
6. New York State Deli is delivering lunch to the University Dining Room.
7. Irina Petrova will take Dr. Liu to University Park Hotel at 4:45 p.m.
8. At 6:00 p.m., Dr. Liu will visit the art museum.

Translation of E-mail Thread 2 (for Reference)

译文：

邮件 2-1

主题：回复：接待刘博士访问的志愿者
发件人：汤姆·格伯
日期：2012 年 2 月 24 日
收件人：伊琳娜·佩特洛娃

伊琳娜，

我想三月二十日晚上带刘博士外出。我总是带来访者参观能看到我市美丽的城区风景和湖边的城区公园。艺术博物馆那天也开到很晚，所以我们也能去博物馆看展览。“湖滨小馆”就在附近，它不但有具有美国特色的餐饮，还有现场音乐表演。

汤姆·格伯
教育系技术员
州立大学
电话：555-555-0145，分机：110

——最初信息——

发件人：伊琳娜·佩特洛娃
日期：2012 年 2 月 24 日周五上午 8:35
收件人：〈教育系全体教职员工〉
主题：接待刘博士访问的志愿者

伊琳娜·佩特洛娃写到：

大家好，

西蒙的提议太完美了，我们请刘博士观光城区景点，享受晚餐，也许还参加一些文化活动。系里将承担所有娱乐活动的花销。

请告知我你们是否能于三月二十日晚参与招待刘博士的安排。另外也请告知我还有什么可带她观光地方。

谢谢，

伊琳娜·佩特洛娃，博士
教育系主任
州立大学
电话：555-555-0145，分机：104

邮件 2-2

发件人：伊琳娜·佩特洛娃
日期：2012 年 3 月 16 日
收件人：〈教育系全体教职员工〉
主题：刘博士访问期间的时间安排

大家好，

谢谢你们的建议和对我们国际教育会议及刘博士的访问的帮助。我期待着这个令人兴奋的星期。我们有关刘教授三月二十日的来访时间安排如下：

上午 **8:00-8:15** 由伊琳娜·佩特洛娃博士在教育系会议室在主持欢迎和介绍仪式。

上午 **8:15-9:30** 由汤姆·格伯、布兰妮·亨特和安吉拉·亚杰陪同参观教育系包括教育科学技术中心。

上午 **9:30-9:45** 休息

上午 **9:45-10:45** 由玛格丽特·格雷博士在教育系会议室作“美国中小学教育政策”的专题报告。

上午 **10:45-11:45** 由西蒙·惠灵顿博士在教育系会议室就中等教育问题作“美国与国际教育政策的比较”专题报告。

11:45-12:00 休息

12:00-1:30 在学校餐厅与系参会人员共进午餐。(由“纽约州熟食店”提供午餐)

下午 **1:30-2:30** 由伊琳娜·佩特洛娃博士在教育系会议室就高等教育问题作“国际教育趋势”专题报告。

下午 **2:30-2:45** 休息

下午 **2:45-3:45** 由马库思·霍华德博士在教育系会议室作“有关美国特殊教育的新研究”专题报告。

下午 **3:45-4:45** 安尼塔·威究博士在教育系会议室作“有关教师交流项目”专题报告。

下午 **4:45** 专题报告结束。报告由伊琳娜·佩特洛娃博士送刘博士回 45 号高峰街“大学公园旅馆”。

晚上 **5:30** 观光活动;汤姆·格伯开车到大学公园旅馆接刘博士并驱车到市区公园。

晚上 **6:00** 与共进晚餐的系教职员工参观中央路 500 号的艺术博物馆。

晚上 **7:00** 刘博士与系教职员工在中央路 713 号的湖滨餐馆共进晚餐。（位子已预订在格伯名下）

晚上 **9:00** 活动完毕；由汤姆·格伯送刘博士回大学公园旅馆。

伊琳娜·佩特洛娃，博士
教育系主任
州立大学
电话：555-555-0145，分机：104

Lesson 13

Web Advertising

网络广告

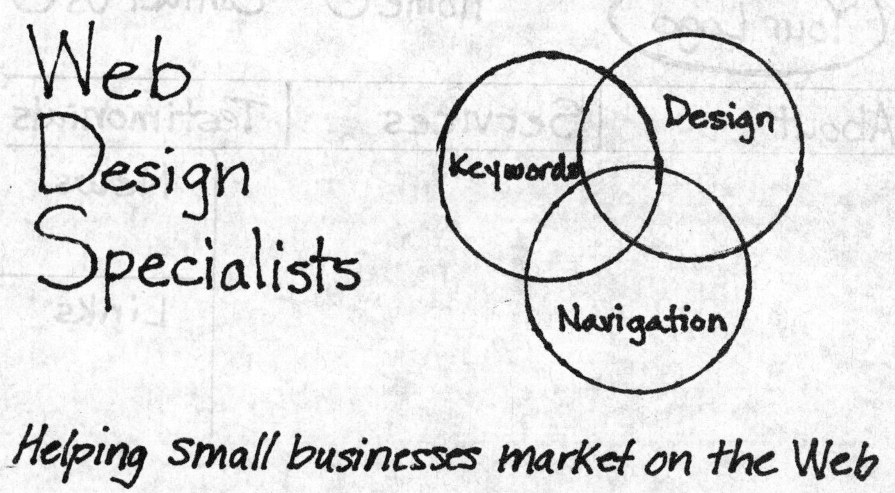

Learning Objectives

In this lesson, you will learn the following:

- Why a small business should have a website
  为什么小公司应有网站或网页
- What features a website can have
  网站的特点
- What the difference is between a blog and social media
  个人博客与社交网

E-mail Thread 1

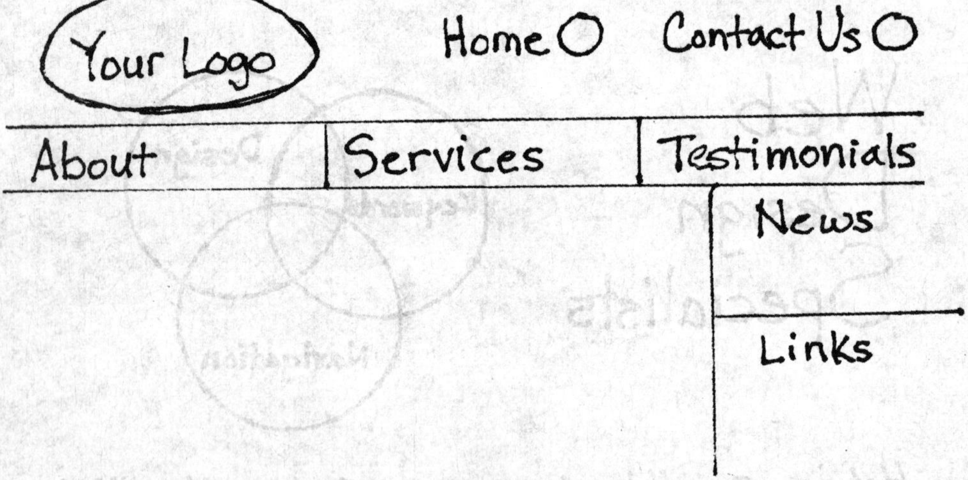

Subject: Inquiry about Website Development
From: RWeber@rwerberediting.com
Date: December 12, 2012
To: Info@webdesignspecialists.com
Dear Sir or Madam: I am a freelance editor with 20 years of experience editing educational materials. I would like to expand my business by developing a website to attract new clients. I found Web Design Specialists after searching the Web for local website developers. I am interested in hiring your company to develop my website. But first, I would like to know how a website would help my business. I would also appreciate a cost estimate for developing and maintaining it. Thank you for your time. Sincerely, Ryan Weber 53 Open Sky Dr. Fort Collins, CO 80521 555-555-0189 RWeber@rwerberediting.com

Subject: Re: Inquiry about Website Development
From: SMartin@webdesignspecialists.com
Date: December 12, 2012
To: RWeber@rwerberediting.com
Dear Mr. Weber:

Thank you for contacting Web Design Specialists. We have 10 years of experience helping small businesses market their products and services on the World Wide Web.

A website can certainly help your business. It will allow you to:

- provide basic information about you and your services, 24/7, worldwide;
- reduce your marketing costs because you won't need to print brochures; and
- stay in contact with your clients and recruit potential clients.

At Web Design Specialists, we use the latest technology to develop well-designed websites. We guarantee that our websites will work on different browsers (such as Safari and Firefox). We ensure that the websites contain the best keywords for search engines to find them. We design easy-to-use navigation so that website visitors can find what they want in one or two clicks.

A basic website costs $500, and the price increases as you add features. A domain name and website hosting cost an additional $150 per year. The cost of maintenance varies depending on how often you update your website.

Thank you for contacting us. Please let me know if you have more questions or would like to schedule a consultation.

Sincerely,

Sally Martin
Account Representative
Web Design Specialists
555-555-0126
SMartin@webdesignspecialists.com
webdesignspecialists.com

New Words 1

1. appreciate [ə'pri:ʃieit] *v.* 感谢

2.	blog	[blɔg]	*n.*	博客；网上日志
3.	brochure	[brəu'ʃjuə]	*n.*	宣传小册子
4.	browser	['brauzə]	*n.*	浏览器
5.	click	[klik]	v/*n.*	点击
6.	consultation	[ˌkɔnsəl'teiʃən]	*n.*	咨询
7.	edit	['edit]	*v.*	编辑
8.	expand	[iks'pænd]	*v.*	扩大；扩充；发展
9.	feature	[fiːtʃə]	*n.*	特点；特色
10.	guarantee	[ˌgærən'tiː]	*v.*	有保证；担保
11.	hire	['haiə]	*v.*	雇用
12.	inquiry	[in'kwaiəri]	*n.*	询问；打听
13.	keyword	[kiː wəːd]	*n.*	关键词
14.	madam	['mædəm]	*n.*	夫人
15.	maintain	[mein'tein]	*v.*	维持；保持
16.	recruit	[ri'kruːt]	*v.*	雇用；聘用
17.	schedule	['skedʒul]	*v.*	日程安排表
18.	technology	[tek'nɔlədʒi]	*n.*	科技
19.	website	['webˌsait]	*n.*	网站
20.	well-designed	[wel- di'zaind]	*adj.*	设计完美的

Phrases and Expressions 1

1.	account representative	客户代表
2.	cost estimate	费用估算
3.	domain name	网域名称；域名
4.	easy-to-use navigation	容易使用的浏览器
5.	educational material	教育材料
6.	freelance editor	自由职业编辑
7.	marketing cost	营销费用；销售成本
8.	potential client	未来客户
9.	search engine	搜索工具
10.	social media	社会化媒体；社交网
11.	website developer	网站开发者

12. website development 网站开发
13. website hosting 网站管理

Proper Names 1

1. Sally Martin 莎莉·马丁
2. Web Design Specialists 网站设计专家

Notes 1

1. *The World Wide Web*, or *the Web*, is a system on the Internet that allows people to find and use information that is held on computers all over the world.
World Wide Web 或 Web 意为万维网或全球资讯网，常被译为网络，它是一种超文本信息系统，使人们可以从中获取更多的信息。想要了解某一个主题的内容只要在这个主题上点一下，就可以进入到包含这一主题的文档上。正是这种多连接性使得人们称它为 Web。Web 前面通常使用的介词“on”。
例：I'll put the news on the Web tomorrow.
我明天将这条消息发到网上。

2. *website* 译为网站，它是一种通信工具，就像布告栏一样，人们可以通过网站来发布自己想要公开的信息或收集想要得到的信息。

3. *Freelance* means to work independently for different companies rather than being employed by one company.
现今通信科技高度发达，网络普及，从而产生了许多自由职业者。
例：1) freelance writer 自由作家
2) freelance translator 自由翻译
3) freelance designer 自由设计师
4) freelance illustrator 自由插图画家
“Freelancer”意思是自由职业者。freelance 与“self-employed”有所不同，self-employed 是从事个体经营某一行业的个体经营者。

4. *browsers*、*search engines* 和 *keywords*: A *browser*, or *web browser*, is a software program that allows the user to locate and display web pages. Safari, Internet Explorer, and Firefox are browsers. A *search engine* is a program that allows the user to enter terms, or *keywords*, to search for relevant web pages. Google and Baidu are search engines.
浏览器、搜索引擎和关键字：一个浏览器或 Web 浏览器，是一个软件程序，允许用户查找和显示网页。Safari、IE 和 Firefox 都是浏览器。一个搜索引擎允许用户输入条款或关键字，搜索相关网页，如谷歌和百度搜索引擎。

5. *Domain names* identify an individual, a computer, or an organization on the Internet. For example, the domain name for the University of International Business and Economics is www.uibe.edu.cn.
在互联网上域名识别个人身份，一台计算机或一个机构。例如，对外经济贸易大学的域名是 www.uibe.edu.cn。

6. *Website hosting* is usually provided by hosting companies or Internet service providers. They support the files, programs, servers, and Internet connections for websites.
网站托管通常是由托管公司或互联网服务供应商提供。他们支持文件、程序、服务器、网站和因特网的连接。

Exercises 1

I. Answer the following questions.

1. What would Ryan Weber like to do?
2. How did Ryan find Web Design Specialists?
3. What would Ryan like to know?
4. How many years of experience does Web Design Specialists have?
5. Identify one thing that a website will allow Ryan to do.
6. What does Web Design Specialists guarantee?
7. How much does a basic website cost?
8. How much does maintenance cost?

II. Write the key points of this e-mail thread.

III. Fill in the blanks.

1. I don't have many clients, so I would like to recruit potential________.
2. Since she had more ________ for me, we scheduled a consultation.
3. If he adds another feature ________ his basic website, will the price increase?
4. My company ________ appreciate a cost estimate for website hosting and maintenance.
5. I would not use that company—it doesn't guarantee that its websites will work ________ different browsers.
6. Did she use the latest technology to ________ the website?
7. Developing a website may be cheap, but how ________ does it cost to maintain it?
8. Her new website is attracting new ________ and expanding her business.

IV. Fill in the missing information.

Dear Ms. Adams,

I would like to develop a website for my business. I am interested in hiring you to develop it. I would appreciate your telling me how much experience you have.

Sincerely,

David Masters

Dear Mr. Masters,

Thank you for contacting me. I have eight years ________ experience as a website developer. I guarantee that my websites will work ________ different browsers. I also ensure that they are well designed and have easy-________-use navigation. Would you like to schedule a ________?

Sincerely,

Mary Adams

V. Choose the correct answer. Only one answer is correct.

1. There's something I _________ to tell you.
   A. had better like B. like C. should like D. would like
2. You're welcome to stay with us as long as you _________.
   A. like B. would like C. should like D. had better like
3. Why don't you get up early _________ you don't have to hurry?
   A. until B. so that C. so as that D. although
4. He's one of the regular _________ in our restaurant. He comes once a week.
   A. clients B. eaters C. customers D. visitors
5. We've bought him a gift _________ his birthday.
   A. in B. for C. against D. to
6. His strong stand on the issue could have _________ him his job.
   A. costed B. lost C. cost D. changed
7. Medical treatment for the disease _________ hospital to hospital.
   A. varies B. differ from C. differs D. varies from
8. It is a beautiful watch. You _________ have spent so much money.
   A. mustn't B. cannot C. may not D. needn't

VI. Translate the following sentences from English into Chinese.

1. You can find our website by entering the keywords "Happy Travel."
2. If you want to hear the sentence, just click on it.
3. An important feature of his painting is the bright colors.
4. I registered three domain names on the Internet last year.
5. Which country is going to host the next World Cup?

VII. Translate the following sentences from Chinese into English.

1. 汤姆现在是一个自由职业插图画家，为多家公司工作。
2. 我很感谢你去年的工作，你真的很棒。
3. 你可以随时访问我的网站。
4. 我们计划在下个月将你们产品放在我公司商品目录上。
5. 你需点击两次才能进入我的网页。

Writing Tips

Hyphenation*	
Adverbs ending in *-ly*	Don't hyphenate adverbs ending in *–ly*: ● *privately held company*
Compound modifiers	Do hyphenate compound modifiers before a noun: ● *well-designed website* ● *low-quality clothing* Don't hyphenate compound modifiers after a noun: ● *The website is well designed.* ● *The clothing has a low quality.*
Fractions and numbers	Do hyphenate spelled-out fractions and numbers from twenty-one to ninety-nine: ● *one-half* ● *three hundred forty-eight*
Multiple hyphens	Do hyphenate a phrase that modifies a noun: ● *easy-to-use navigation* ● *100-year-old eggs*
Prefixes	Don't hyphenate most prefixes: ● *multinational corporation* ● *nonviolent* Do hyphenate prefixes before a capitalized term or a number. Also insert a hyphen between two *i*'s or *a*'s that form when the prefix is added: ● *pre-Han history* ● *pre-1949* ● *anti-inflammatory*
Readability, pronunciation,	Do hyphenate if it will increase readability, clarify pronunciation,

and ambiguity	or reduce ambiguity. For example, use a hyphen to distinguish between words such as these: ● *recreation* (a sport or hobby) and *re-creation* (something created again) ● *coop* (a small cage or building) and *co-op* (a cooperative organization owned and run the people who use it) Don't use a hyphen when the term is well known: ● *high school graduation* ● *first aid kit* ● *health care policies*

*Hyphenation is troublesome even for native English speakers. Consult a dictionary first, and if the term isn't there, then follow these rules.

E-mail Thread 2

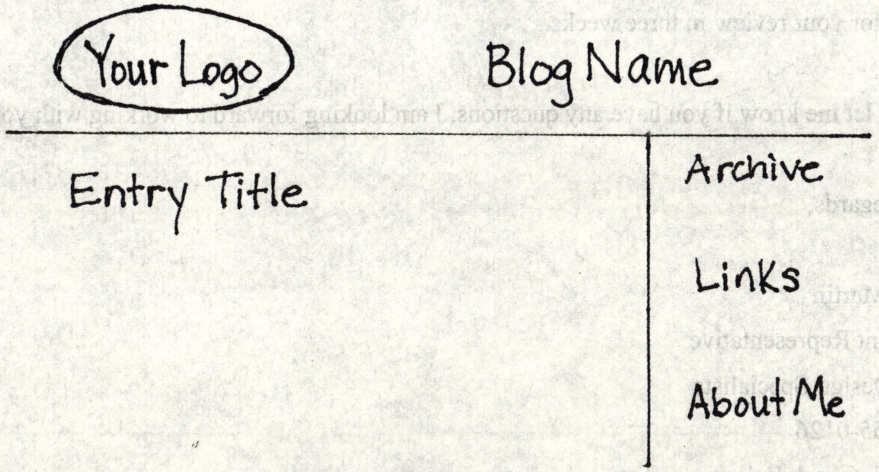

Subject: Consultation Summary
From: SMartin@webdesignspecialists.com
Date: December 19, 2012
To: RWeber@rweberediting.com

Dear Ryan,

It was nice meeting you last week and discussing your website. I would like to confirm that your website will have the following basic features:

- Domain name (www.WeberEditorialServices.com)
- Contact page listing your address, phone number, and a link to send you e-mail
- About page listing your experience
- Services page listing the services you provide and their costs
- Testimonials page listing recommendations from your clients

We will design navigation buttons for each feature. In addition, we will design a logo for your company. As we discussed, you will write the text for each feature. The website will be ready for your review in three weeks.

Please let me know if you have any questions. I am looking forward to working with you.

Best regards,

Sally Martin
Account Representative
Web Design Specialists
555-555-0126
SMartin@webdesignspecialists.com
webdesignspecialists.com

Subject: Consultation Summary and Questions
From: RWeber@rweberediting.com
Date: December 19, 2012
To: SMartin@webdesignspecialists.com

Dear Sally,

Thank you for the summary; I think our consultation was very productive.

This e-mail confirms that I would like my website to include all the features you noted in your last e-mail.

I have a few questions for you. I would like to interact more with my clients and potential clients. Should I add a blog feature to do this? A blog would allow me to use my website to write about my business. Or should I add a link to a social media account like Facebook or Twitter? Do you think more people will find me through social media? Also, is there difference in cost between adding a blog and a link?

Thank you for your help.

Best,

Ryan Weber
53 Open Sky Dr.
Fort Collins, CO 80521
555-555-0189
RWeber@rweberediting.com

New Words 2

1.	interact	[ˌintəˈrækt]	*v.*	互动
2.	link	[liŋk]	*n.*	连接

3.	logo	['lɔgəu]	*n.*	标记；标志
4.	productive	[prə'dʌktiv]	*adj.*	有成果的，多产的
5.	recommendation	[ˌrekəmen'deiʃən]	*n.*	推荐信，介绍信

Phrases and Expressions 2

1.	consultation summary	咨询总结
2.	contact page	联系页面
3.	navigation button	网站导航索引按钮
4.	potential clients	未来客户
5.	services page	服务页面
6.	social media account	社会化媒体账户；社交网账户
7.	testimonials page	推荐页面；审核页面

Proper Names 2

1.	Facebook	脸谱网
2.	Fort Collins (Colorado; CO)	柯林斯堡
3.	Open Sky Dr.	通天路
4.	Twitter	推特
5.	Weber Editorial Services	网站编辑服务

Notes 2

1. 在一个网站中会设立一个网站导航索引系统，英语是“navigation”，借助这个导入系统可进入多个网页，英语用 page 一词。在这里有：

例：1) domain name　意思是域名，机构或者个人在网上注册的名称，是机构与个人间相互联络的网络地址。

2) contact page　注册网页，　该网页提供联系你的信息。

3) service page　该网页提供你的服务及价格。

4) testimonials page　该网页提供第三者所写的关于你的介绍和评价。

此外机构与个人还设有其他一些网页。

例：1) On a blog page, users want to share their views with others on a daily basis.
博客页面用户每日与他人分享日常生活。

2) A home page is the first page of a website, which often contains links to other pages on that website.
首页是网站第一页用于连接网站其他网页。

2. *Blog* is an abbreviation for *weblog* (created from *web* + *log*). It is a website or part of a website where a person or company posts thoughts, photographs, and other interests, and other people can comment on them. The most-recent posts appear first. *blog* can also be used as a verb, for example, "I like to sit at the coffeehouse and blog." A person who writes a blog is a "blogger."
Blog 是 weblog 的缩写，中文意思是"网络日志"。blog 是以网络作为载体，简单而又迅速地发布自己的信息和心得，及时有效轻松地与他人进行交流。blog 一词也可以用作动词"to blog"。"blogger" 是指撰写 blog 的人，也被译为"博客"。

3. *Social media* refers to a variety of technologies on the World Wide Web that allow many people to interact. Examples are Facebook, Twitter, and YouTube. Users can search a social media site to find people, jobs, or other things they are interested in.
social media 意思是社交媒体或社交网络，它使用非常方便的通信技术使得网上交流变为互动对话，因此也被译为社交媒体。

Exercises 2

I. Answer the following questions.

1. Did Ryan Weber and Sally Martin have a consultation?
2. Name one feature that will be on Ryan's website.
3. What will Web Design Specialists design for Ryan's company?
4. What will Ryan do?
5. When will the website be ready for Ryan's review?
6. Does Ryan want his website to have all the features Sally listed in her e-mail?
7. What else would Ryan like to do?

8. What two features could Ryan add to create more interaction?

II. Write an e-mail that lists the features you would like to have on your website.

Key to E-mail Thread 1 Exercises (for Reference)

I. Answer the following questions.

1. Ryan Weber would like to expand his business by developing a website to attract new clients.
2. Ryan found Web Design Specialists by searching the Web for local website developers.
3. Ryan would like to know how a website would help his business.
4. Web Design Specialists has 10 years of experience.
5. A website will allow Ryan to 1) provide basic information about himself and his services, 24/7, worldwide; 2) reduce his marketing costs because he won't need to print brochures; and 3) stay in contact with his clients and recruit potential clients.
6. Web Design Specialists guarantees that its websites will work on different browsers.
7. A basic website costs $500.
8. The cost of maintenance varies depending on how often Ryan updates his website.

II. Write the key points of this e-mail thread.

- Ryan Weber would like to expand his business by developing a website to attract new clients.
- Ryan found Web Design Specialists after searching the Web for local website developers.
- Ryan is interested in hiring this company to develop his website.
- Ryan would like to know how a website would help his business. He also would appreciate receiving a cost estimate for developing and maintaining it.
- Sally Martin replied to Ryan's e-mail.
- Sally said a website would allow Ryan to 1) provide basic information about himself and his services, 24/7, worldwide; 2) reduce his marketing costs because he won't need to print brochures; and 3) stay in contact with his clients and recruit potential clients.
- Sally said Web Design Specialists used the latest technology to develop well-designed websites. She listed other things the company did and guaranteed.

- Sally gave Ryan the costs for developing, hosting, and maintaining a basic website.

III. Fill in the blanks.

1. I don't have many clients, so I would like to recruit potential clients.
2. Since she had more questions for me, we scheduled a consultation.
3. If he adds another feature to his basic website, will the price increase?
4. My company would appreciate a cost estimate for website hosting and maintenance.
5. I would not use that company—it doesn't guarantee that its websites will work on different browsers.
6. Did she use the latest technology to develop the website?
7. Developing a website may be cheap, but how much does it cost to maintain it?
8. Her new website is attracting new clients and expanding her business.

IV. Fill in the missing information.

Dear Mr. Masters,

Thank you for contacting me. I have eight years of experience as a website developer. I guarantee that my websites will work on different browsers. I also ensure that they are well designed and have easy-to-use navigation. Would you like to schedule a consultation?

Sincerely,

Mary Adams

V. Choose the correct answer. Only one answer is correct.

1. D 2. A 3. B 4. C 5. B 6. C 7. D 8. D

VI. Translate the following sentences from English into Chinese.

1. 你可以通过输入关键词‘Happy Travel’找到我们网站。
2. 如果你想听到这句话的发音，就点击一下该句子。
3. 他这张画的一个特点是明快的颜色。
4. 我去年在网上注册了三个域名。
5. 明年的世界杯由谁来主办?

VII. Translate the following sentences from Chinese into English.

1. Tom has become a freelance illustrator, working for several companies.
2. I really appreciate your work last year. You did very well.
3. You can visit my website any time.
4. We plan to put your products in our company's brochure next month.
5. You can enter my page by clicking twice.

Translation of E-mail Thread 1 (for Reference)

译文:

邮件 1-1

主题：网站需求
发件人：瑞恩・韦伯
日期：2012 年 12 月 12 日
收件人：info@webdesignspecialists.com
尊敬的先生，女士，

我是一个有着二十年编辑教育材料经验的自由职业编辑。我想用建立网站来吸引更多新客源并扩大我的业务。

在搜索本地网站开发网页设计专家后，我发现了 “网站设计专家”。我有意雇用你们公司建立我的网站。但首先，我想了解这样的网站是如何使别人了解我的业务的。并请告知建立和更新这一网站的费用是多少。

感谢你花费了时间，

真诚的，

瑞恩・韦伯
科罗拉多州柯林斯堡

通天路 53 号，邮编 80521
电话：555-555-0189
RWeber@rweberediting.com

邮件 1-2

主题：回复：网站需求
发件人：SMartin@webdesignspecialists.com
日期：2012 年 12 月 12 日
收件人：RWeber@rweberediting.com

亲爱的韦伯先生，

感谢你与"网页设计专家"联系。在万维网上我们有十年帮助小企业营销他们的产品和服务的经验，网站定会帮助你扩大的业务。

它可以使你：

全天候向世界各地提供有关你和你服务的基本信息；
由于你将不需要打印业务宣传册，所以会降低经营成本；
能使你随时与现有及未来客户保持联络。

我们"网页设计专家"使用最新的技术精心设计开发网站。我们保证我们开发的网站将适用于不同的浏览器（如 Safari 和 Firefox）。我们确保该网站有能找到搜索引擎所需要的关键字。我们的设计易用，网站的访问者仅需点击一两次，就可以找到他们想要的东西。

开发网站的基本费用为 500 美元，如添加功能另外收费。域名和网站托管费用每年为 150 美元。维护费用则根据多久更新一次你的网站而定。

感谢你与我们联系。如有问题或想安排咨询请告知。

此致，
莎莉•马丁

客户代表
“网页设计专家”
电话：555-555-0126
SMartin@webdesignspecialists.com
webdesignspecialists.com

Key to E-mail Thread 2 Exercises (for Reference)

I. Answer the following questions.

1. Yes, Ryan Weber and Sally Martin had a consultation.
2. Ryan's website will have the following features: 1) domain name, 2) contact page, 3) about page, 4) services page, and 5) testimonials page.
3. Web Design Specialists will design a logo for Ryan's company.
4. Ryan will write the text for each feature.
5. The website will be ready for Ryan's review in three weeks.
6. Yes, Ryan wants all the features that Sally listed.
7. Ryan would like to interact more with his clients and potential clients.
8. Ryan could add a blog feature or a link to a social media account.

Translation of E-mail Thread 2 (for Reference)

译文：

邮件 2-1

主题：咨询总结
发件人：SMartin@webdesignspecialists.com
日期：2012 年 12 月 19 日
收件人：RWeber@rweberediting.com

尊敬的瑞恩，

非常高兴上周认识你和与你讨论你的网站。我想与你确认，你的网站将有以下基本特点：

网名 (www.WeberEditorialServices.com)

联系页，列出你的地址，电话号码和发送电子邮件连接

网页显示你的工作经验

服务页上列出你提供的服务及费用

你客户推荐信网页

我们将为每个功能设计巡视按钮。此外，我们将为贵公司设计一个徽标。正如我们讨论过的，你将为每个功能书写文本。我们将在三周内建好该网站请你过目。

如果你有任何问题，请通知我。我期待着与你的合作。

此致，

莎莉·马丁
客户代表
“网页设计专家”
电话：555-555-0126
webdesignspecialists.com

邮件 2-2

主题：咨询总结和问题
发件人：RWeber@rweberediting.com
日期：2012 年 12 月 19 日
收件人：SMartin@webdesignspecialists.com

亲爱的莎莉，

谢谢你的总结，我觉得我们的探讨非常有成效。

我想以此电子邮件确认我的网站，包括在你最后的电子邮件中提出的所有功能。

我仍有几个问题想请教。我想与我的客户和未来客户交流。要做到这一点，我是否应该添加一个博客功能？博客将允许我使用自己的网站写出我的服务业务。还是应该连接到社会媒体，如“脸谱”或“推特”账户？你觉得更多的人会通过社会媒体找到我的服务吗？

此外，增加一个博客和链接有没有费用上的差异？

感谢你的帮助。

最好的，

瑞恩·韦伯
科罗拉多州柯林斯堡
通天路 53 号，邮编 80521
电话：555-555-0189
RWeber@rweberediting.com

Glossary

1.	accept	[ək'sept]	*v.*	接受
2.	access	['ækses]	*v.*	使用；取得
3.	account	[ə'kaunt]	*n.*	账单；账户
4.	accounting	[ə'kauntiŋ]	*n.*	会计；会计学
5.	acknowledge	[tuːək'nɔlidʒ]	*v.*	对……打招呼
6.	addition	[ə'dɪʃən]	*n.*	附加
7.	address	[ə'dres]	*n.*	住址，地址
8.	adjourn	[ə'dʒəːn]	*v.*	休会；闭会；中止活动
9.	adventure	[əd'ventʃə]	*n.*	令人激动的活动
10.	affect	[ə'fekt]	*v.*	对……影响；改变
11.	although	[ɔːl'ðəu]	*conj.*	虽然
12.	analysis	[ə'næləsis]	*n.*	分析；分析报告
13.	apparel	[ə'pærəl]	*n.*	衣服；服装；衣着
14.	appreciate	[ə'priːʃieit]	*v.*	感谢；感激
15.	assistance	[ə'sistəns]	*n.*	助理；协助
16.	assume	[ə'sjuːm]	*v.*	承担；就任
17.	attach	[ə'tætʃ]	*v.*	附加
18.	attachment	[ə'tætʃmənt]	*n.*	附属物；附件
19.	attend	[ə'tend]	*v.*	参加；出席
20.	attendee	[ə'tendiː]	*n.*	出席者
21.	authenticity	[ˌɔːθen'tisiti]	*n.*	真实性；可靠性
22.	automatically	[ɔːtə'mætikəli]	*adv.*	自动地
23.	available	[ə'veiləbl]	*adj.*	有空的；可用的；可得到的
24.	benefit	['benifit]	*n.*	好处；福利
25.	bill	[bil]	*v.*	付账；付款
26.	blog	[blɔg]	*n.*	博客；网上日志
27.	board	[bɔːd]	*v.*	登（车，船，飞机）
28.	brand	[brænd]	*n.*	商标；牌子
29.	brochure	[brəu'ʃjuə]	*n.*	宣传小册子

30.	browser	['brauzə]	*n.*	浏览器
31.	careerwise	[kə'riəwaiz]	*adv.*	从事业上来说
32.	casually	['kæʒjuəli]	*adv.*	非正式地；漫无目的地
33.	chair	[tʃεə]	*n.*	主持人；系主任
34.	challenge	['tʃælindʒ]	*n.*	挑战
35.	championship	['tʃæmpiənʃip]	*n.*	冠军赛，锦标赛
36.	check	[tʃek]	*n.*	支票
37.	check	[tʃek]	*v.*	检查；检验；核对
38.	cheers	[tʃiəs]	*n.*	祝贺；干杯
39.	choose	[tʃu:z]	*v.*	选择；挑选
40.	click	[klik]	v.&*n.*	点击
41.	commitment	[kə'mitmənt]	*n.*	承诺
42.	confirm	[kən'fə:m]	*v.*	批准；确认
43.	confirmation	[ˌkɔnfə'meiʃən]	*n.*	确认；认可
44.	congratulation	[kənˌgrætju'leiʃən]	*n.*	庆贺；祝贺
45.	consultation	[ˌkɔnsəl'teiʃən]	*n.*	咨询
46.	consumer	[kən'sju:mə]	*n.*	消费者；顾客
47.	contact	['kɔntækt]	*v.*	联系；联络
48.	contain	[kən'tein]	*v.*	包含；包括
49.	contribute	[kən'tribju:t]	*v.*	提供；捐助
50.	coordinate	[kəu'ɔ:dneit]	*v.*	调节；协调
51.	corner	['kɔ:nə]	*n.*	街角；拐角处
52.	cuisine	[kwi'zi:n]	*n.*	菜肴
53.	culture	['kʌltʃə]	*n.*	文化
54.	cutie	['kju:ti]	*n.*	可爱的孩子
55.	deadline	['dedlain]	*n.*	截止期限；最后限期
56.	departure	[di'pɑ:tʃə]	*n.*	启程；离开；出发
57.	design	[di'zain]	*v.*	设计；构思；绘制
58.	despite	[di'spait]	*prep.*	尽管；不论
59.	details	['di:teils]	*n.*	具体细节；详细情况
60.	direction	[di'rekʃən]	*n.*	方向；方位
61.	director	[di'rektə]	*n.*	主管
62.	discount	['diskaunt]	*n.*	折扣；打折扣

63.	donation	[dəu'neiʃən]	*n.*	捐款；捐献；捐赠
64.	edit	['edit]	*v.*	编辑
65.	efficiently	[i'fiʃəntli]	*adv.*	效率高地
66.	electronically	[ilek'trɔnikəli]	*adv.*	电子地
67.	eligibility	[elidʒə'biliti]	*n.*	合格；资格
68.	eligible	['elidʒəbl]	*adj.*	合格的；适宜的
69.	employee	[ˌemplɔi'iː]	*n.*	受雇者；员工
70.	encourage	[in'kʌridʒ]	*v.*	鼓励；激发
71.	enrollment	[in'rəulmənt]	*n.*	注册人数；招生
72.	ensure	[in'ʃuə]	*v.*	保证；确保
73.	enter	['entə]	*v.*	登录；将……输入
74.	estimate	['estimeit]	*v.*	估计；判断
75.	exception	[ik'sepʃən]	*n.*	例外；被除外
76.	excite	[ik'sait]	*v.*	使兴奋；使激动
77.	exhibit	[ig'zibit]	*n.*	展品
78.	expand	[iks'pænd]	*v.*	扩大；扩充；发展
79.	expert	[ˌekspəːt]	*n.*	专门技术或知识人材
80.	expertise	[ˌekspəː'tiːz]	*n.*	专门技能；专门知识
81.	expire	[iks'paiə]	*v.*	终止；期满；无效
82.	explore	[iks'plɔː]	*v.*	探索；探究
83.	extension	[iks'tenʃən]	*n.*	电话分机
84.	extraordinary	[ekstrɔːdiː'nɛə]	*adj.*	杰出的
85.	faculty	['fækəlti]	*n.*	（大学）全体教职员
86.	fall	[fɔːl]	*n.*	秋天
87.	fascinating	['fæsineitiŋ]	*adj.*	迷人的；醉人的
88.	feature	[fiːtʃə]	*n.&v.*	特征；特色
89.	fee	[fiː]	*n.*	费用
90.	festivity	[fes'tiviti]	*n.*	庆祝活动
91.	following	['fɔləuiŋ]	*adj.*	下面的，下述的
92.	forward	['fɔːwəd]	*v.*	发送；递送
93.	freelance	['friː'lɑːns]	*adj.*	自由的；独立的
94.	freelancer	['friːlænsə]	*n.*	自由职业者
95.	frequently	['friːkwəntli]	*adv.*	频繁地；经常

96. funeral	['fju:nərəl]	*n.*	葬礼
97. generosity	[ˌdʒenə'rɔsiti]	*n.*	慷慨行为
98. gift	[gift]	*n.*	礼物；赠品
99. graciously	['greiʃəsli]	*adv.*	亲切地；仁慈地
100. guarantee	[ˌgærən'ti:]	*v.*	有保证；担保
101. handle	['hændl]	*v.*	对待；处理
102. head	['hed]	*v.*	出发(向某个方向)
103. help	[help]	*n.*	帮助；协助
104. hesitate	['heziteit]	*v.*	犹豫；有顾虑
105. hire	['haiə]	*v.*	雇用；聘用
106. honor	['ɔnə]	*v.*	给……以荣誉
107. host	[həust]	*v.*	主持；操办；主办；举办
108. impress	[im'pres]	*v.*	留下印象；印象
109. incomplete	[ˌinkəm'pli:t]	*adj.*	不完善的；不完整的
110. inquiry	[in'kwaiəri]	*n.*	询问；打听
111. interact	[ˌintə'rækt]	*v.*	互动
112. intimate	['intimit]	*adj.*	亲切；舒适的
113. introduce	[ˌintrə'dju:s]	*v.*	介绍，引见
114. issue	['iʃju:]	*n.*	问题；争议
115. item	['aitəm]	*n.*	商品；货物
116. keyword	[ki:wə:d]	*n.*	关键词；关键字
117. latex	['letεks]	*n.*	天然橡胶；乳胶
118. layoff	['leiɔ:f]	*n.*	解雇
119. league	[li:g]	*n.*	俱乐部联合会
120. legally	['li:gəli]	*adv.*	法律上；合法地
121. librarian	[lai'brεəriən]	*n.*	图书馆员
122. library	['laibrəri]	*n.*	图书馆；图书室
123. link	[liŋk]	*n.&v.*	结合；连接
124. list	[list]	*v.*	列表；列在
125. logo	['lɔgəu]	*n.*	标记；公司标志
126. madam	['mædəm]	*n.*	夫人
127. maintain	[mein'tein]	*v.*	维持；保持
128. Mandarin	['mændərin]	*n.*	汉语；普通话

129. memorial	[mi'mɔːriəl]	*n.*	纪念活动
130. message	['mesidʒ]	*n.*	信息；消息
131. modify	['mɔdifai]	*v.*	更改；修改
132. munchies/snacks	['mʌntʃiz/snæks]	*n.*	点心；零食
133. museum	[mjuː'ziəm]	*n.*	博物馆；展览馆
134. musician	[mjuː'ziʃən]	*n.*	音乐家
135. nonrefundable	[nʌnri'fʌndəbl]	*adj.*	不退还的
136. nonstop	[nɔn'stɔp]	*adj.*	直达的；不停的
137. note	[nəut]	*v.*	注；注释
138. note	[nəut]	*n*	笔记；便条；注释
139. notice	['nəutis]	*v.*	意识到；注意
140. objective	[əb'dʒektiv]	*n.*	目的，目标
141. offer	['ɔːfə]	*v.*	给予；提供
142. opinion	[ə'pinjən]	*n.*	见解；主张
143. opportunity	[ˌɔpə'tjuːniti]	*n.*	时机，机会
144. optional	['ɔpʃənəl]	*adj.*	可选的；非必需的
145. order	['ɔːdə]	*v.*	订购；订货
146. original	[ə'ridʒənl]	*adj.*	最初的；本来的
147. ounce	[auns]	*n.*	盎司
148. outlet	['autlet]	*n.*	销路；厂家直销店
149. parent	['pɛrənt]	*n.*	父亲；母亲；家长
150. participate	[pɑː'tisipeit]	*v.*	参与；分担
151. passport	['pɑːsˌpɔːt]	*n.*	护照
152. payable	['peiəbl]	*adj.*	应支付的
153. permanent	['pəːmənənt]	*a.*	永久的；常在的
154. phrase	[freiz]	*n.*	短语
155. position	[pə'ziʃən]	*n.*	位置；立场
156. present	['preznt]	*v.*	提交；呈递
157. previously	['priːvjəsli]	*adv.*	以前
158. process	['prəuses]	*n.*	步骤；程序；工序
159. productive	[prə'dʌktiv]	*adj.*	多产的
160. profile	['prəufail]	*n.*	资历；个人概况
161. prominent	['prɔminənt]	*adj.*	显著的；重要的

162. publish	['pʌbliʃ]	*v.*	出版；发行
163. publisher	['pʌbliʃə]	*n.*	出版商；出版公司
164. purchase	['pɚtʃəs]	*n.*	买；购买
165. qualify	['kwɔlifai]	*v.*	有资格
166. quality	['kwɔliti]	*n.*	质量
167. rare	[rɛə]	*adj.*	稀有的；罕见的
168. rate	[reit]	*n.*	价格；比率
169. recommend	[rekə'mend]	*v.*	推荐；介绍
170. recommendation	[ˌrekəmen'deiʃən]	*n.*	推荐信，介绍信
171. recruit	[ri'kruːt]	*v.*	雇用；聘用
172. regard	[ri'gɑːd]	*n.&v.*	问候；致意
173. regional	['riːdʒənəl]	*adj.*	地方的；区域的
174. regretfully	[ri'gretfəli]	*adv.*	遗憾地；抱歉地
175. related	[ri'leitid]	*adj.*	有关的
176. replacement	[rɪ'pleismənt]	*n.*	代替者；代替物
177. request	[ri'kwest]	*n.*	要求；需求
178. research	[ri'səːtʃ]	*n.*	研究
179. reserve	[ri'zəːv]	*v.*	预约；预订
180. residential	[rezi'denʃəl]	*adj.*	居住的；住宅的
181. resolve	[ri'zɔlv]	*v.*	解决；解答
182. response	[ri'spɔns]	*n.*	回答；答复
183. responsibility	[riˌspɔnsə'biliti]	*n.*	职责；义务
184. résumé	[ri'zjuːm]	*n.*	个人简历
185. retailer	['riːteilə]	*n.*	零售商；零售店
186. return	[ri'təːn]	*v.*	返回
187. review	[ri'vjuː]	*v.*	复习；浏览
188. reward	[ri'wɔːd]	*n.*	奖赏；奖励
189. rumor	['ruːmə]	*n.*	谣传；传闻
190. sale	[seil]	*n.*	卖；出售
191. schedule	['skedʒul]	*v.*	安排；预定
192. search	[səːtʃ]	*v.*	找；查找
193. season	['siːzn]	*n.*	季；季节
194. select	[si'lekt]	*v.*	选择；挑选

195. service	['sə:vis]	*n.*	服务
196. share	[ʃεə]	*v.*	交流；分享
197. ship	[ʃip]	*v.*	运货；交货
198. shipment	['ʃipmənt]	*n.*	货物；物品
199. shipper	['ʃipə]	*n.*	发货人；运货人
200. sightseeing	['sait,si:iŋ]	*n.*	观光；游览
201. silicone	['sɪlɪ,kon]	*n.*	硅胶
202. sincerely	[sin'siəli]	*adv.*	真诚地；诚恳地
203. snowshoe	['snəuʃu:]	*n.*	雪鞋
204. snowstorm	['snəustɔ:m]	*n.*	暴风雪
205. spam	[spæm]	*n.&v.*	垃圾电子邮件
206. staff	[stɑ:f]	*n.*	职员；工作人员
207. store	[stɔ:]	*n.*	商店
208. store	[stɔ:]	*v.*	保管；容纳
209. streamline	['stri:mlain]	*v.*	精简机构；提高效率
210. subject	['sʌbdʒikt]	*n.*	主题；题目
211. supermarket	['sju:pə,mɑ:kit]	*n.*	超市
212. supply	[sə'plaɪ]	*n.*	生活用品；供应品
213. surprise	[sə'praiz]	*v.&n.*	意外；使惊讶
214. survey	[sə:'vei]	*n.*	调查；向……作调查
215. tax	[tæks]	*n.*	税；税金
216. technology	[tek'nɔlədʒi]	*n.*	科技
217. temperature	['tempritʃə]	*n.*	温度；气温
218. terminology	[tɚmə'nɑlədʒɪ]	*n.*	术语；专门用语
219. thunderstorm	['θʌndɚ,stɔ:m]	*n.*	大雷雨；雷暴
220. toe	[təu]	*n.*	脚趾头
221. tour	[tuə]	*n.*	旅游
222. track	[træk]	*v.*	跟踪；追踪
223. T-shirt	[ti-ʃɚt]	*n.*	短袖圆领运动衫；T 恤衫
224. turnout	['tə:n'aut]	*n.*	出席者
225. under	['ʌndə]	*prep.*	在……下面，在……下方
226. unexpectedly	['ʌnik'spektidli]	*adv.*	未料到地；意外地
227. unfortunately	[ʌn'fɔ:tʃənitli]	*adv.*	遗憾地；可惜地

228. upcoming	['ʌpˌkʌmiŋ]	*adj.*	即将来临的
229. update	[ʌp'deit]	*n.*	最新的情况，最新的信息
230. urge	[əːdʒ]	*v.*	极力主张；催促
231. username	['juːzə neim]	*n.*	用户名
232. vacation	[vei'keiʃən]	*n.*	休假
233. valid	['vælid]	*adj.*	合法的；有效的
234. value	['væljuː]	*n.&v.*	价值；重要性
235. various	['vɛəriəs]	*adj.*	各种各样的
236. via	['vaiə]	*prep.*	通过；凭借
237. view	[vjuː]	*n.*	景色；视野
238. view	[vjuː]	*v.*	察看；观看
239. volunteer	[ˌvɔlən'tiə]	*n.*	志愿者
240. website	['webˌsait]	*n.*	网站
241. welcome	['welkəm]	*v.*	欢迎
242. well-designed	[wel- di'zaind]	*adj.*	设计完美的
243. wonderful	['wʌndəfəl]	*adj.*	极好的